Creating Value Through Effective Relationships

John Churchill, Ph.D.

ISBN-13 978-1456469788
ISBN-10: 1456469789

Published by C*Port Financial Education Services
Port Williams, Nova Scotia
Canada B0P 1T0

www.CPortFinancialEducation.com

CONTENTS

THE AUTHOR

John Churchill, B.A., B.D., M.A., M.B.A., Ph.D., has developed financial courses and programs, written textbooks and other course material, and taught seminars for the Institute of Canadian Bankers, the Canadian Securities Institute, the Omani Institute of Banking, and the Saudi Arabian Institute of Banking (IOB), as well as a number of financial corporations. Until his retirement in 2007 as professor of finance at Acadia University, Nova Scotia, Canada, Dr. Churchill specialized in personal finance, pension fund management, and portfolio management. Complementing his degrees in business is a Masters degree in Psychology. His particular interest is the convergence of relationship principles and financial theory in the context of financial advising. He is now President and Principal Consultant of C*Port Financial Education Services: **www.CportFinancialEducation.com**

ACKNOWLEDGEMENTS

The author thanks those who contributed to the creation, refinement, and presentation of the ideas in this book. The first edition was published in 2000 and it and this revision have benefited greatly from the help of several people, including:

- Kendra Carmichael, communication expert and keen-eyed editor, whose comments strengthened this work and helped to make it linguistically credible.
- Dr. Doug Baldwin, historian, editor always at the *top of his game,* and fellow trekker through the inscrutable.
- Lana Churchill, whose patience in reading this book numerous times always caught something, and whose suggestions made sure vague ideas and *things* were better explained.
- Ernie Buist, valued colleague, who proves that when two people don't always agree, creativity occurs.
- Jonathan Campbell, author, man of letters, and editorial consultant who helped to navigate the treacherous shoals of jagged logic.
- Dr. Rosaire Couturier, former CEO of the Institute of Canadian Bankers, conceptual architect.
- Dr. Hadi Belazi, Adel Al-Ateeq, Steve Dorvic, Mohammed Hammoudah, and Maher Al Yousif – IOB program directors, who *managed* the development of the Interpersonal Relationships Skills course for the Saudi Arabian Institute of Banking and have kept it running smoothly. The first versions of this book were written for that course, which is part of IOB's Certified Financial Planning Program.
- Former students, who have urged me on to *get it right* (that is, theoretically sound, clear, and useful).

PREFACE

While teaching university students for the past twenty years, I have also had the pleasure of instructing financial services professionals in numerous courses, seminars, and workshops. The first group challenged my ability to make theory clear; the second group demanded relevancy. It is my hope that this book is both clear and relevant. I believe that there is nothing more relevant than good theory, thus, the concepts in this book are backed by research and theories emanating from such academic areas as personality study, counselling, cognitive psychology, and educational psychology. The practical context is based on my experience and that of many professional financial advisors in the West and the Middle East with whom I have worked. It has been delightfully surprising to see how the concepts in this book are universally applicable. This does not mean that cultural differences do not matter – they do and at times, they override common shared experiences – however, my experience is that all clients of financial services want advisors who understand their concerns and aspirations and whom they can trust to create value for them. My educational hope, and experience, is that the requisite knowledge and skills needed to deliver this type of service can be learned – or improved upon.

I have worked equally with male and female professionals and honour all of their experiences (some of which appear in this book and the accompanying Participants' Manual.) I have avoided the awkward and outmoded *he/she* form and have generally used the plural *they*. I have been gender-specific, especially in examples, where clients have been given an identity (although false) to enhance realism.

This book is written to help educate those who give personal financial advice. I define education as *the awareness of options and the power to select and employ the most appropriate ones for the situation*. This book presents a wide range of concepts and strategies that advisors can use to help build or turn around client relationships. Like a medical doctor's kit bag, the ideas in this book are available for selective use by educated advisors who understand their purpose and situational appropriateness.

After giving my *education-as-power* speech, Hossam, a seminar participant, asked me, *Can you really teach these skills?* My response was: *That is the objective.* At the end of the course, he paid me the supreme compliment: *You met the challenge.* Based on my experience and that of others, I believe it can happen and I hope it will happen as you read this book or participate in a course of which this book is a part.

INTRODUCTION

The focus of this book is the communication and relationship skills needed to create dynamic advisor-client relationships in which clients come to trust their advisors' ability to care and create value for them. Many surveys point to troublesome personal relationships and inadequate communication as the main causes of client dissatisfaction and lack of loyalty. Many financial programs and courses recognize these realities but do little to help develop the required competencies. It is important to go beyond paying lip service to the importance of these skills to understand the concepts that underlie them and how they can be developed and operationalized in the context of selling financial services.

There are many aspects to communication and relationship competency. The structure of this book identifies those dimensions and elaborates their key conceptual and skill-based components. It also recognizes that in practice these components interact and that an integrated approach towards client relationships is the key. This integrated approach is exhibited in the conceptual discussions and in examples in the following pages. They are also highlighted in the questions, exercises, and case studies contained in the Participants Manual.

This book begins with an overview of the financial advisor's role and objective. Much can be learned by juxtaposing the advisor's instincts and tendencies with a renewed vision of what it means to offer financial advice. A key theme of the book is **value creation.** Advisors should view their most important contribution as creating value for clients – certainly not selling products. This leads to the important distinction between a client-centred and a product-centred approach (Chapter 1). For completeness, the various roles financial service representatives play as transaction facilitators, counsellors, and financial planners are described and distinguished. To set the complete context within which financial representatives service clients, the financial planning process is outlined in some detail (Appendix 1A). The key competencies identified for delivering this type of service are technical, relational, and character-based. The development of technical competency is left to other books and courses. This book focuses on relational competency and character (Chapter 2) – key components for creating value for clients and for securing their business.

A major part of relational competency is the ability to communicate skilfully, which requires an understanding of the nature of the communication process, and how to avoid or *fix* problems that threaten to derail it (Chapter 3). What we communicate depends to a large extent on how we perceive the *facts*. Our perceptions influence the way we gather and communicate information (Chapter 4). Only part of a message is communicated verbally. Nonverbal communication contains valuable information advisors must be able to *read* (Chapter 5).

There are specific skills advisors can learn to be more relationally effective. These include the critically important abilities of active listening, empathy, and questioning (Chapter 6). As well as managing relational dynamics, competent advisors must be able to administer the structure and flow of an interview by adopting a *semi-structured* approach and viewing the interview as a series of *phases* (Chapter 7). The proof that advisors have listened attentively to client concerns is the appropriateness and attractiveness of their proposals. To enhance client willingness to be open to and respond positively to product presentations, advisors need to use effective presentation skills (Chapter 8.) The better advisors understand the dimensions of clients' personalities, the better they can add value to their clients' situations and develop stronger working relationships. The advisor must be familiar with clients' beliefs and values, as well as the way they receive and process information (Chapter 9). It is also highly useful if the advisor is aware of the decision-making process clients proceed through as they search out and buy financial services. The rational decision-making model must be balanced with some of the irrational aspects of decision making, especially those related to investing (Chapter 10). The cultural and social contexts of people's lives have a major influence on what they want from financial services and how they will respond to recommendations (Chapter 11). Some personality types present challenges to advisors who must be able to handle them and attempt to turn the more troublesome types into allies. Some clients have special needs. In particular, the elderly and those grieving a death need to be approached with an understanding of their dynamics and the particular strategies that will accommodate their needs (Chapter 12). Perhaps the supreme challenge of building client relationships is the management of conflict. Advisors must understand the nature of conflict and be skilled in working through it to find a resolution (Chapter 13).

The following table depicts the knowledge and skills competent financial advisors must master in order to create value for clients. (The relevant chapters are designated.) Competency extends over four domains: (1) knowledge of the context of financial advising; (2) understanding the advisor's objectives and role; (3) understanding and mastering communication and relationship building processes; and (4) understanding internal and external forces that influence client attitudes and behaviour.

Domain	Topics	Chapters
Context	Foundational Concepts	1
The Advisor	The Financial Planning Process	1A
	The Financial Advisor's Character	2
The Interaction	The Communication Model	3
	Nonverbal Communication	5
	Effective Relationship Skills	6
	The Interview Agenda	7
	Designing and Presenting a Proposal	8
	Managing Conflict	13
The Client	Perceptions	4
	Personality Dimensions	9
	Rational and Irrational Aspects of Decision Making	10
	Cultural and Social Dimensions of Personality	11
	Managing Challenging Relationships	12

This book's objective is to help financial advisors distinguish themselves by the value they create for clients as they use their technical and relational skills with character to help clients fulfil their needs and goals. The content of this book should be of interest to two groups of financial services professionals: (1) those who create comprehensive financial plans, and (2) those who work on aspects of clients' overall financial strategies by providing specific products, services, and advice.

This book refers to the different functions financial services professionals undertake: performing transactions, giving advice, and creating comprehensive financial plans – but the generic term *advisor* is used to refer to all financial services professionals despite the role they play and the nature of their business relationship with clients.

MODULE I

CREATING VALUE FOR CLIENTS

CHAPTER 1

FOUNDATIONAL CONCEPTS

1.0 INTRODUCTION

I once asked a small boy what his father did. His unashamed, straight-forward answer was, *He makes money in a sneaky, but legal way.* (Some advisors fear the boy's caricature of his father reflects a popular perception of all financial advisors.) If I were to ask financial advisors the same question, I would expect a range of answers that highlighted products and services and emphasized selling.

- o   *I manage client accounts.*
- o   *I review investment portfolios and make recommendations.*
- o   *I sell mutual funds.*
- o   *I open accounts, help clients apply for credit, and meet their daily banking needs.*
- o   *I sell a wide-range of structured products to high net-worth clients so they can achieve their investment objectives with a minimum of risk.*

1.1 Creating Value

The above answers are all *functional* – that is, they describe the tasks advisors perform. We need a more general, conceptual answer, which ties together a variety of day-to-day activities and indicates what advisors actually hope to achieve for their clients. The job description adopted in this book is this: **financial advisors create value for clients.** Despite the products, regardless of clients' requests, in addition to analysis and strategizing, advisors should see their role as creating value for their customers. In helping create value, advisors provide a valuable service and at the same time achieve their own business plans. To be more specific:

> **Value is created when advisors, with an understanding of their clients' concerns, provide products and services in a competent and ethical manner, which meet their clients' needs and help them achieve their goals.**

All financial institutions provide the same basic products and services, so the distinguishing feature between providers is the value they can add to their clients' situations. Charlotte Beyer, CEO of The Institute for Private Investors suggests

The most successful firms of the future will be those that focus on providing a first-rate service (as distinct from selling the best products) and those that concentrate on understanding how investors behave and tailor their services accordingly (Beyer, 2009, p.13).

Customers are not interested in buying financial products and services; they want assistance in making choices that help them satisfy their financial needs and achieve their goals. Purchasing an investment has no satisfaction in itself, but clients hope it will either meet a need, such as securing a higher investment return, or that it will be a step towards achieving a goal, such as the establishment of a child's educational fund. Products are merely means to an end. Opening a current account or exchanging foreign currency are not particularly pleasurable activities, but they are steps towards meeting needs and achieving goals. **Financial institutions and advisors who compete successfully in the marketplace will be those who see their roles as doing more than selling products and services.** They are the ones who view their roles as providing products and services that help clients deal with their concerns, and, overall, create value for them.

Creating value for clients is the key to enhancing business and fostering loyalty. The adoption of value creation as an objective has several benefits. When customers feel value has been created,

- fees are viewed as costs incurred to achieve future benefits
- long-term relationships are developed and opportunities are created for selling a range of financial products over time
- customer satisfaction is created, trust is enhanced, and loyalty is developed

In order to create value for clients, advisors must be equipped with specific knowledge and skills. They must have

- technical competency
- relational competency
- an ethical character

1.1.1 Technical Competency
Effective advisors are knowledgeable about a range of personal financial issues: the technicalities of wealth assessment, debt and cash management, investment planning, risk management, asset valuation, taxation, and estate planning. And they use that knowledge to analyze their clients' financial situations and recommend strategies and products that improve their clients' financial positions. The ability to create value varies across and within institutions because some advisors are more technically competent than others as a result of differences in formal education, training, or experience.

1.1.2 Relational Competency
Neal Van Zutphen 2007), a credentialed financial advisor points out that in the industry

practicing financial planners have achieved and demonstrated a base level of technical expertise. But there's a gap in our training...: it's in...the development of interpersonal communication skills.....Financial planners must possess technical expertise...But consumers also seek client-centred relationships....If a planner has little or no ability to establish a personal rapport or connection with the client, plan implementation and compliance suffer....demand of client-centred relationships means a demand for advisors to place greater focus on, and develop, their interpersonal communication skills.

Effective advisors are competent in establishing and managing relationships. They have mastered the knowledge and skills related to communication theory, interpersonal dynamics, interviewing, and effective presentations. And they are able to develop strong working relationships in which clients feel their needs are met. This implies that the advisor will not try to sell products that are unsuited to their clients' needs or that are inferior – even if the advisor is under pressure to meet targets. A *hard-sell* approach may damage relationships and, furthermore, it is unnecessary because a value creation approach is better able to build the advisor's business.

The advisor is *in-between* – between client needs and employer requirements. In this precarious position, the advisor must find a balance, a way to satisfy the requirements of each. The anxiety produced from being in the middle is reduced by the knowledge that as the advisor builds satisfying relationships with clients and gains their loyalty, it is easier to sell a range of products. Thus, over time, the requirements of both customers and employers will be met.

Charlotte Beyer (2009) provides a helpful way to view the blend of skills required to create customer satisfaction. She depicts it as an intersection of technical competency and emotional intelligence (based on Daniel Goleman's *Emotional Intelligence*, 2005). Figure 1.1 shows the framework that can be used to assess an advisor's balance of necessary competencies.

Figure 1.1
A Framework for Understanding Advisor Competency

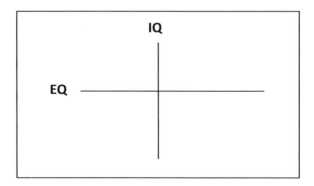

The vertical axis IQ, represents the knowledge, intelligence and expertise of the advisor. The horizontal axis, EQ, is the emotional intelligence, and empathetic skills of the advisor. Beyer suggests that the most satisfied clients are those whose advisors are in the in the upper-right quadrant where the advisor displays technical competency and the ability to understand and care about the client. Clients doomed to dissatisfaction have advisors who lie in the lower-left quadrant with little skill or interest in understanding the client.

1.1.3 Ethical Character
Clients must trust the advisor to look after their best interests. Without this assurance, customers will be wary of seeking advice. The financial advising profession should be known equally for its competence and ethics. Ethical conduct advances the interests of both customers and financial institutions. Charlotte Beyer in an article calling for the development of a new science with new theories to undergird the foundation of private client relationships suggests this new science would examine how trust and faith are at the core of the private client-advisor relationship. *A client's level of trust and faith is critical for an adviser [sic] because it has a correlation of 1 with client retention* (Beyer, 2009).

The management firm A.T. Kearney reported in *AME Info.Com*, a Middle-Eastern business publication, on the results of a study they conducted to identify the components of good customer service. One of its findings was that good communication and relationship building skills and clear ethical practices are paramount to customer satisfaction and business growth. The link between satisfaction and growth is found in their reported statistic that a 5% increase in customer retention increased product profitability by 20% to 80% (Buchta *et al.*, 2008*)*.

1.1.4 All Three are Necessary
All three dimensions – technical competency, relational competency, and ethical character – are essential for creating value and satisfied customers. Good relationships cannot make up for the lack of sound technical knowledge, and technical competency cannot make up for the lack of good relational skills or ethical conduct. The A.T. Kearney study concluded that *highly satisfied customers are almost twice as likely to ... purchase another product as are dissatisfied customers* (Buchta *et al*, 2008*)*.

Figure 1.2 captures the critical links.

Figure 1.2
Creating Value for Customers

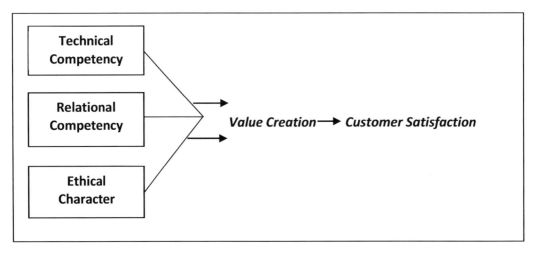

The A.T. Kearny study asserts that despite growth in profitability and asset size, GCC (Gulf Cooperation Council) banks are losing millions as the result of poor customer service to which a number of factors contribute, as listed below.

- Too few skilled resources. Given the recent and rapid expansion of product lines, customers depend on advisors to help them choose the right products; however, advisors are often ill-equipped for the role. Some lack even the basic technical knowledge and skills.
- Lack of product transparency at the time of sale. Customers are not fully informed of all relevant costs or unfavourable product features, and usually find out about them later.
- Lack of responsiveness and follow-up of customer requests in a timely manner, especially with regard to website contacts.

It is shocking that more than half of all UAE nationals consider their customer service experience negative or neutral. This figure is above 90% for Western expatriates.

Subsequent chapters of this book go beyond general statements about customer satisfaction and look at specific knowledge, skills, and strategies that create it.

1.2 A CLIENT-CENTRED APPROACH

Advisors are tempted to see themselves narrowly as product sellers. Many things explain this view including product-centred training, the constant concern for institutional economic viability and shareholder return, and competitive pressure. But at the heart of a value-creation focus is a client-centred approach. Customers' concerns are downplayed when products become central and relationships are ignored.

According to financial advisor Jamie Williams,

> Successful financial advisors emphasize people skills, not product offerings....The value that an advisor brings to the relationship with a client cannot be the product....It is just one solution (in Moulton, 2008, p.B12).

Michael Callahan says there has been a shift in focus.

> Not so long ago, the industry [financial services] was much more commission and transaction oriented, with the primary focus being on the markets and their next move. These days, the focus has shifted to people and relationships (Callahan, 2008, p.37).

The product-centred approach views customers as sales targets. By contrast, the client-centred approach puts client concerns at the forefront. The advisor's pre-eminent skills are the ability to listen to clients, understand their concerns, and devise strategies that use the institution's products and services to help meet their clients' needs and goals. The focus of the client-centred approach is not the immediate sale, but a long-term relationship over which the advisor can create value for clients and generate satisfaction by supplying the right products and services to meet their changing circumstances. Figure 1.3 illustrates the contrast between the two approaches.

Figure 1.3
A Client-Centred Vs. Product-Centred Approach

	CLIENT-CENTRED	**PRODUCT-CENTRED**
FOCUS	Customer needs and goals	Products
OBJECTIVES	Help customers meet their needs and achieve their goals	*Close the deal*
TIME HORIZON	Long-Term	Short-Term
STRATEGY	To add value to the customer's situation	To influence customers to buy

The product approach has many shortcomings.

- The product the advisor feels pressured to sell is not always the best one for the client.
- Customers are left without a comprehensive understanding of their needs or a plan to achieve their goals.
- Advisors are often put in a conflict between their client's best interests and their employer's requirements.

The client-centred advisor still must have in-depth product knowledge, but in this context **selling is matching.** Products are presented as solutions matched to needs.

In 2003, Blomfield and Hamil, using research conducted by CEG Worldwide and Oppenheimer Funds, concluded that becoming a truly client-centred advisor was the best way to be set apart from the competition. (It is interesting that all the advisors who responded to the research questionnaire claimed they were client-centred, but according to CEG's definition, only 13.8% were truly focused on their clients. CEG designated the others *investment-centred*.)

The research studied how both types of advisors (client-centred and investment-centred) fared over a six-month period in the first-half of 2001. Despite a market downturn, Blomfield and Hamil found that client-centred advisors enjoyed substantial success over investment-centred advisors. Table 1.1, summarizes the most important findings.

Table 1.1
Client-Centred and Investment-Centred Advisors Performance During Q1 and Q2, 2001

	Client-Centred Advisors	Investment-Centred Advisors
Average number of new clients gained	6.8	1.3
Average amount of assets brought by each new client	$269,000	$51,000
Average number of existing clients bringing additional business	7.3 clients	Less than 1
Average amount of additional business brought by existing clients	$64,000	$13,000
Average total new assets per advisor	$2,300,000	$76,700

Client-centred advisors, who focused on building client relationships and keeping contact during a rough market, brought in 30 times more assets than investment-centred advisors.

The following example of client-centred advising is extracted from a promotional brochure distributed by one of Canada's successful financial service advisors. Excerpts highlight the importance of a commitment to understanding clients' concerns, constant communication, value creation, and product recommendations that match client profiles.

You should expect three things from your financial advisor:
o *First, a financial plan that is tailored to your specific objectives and circumstances.*
o *Second, an investment strategy that provides long term growth with emphasis on capital preservation.*
o *Third, consistent and regular communication.*
What kind of Investments do you recommend?
My recommendation depends on your personal financial goals and your risk tolerance.
How often will I hear from you?
Every client receives a semi-annual statement and regular newsletters. I will also phone you every six months.... I also meet with clients periodically to update and review their situations. However, if there are any upcoming changes in your situation or needs, I expect to hear from you.

- Extracted from a promotional brochure of Brightside Financial Services Inc., Mississauga, Ontario, Canada, Rick Sukhu, financial advisor.

1.2.1 Difficulties in Selling and Purchasing Financial Services

In addition to its distinct advantages, a client-centred approach is critical because of the nature of selling and purchasing financial services. Offering financial services is considerably different from selling tangible goods, such as cars or appliances. The difference creates difficulties for financial representatives who sell them, and for customers who evaluate and purchase them. The strategy that consistently overcomes these problems is a client-centred approach.

1.2.1.1 Difficulties for Providers. Most tangible goods are produced and stored before sale. Services cannot be created ahead of time; they are *produced* in the customer's presence. No dentist can stock up on root canals or car mechanics on engine tune-ups. The quality of a service can be influenced by the performance and even the mood of the provider on a particular day. The quality of advice and service may vary from time to time, and from advisor to advisor. The advisor's own personal issues may also be internally distracting at a particular time and interfere with full concentration on clients' concerns.

The quality of the service also depends on the customer's cooperation. If the customer is resistant or highly critical, the advisor works under a handicap and the quality of the outcome will be affected. The final result of the client-advisor interaction depends not only on how well the advisor performs, but also on how freely the customer joins in.

1.2.1.2 Difficulties for Consumers. The nature of financial products and services makes it difficult for customers to evaluate their quality prior to purchase. The performance of a financial product or service cannot be fully evaluated until after its purchase – as with a vacation or a haircut. An advisor may recommend a particular investment, but the client's satisfaction depends upon its subsequent performance. There is no *test drive*. No wonder customers feel they are taking a risk in purchasing a financial service. This helps to explain the hesitancy of some clients to commit to a purchase.

Because of the difficulty of offering and purchasing financial services, clients may feel they are taking a chance in seeking an advisor's help. Trust in the advisor's competency and character is a central issue for clients. A key question for advisors is: *how can I gain my clients' trust and convince them of my trustworthiness?* The major part of the answer is to be client-centred.

Trust is developed and client loyalty secured as clients come to believe that the advisor understands their concerns and has the ability to recommend effective solutions. If clients prize their relationships with their advisors, even when unexpected shocks derail their expectations, they trust that the advisor stands ready to make the needed adjustments. Trust is enhanced as clients feel their situations and concerns are understood and respected by the advisor.

1.3 TRANSACTIONS VS. COUNSELLING VS. PLANNING
Let us return to the question of what advisors do for clients.

> Mr. Galen entered the branch and asked to talk with someone about a credit card. He was led into an advisor's office. The advisor asked Mr. Galen a series of questions and proceeded to fill out the application....

It would be interesting if we could press *pause* and ask the advisor some questions.

- What is your objective with this client?
- How will you know if you have been successful?
- How much time will you spend getting to know Mr. Galen's personal and financial situation?
- Do you look at this as a transaction that ends when Mr. Galen signs the application and after you have tried to cross-sell other products and services?
- Do you see this as the beginning of a longer-term relationship during which you can help Mr. Galen with a range of concerns?

The advisor can choose from a number of roles in response to the client's concerns and requests. Each role takes the conversation in a different direction and towards a different objective. As the advisor proceeds with the credit card application, the type of service offered will depend on the client's personality and needs, and the advisor's objectives and skills. There are three possibilities: a **transaction** role, a **counselling** role, and a **financial planning** role. The three approaches differ with regard to the amount of personal information the advisor needs from the client, how central products are in the discussion, the time spent discussing the client's needs and goals, the advisor's objectives, and how the client perceives the advisor. The three approaches have markedly different agendas, time lines, and outcomes.

But before we distinguish further between the three approaches, we need to be clear about the differences between financial ***needs*** and financial ***goals***. Financial needs are basic and common to all clients. They are about the efficient management of one's personal financial resources to get the most from them. They result from the desire for such things as more income, decreased expenses, increased returns with more acceptable levels of risk, reduced fees, effective cash and debt management, after-tax maximization, personal risk management and insurance, wealth preservation, and estate planning. Financial needs motivate people to seek improvements to the way they manage their finances.

The following is a conversation about a client's needs. The client has a time deposit that soon matures and the client and advisor are discussing re-investment options. The client has asked about a particular investment – a National Investment Fund.

> **Advisor:** *Sir, before we talk about the national fund, would you tell me more about your needs?*
> **Client:** *My needs are very simple; I want a better rate of return.*
> **Advisor:** *That is great. What about other needs?*
> **Client:** *What do you mean by "other needs?"*
> **Advisor:** *What I meant was how often do you need to withdraw from your capital?*
> **Client:** *I don't need to withdraw from my capital at all. I want it to stay intact. All I need is a monthly income. So what is the best product you can offer me?*

The client outlined his needs: a good rate of return, capital preservation, and monthly income. With this information, the advisor can recommend the appropriate product. We don't know why the client needs these features, but the client perceives them as necessary to achieve specific goals.

Compared to financial **needs**, financial **goals** are conditions or ends people want to accomplish, such as a new car, an increased number of vacations per year, early retirement, or securing the education of children. Satisfying financial needs is never an end in itself. The satisfaction of needs is always *in order to* bring about a larger objective – the achievement of financial goals. Obtaining a higher investment return is a need; accumulating enough money for children's future education is a goal. Someone might *need* a higher return to provide a college education for children. Liquidity is a need. The goal might be the establishment of an emergency fund that will help pay bills in the event of sickness or a disability that renders a person unable to work.

Generally, transactions are focused on needs, while planning is focused on goals, and counselling is in between. In the transaction mode, the advisor's objective is to fulfil client requests and to make immediate sales. Carrying out a financial planning role, advisors focus on their client's financial and personal circumstances and assess whether their clients' finances are adequate to fund their goals. The objective of the process is to create a coherent, comprehensive financial plan that will help clients achieve their financial goals using the institution's products and services.

1.3.1 Transactions

A transaction-based service is predominantly concerned with standard financial products and requires the least amount of discovery of the client's personal and financial circumstances. There are times when transaction-based discussions are appropriate: when it is clear the client is looking for a specific product or service to fulfil a specific need, or when the client requires specific information. For clients with unlimited financial resources who can afford any goal, their only interest may be to secure the *best deal*.

I recently had a conversation with a financial services representative about her institution's airlines affinity credit card. (I have a major complaint about my current one that accumulates air miles for credit card purchases – it is too restrictive.) The representative highlighted the benefits of her institution's card – something I would expect her to do. I had no need of a discussion of my broad goals and I was satisfied with the specific information she gave me. I used that information and other information I had gathered to make a decision – I decided not to change.

1.3.2 Counselling

A counselling-based service requires more personal information from the client. In my discussion with the financial services representative about affinity credit cards, I was not looking for advice and the representative did not offer any. If I had asked for the representative's help to assess the possibilities, the discussion would have been a counselling one. Sometimes clients do not ask for counselling help because they fear advisors might be biased, especially when it appears they are under pressure to sell. The representative offered me a website where I could view the different options offered by various financial institutions, but this is not the same as offering to help me sort through and choose from the options. To have entered into the realm of counselling, the representative would have had to become more involved with me and have asked a number of questions about my needs, travelling habits, and financial situation. Counselling is appropriate when the client asks for it or the representative decides it is appropriate, as in the following examples.

> My wife and I bought our first house soon after we were married. A large encouragement to purchase was the advice given by a real estate agent. This could have been a transaction event with the agent simply driving us around and showing us different properties. However, the agent turned counsellor when he offered us some advice about the economics of purchasing a house at this stage in our lives and suggested some important criteria to consider. We trusted his advice because some of it was not entirely in his best interest.

> Mr. Hashesh is a pharmacist who has just suffered a stroke. The possibility of returning to work is minimal. This is a large worry; he may not be able to live on his investments and the two small pensions he will receive. The financial advisor offered to do a financial review to assess how he might use his current and future resources to provide adequate cash flow if he should become disabled.

The assistance the advisor offered Mr. Hashesh comes close to planning, but because the exercise will be limited and focused on income generation and expense coverage, it is a counselling relationship.

Counselling assistance lies between a transaction and a planning approach. Counselling discussions range over a number of issues, including needs and goals, and personal finances and product features, but always with the objective of advising the client on product features and options, and recommending the best fit.

1.3.3 Financial Planning

The objective of financial planning is to **help clients articulate their goals, ascertain the financial resources needed to achieve them, create a plan that balances goals and finances, and then identify the specific products and services that will support the plan.** The Financial Planners Standards Council of Canada (FPSC), licensee of the Certified Financial Planning (CFP) designation, defines financial planning as *a process that determines how you can best meet your life goals through the proper management of your financial affairs* (FPSC website). In the planning process, a financially feasible, comprehensive plan is worked out to help clients achieve their goals. Products are solutions to problems, tools to reach financial goals. A financial planning discussion may begin with a transaction or counselling conversation and then lead into a consideration of the client's goals. (Chapter 7 presents a strategy for leading clients from a transaction or counselling discussion into the subject of goals.)

The financial planning role requires the most of the advisor, provides opportunity for the greatest involvement with clients, and as it uncovers a host of needs and goals, presents the opportunities for offering a range of products and services. Not all client contacts are financial planning sessions, either because the client is not interested or the advisor decides it is not appropriate.

1.3.4 A Comparison of the Roles

To illustrate the distinctions between the three approaches, let us return to our example about the credit card. If the incident is handled as a transaction, the advisor will obtain the information needed to complete the credit card application in a friendly and efficient manner and, perhaps, make a pitch to the client about other products and services. Handled as a counselling service, the advisor will ask the client for personal information including the need for a credit card. The advisor may point out the features of other cards, help the client evaluate them, and then help the client choose the most appropriate one.

If the brief encounter has potential for more involvement, the advisor will ask probing questions about the client's need for a card and how this fits with some of the client's other financial needs and goals. The advisor will introduce the idea of an overall financial plan in which to view needs and goals and may possibly offer assistance to create a comprehensive plan.

Even though the financial planning model holds out the most promise for sales over time, it is not always appropriate. It is time consuming and the advisor must decide when it is profitable to offer the service. (A detailed presentation of the financial planning process is contained in Appendix 1A.)

Sometimes, the client and advisor may not have the same objective. The client may simply want a transaction executed while the advisor may want to probe the client's situation to see if the client has an interest in a more comprehensive service. The following example illustrates the possibility.

The client was convinced that investing in the bank's *ALN* fund was the right thing to do, just as his nephew had done. The advisor wanted to make sure the client understood the technical features of the fund before selling it to the client.

Advisor: *But before you purchase the fund, I want to make sure you have the full picture about ALN so you can decide whether it is right for you.*
Client: *Fine, but I am in a hurry to make another meeting.*
Because time was limited, the advisor talked briefly about the product features. The client, in whose office they were meeting, was continually distracted by a ringing phone and his secretary passing papers in front of him to sign.

The advisor did not see any expression of interest in the fund's technicalities and when the advisor asked the client for feedback, the client immediately asked for the documents to sign. The advisor decided to do just what the client wanted and closed the deal.

Two years later, in an agitated state, the client withdrew his money from the fund because he had not understood that a large part of the yearly fee went to cover the plan's insurance benefit.

Some transactions do not require extensive conversations, but if the advisor wants to act in the client's best interests, the advisor will have to assure the product or service is best suited to the client and some degree of counselling will have to occur. In addition, the advisor may decide that the client's requests are best considered in the context of the client's overall financial situation and may try to engage the client in an extensive discussion of it.

1.4 CONCLUSION

Regardless of the advisor's role, creating value should be the advisor's main preoccupation. The total approach to the delivery of financial services **requires that advisors listen carefully and understand their customer's complete concerns and unique circumstances** before proposing solutions.

Creating value for clients is a win-win situation – the client's needs and goals are met and the advisor's business objectives are advanced. To be able to do this requires that advisors adopt a client-centred approach and prepare themselves with the knowledge and skills to be technically and relationally competent, and to always act ethically, with a commitment to looking after their clients' best interests.

Appendix 1A presents a more developed model of the financial planning process. Even though not all advisors function as planners, familiarity with the comprehensive model is instructional because it sets the context in which client requests are handled. A client may only ask for a credit card, but in the context of the customer's overall finances and goals, it plays a part. Knowing that context allows the advisor to offer a more effective service, and to find the door that leads to a fuller discussion of the client's more complete financial concerns and need for a wider range of products.

KEY TERMS

Client-centred approach. Making client concerns the main focus of a financial services relationship. Products are a secondary concern and the way in which client's needs and goals are fulfilled and achieved.

Counselling relationship. Working with clients to help them choose the best products and services that fit their needs.

Financial goals. Ends that people want to accomplish that require financial resources.

Financial needs. Basic desires to manage one's finances more efficiently and effectively.

Financial planning relationship. Relationships with clients in which advisors help clients create financial plans that accomplish their goals in line with their financial resources.

Product-centred approach. A relationship with clients in which products are the main focus.

Transactional relationship. Working with clients to provide the immediate service they request, such as filling an order, providing access to the institution's products and services, or supplying information.

Value creation. When advisors, with an understanding of their clients' situations, provide products and services in a competent and ethical manner, which meet their clients' needs and help them achieve their goals.

APPENDIX 1A

THE FINANCIAL PLANNING PROCESS

1A.0 INTRODUCTION

Financial planning is the process of devising strategies to help clients achieve their financial goals through the management of their current and future financial resources. Planning is the ultimate interaction between advisors and clients requiring the highest level of technical and relational skills to

- gather relevant personal and financial information while gaining the client's cooperation, confidence, and trust
- analyze the client's qualitative and quantitative information
- devise plans that help clients attain their financial goals within their financial capabilities

Financial planning is a comprehensive exercise. Its component activities are described in an excerpt from an American financial institution's promotional material.

> *Our first task is to understand your financial goals and objectives.*
>
> *Next, we help you build your personal financial strategy. In doing so, we consider many factors, including anticipated spending levels and obligations, future major purchases, the financial needs of children and parents, charitable contribution plans, desired retirement income, and ultimately, the important issues that affect the disposition of your estate.*
>
> *The financial strategy we help you develop is dynamic. It functions as a road map towards achieving your financial objectives. It contains short-term and long-term goals. When you inform us that there are significant changes in your circumstances, or we find new investment opportunities appropriate to your financial goals, your team will help you reassess and, if necessary, modify your strategy* (Adler, 1995).

In addition to understanding the steps of the planning process, planners must be able to conceptualize their clients' situations within a larger framework. This larger perspective gives planners a sense of their clients' concerns, their financial resources – current and future – and possible solutions. Two conceptual frameworks are considered here: the financial timeline and the generic lifestyle/capacity positions.

1A.1 THE FINANCIAL TIMELINE

Figure 1A.1 is a timeline of general financial issues clients manage over their lifetimes.

Figure 1A.1
The Financial Timeline

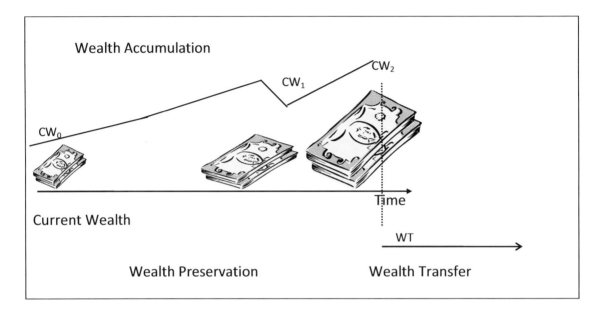

Figure 1A.1 is constructed on the assumption that individuals want to grow their wealth over time. In Figure 1A.1, current wealth is represented on the time line at point CW_0. Over time the wealth line will rise and fall. Wealth accumulates as investments earn a return, and as savings – the result of reduced expenses or increased income – are added. On the other hand, wealth lessens as investment returns decrease, expenses increase, income decreases, or assets are liquidated and cash spent. At CW_1, current wealth is pictured as haven fallen; perhaps funds have been withdrawn to accomplish a goal such as the funding of a child's education, or cash has been drawn down to fund retirement. By point CW_2, two things have occurred: wealth has grown beyond CW_1 and it has been passed on or transferred. The transfer of wealth (WT) usually occurs upon death, but it may take place earlier as part of a planned estate management strategy.

A major decision most individuals face is whether to consume their wealth during their lifetime or to preserve it for the next generation. This crucial decision has major implications for retirement. Some individuals will choose to live a thrifty retirement lifestyle and have their heirs benefit from their frugality, while others will be more interested in encouraging their children's resourcefulness and independence so parents can consume their own wealth in their own lifetime. Mark Twain, the American humourist, commenting on those who decide in favour of estate preservation, is reported to have said, *Thrift is a wonderful virtue, especially in ancestors.*

Those who have relied upon work-related income may have to draw down their wealth in retirement. For those with significant amounts of investment and/or continuing business income, wealth may still continue to grow after retirement.

Throughout a person's lifetime, potential wealth-eroding risks must be identified and managed. These risks come in the form of perils that cause an interruption in income, major unexpected expenses, or decreased market value of real and financial assets. The usual protection against such risks is insurance – life, disability, medical, liability, and property. The financial advisor must assess clients' needs for risk management strategies and make suggestions or referrals when appropriate. Advisors will also be concerned about the preservation of the value of clients' portfolios and will counsel asset allocation, and suitable diversification and hedging strategies.

Wealth accumulation, maximization of savings through budgetary control, tax planning, retirement management, estate planning, and risk management are all individual personal concerns with which the financial advisor must be knowledgeable. The total financial planning approach recognizes that clients have a range of concerns that extend over time, and advisors must be skilfully equipped to coordinate needs, goals, and finances over clients' lifetimes.

1A.2 GENERIC LIFE STYLE/CAPACITY POSITIONS
Another way of viewing the range of client concerns is to consider the interaction between lifestyle aspirations and financial capacity. In basic terms, the generic lifestyle assessment describes the amount of money people spend beyond necessities on luxuries in order to – in the words of economists – maximize their utility (enjoyment). We can categorize lifestyles as ranging from *frugal* to *lavish*.

The relationship between lifestyle and financial capacity is reciprocal. Lifestyle choices impact one's finances, just as finances set the parameters for lifestyle choices. The financial condition of some people is the result of lifestyle choices, while, for others, finances dictate lifestyle options. For example, if people want the latest clothing and electronic equipment, but only have a modest income, their budget will be strained or they will have to make sacrifices.

The relationship between lifestyle and finances differs amongst individuals, but, structurally, there are some commonalities. Figure 1A.2 shows three generic relationships: **balancing**, **maintaining**, and **increasing**.

Balancing. Over the medium to long-term, individuals must balance their lifestyle and financial capacity. People cannot live beyond their means for too long. People who are out of balance can restore equilibrium by either decreasing their lifestyle expenditures or increasing their cash flow. In Figure 1A.2, being out of balance is depicted as being located above the 45-degree line. The goal is to be in balance – to come back to the line – and those with few resources or excessive lifestyles may require help to achieve equilibrium.

Maintaining. Individuals who are in balance (*on the line*) desire, at the minimum, to maintain that balance. They would like to be at least as well off in the future as they are in the present, so identifying and managing risks that might upset their equilibrium is important.

Increasing. Some individuals may be in the enviable position where their financial capacity is more than adequate to fund their current lifestyle so they have the potential to enhance their lifestyle. In Figure 1A.2, they are positioned *below the line*. One family familiar to the author solved this *problem* by selling their house, moving into an apartment, and donating surplus money to charity. Another option is to set aside wealth for future generations.

Figure 1A.2
Life Style and Financial Capacity

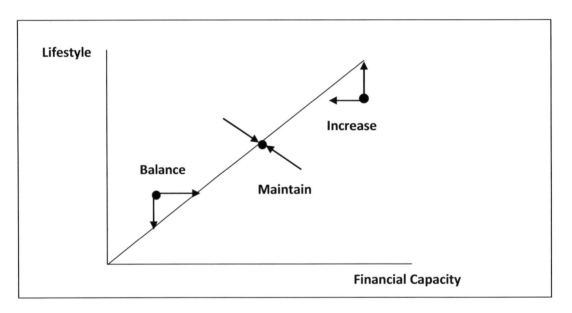

Financial services professionals must understand the interplay between finances and lifestyle in order to offer the proper product solutions. The following incident illustrates this.

> Mr. Roget decided he was ready to leave apartment dwelling and buy a house. He approached a financial institution about a mortgage and was quickly told his modest salary would not qualify him. Incensed over the abrupt nature of the rejection, he approached another institution, and it approved a mortgage. In addition to a mortgage, he now has a car loan, line of credit, and investment portfolio with this institution.

The difference between the two institutions was not their credit standards, but the approach of their financial advisors. The advisor at the first institution knew that financial capacity and lifestyle must coincide, but failed to interview the client long enough, and in the right manner, to discover that his financial situation also included a portfolio of investments worth $500,000, inherited from his father's estate. The second advisor learned the complete financial situation and decided the client's challenge was not that of balancing lifestyle and financial capacity, but of being in a position to improve his lifestyle. With the second advisor's help, the client worked out a solution that used some of his investments for a down payment and his salary easily covered the mortgage payments.

Table 1A.1 below summarizes potential financial strategies for different generic positions.

Table 1A.1
Generic Positions and Financial Strategies

Generic Lifestyle/Financial Positions	Financial Strategies
Balance	·decrease lifestyle ·seek additional sources of income ·cut expenses ·liquidate assets ·borrow

Maintain	·risk management
	  - insurance
	  - portfolio diversification
	·build liquid reserves

Increase	·spend more on lifestyle ·dispose of, or set aside wealth

1A.3 STEPS IN THE FINANCIAL PLANNING PROCESS

Clients may seek the help of financial advisors to design a comprehensive financial plan or simply to help with specific concerns, such as educational or retirement savings. Figure 1A.4 outlines the nine steps in the complete financial planning process. It is presented here to encourage advisors to become more involved in the complete planning process or, at least, to see where their specific interventions fit within the overall process. The double-headed arrows in Figure 1A.4 indicate the recirculation of information between the advisor and the client. The advisor must continually seek feedback and verification to make sure that plans are acceptable to clients and fit their financial and personal situations. The other steps outlined in the diagram are critical to ensuring that the institution's needs are met.

Figure 1A.4
Steps of the Planning Process

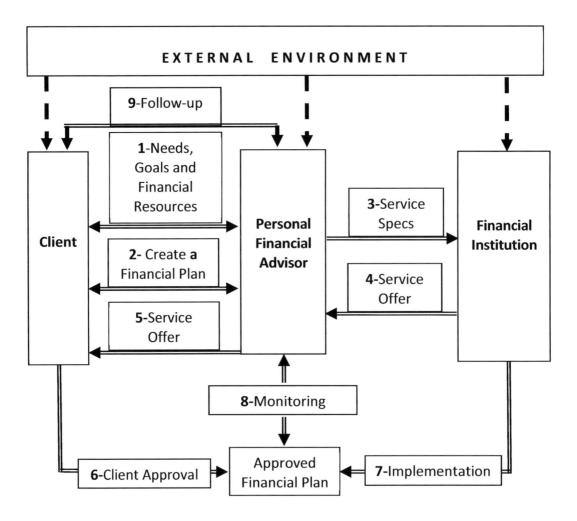

The nine-step financial planning process moves from the acquisition of relevant personal and financial information about the client's needs, goals, and financial resources to an assessment of that information (1), to creation of a financial plan based on that information (2). After the advisor and client work out a plan, the advisor may need to negotiate with the institution to make sure that product and service specifications that fit the client's situation are within the institution's capabilities and willingness to provide (3). For example, special permission may be needed to allow a client to invest less than the stated minimum amount in an investment vehicle, or a structured product with an insurance component may need to be created. The end result of the process is a service the institution can deliver and is acceptable to the client (4). The plan is then presented to the client as a service offer (5). After the client approves and signs the relevant documents (6), the plan is put into operation (7). Now, the planner and institution must monitor the plan with its built-in promises and assumptions (8). When the client's circumstances change, or unanticipated results occur, the planner will follow-up and initiate necessary modifications (9).

At all stages of the process, the advisor's technical and relational competency, and ethical character are critical. The mastery and application of the planner's knowledge and skills will determine if the customer feels value has been created and becomes a satisfied and loyal customer.

Throughout the planning process, the advisor must be skilled at gathering all relevant quantitative and qualitative information. Qualitative data in the form of beliefs, values, past experience, family configuration, hobbies, special needs, age, and health will have a major influence on the kind of concerns clients have, the kind of help they will welcome, and the kind of constraints imposed on possible solutions.

1A.4 THE PLANNER'S AGENDA

In the general planning model in Figure 1A.4, we will focus our attention on the activities on the left part of the diagram that call for the application of the advisor's skills in conversation with clients. The four steps numbered 1, 2, 5, and 6 in Figure 1A.4 require several sub-activities before a plan is finalized. These sub-activities are presented below.

1 - Needs, Goals, and Financial Resources Assessment
Gather Personal Information
- Qualitative and quantitative
- Complete and accurate – verify with client

Prepare a client profile and financial statements
- Profile:
  - Goals (monetary objectives and time frame)
  - Lifestyle preferences
  - Values
  - Critical facts and assumptions
  - Risk tolerance
  - Investment knowledge
- Financial Statements
  - Personal balance sheet
  - Personal income statement

Analyze current financial situation
- Liquidity, debt ratios, and standard norms analysis – calculation and evaluation
- Investment strategy assessment – real and financial
- Risk assessment and insurance – property, liability, disability, and life

Quantify Goals
- Use time value of money methods to quantify the one-time or on-going cost of goals

Prepare proforma financial statements
- Prepare a budget projecting future cash flows
- Include known changes and cost of goals quantified in previous step

2- Create the Financial Plan
- Identify feasible alternatives that will balance the budget subject to client constraints (values, lifestyle preferences, time, etc.)
  - Reduce expenses (based on norms)
  - Increase income (extra work, investment income)
  - Borrow (in line with capacity)
  - Liquidate assets
  - Adjust or prioritize goals

3 – Present the Plan and Service Offer

4- Secure the Client's Approval

1A.5 PLANNING – A PROBLEM-SOLVING EXERCISE

Formulating a financial plan is essentially a problem-solving exercise. When an advisor works with clients to create a plan to achieve their goals, what is being offered is a solution to a problem – getting financially from *here to there*. A problem-solving orientation is the opposite of a product-centred approach. It conveys a desire to collaborate in defining a mutual problem and seeking its solution. It communicates that the planner has no preconceived solution, attitude, or product to impose upon the client.

The advisor manages the process and moves the client towards a solution by engaging in ***sequential problem* solving**, that is, mathematically searching for a balance between a client's financial capacity and the cost of goals until an equilibrium has been found. Throughout the process, the advisor must encourage the client's feedback and adjust the plan in line with the client's preferences. This may require a number of iterations before it is accomplished.

> Mr. Fourdraine has a number of goals he wants to accomplish. He wants to buy a house, educate his children in the finest schools, travel, and upgrade to a better car.

In working with Mr. Fourdraine, the planner will complete a number of activities.

- Help specify the cost and timing of the client's goals.
- Gather personal information to construct a profile.

- Guide the client in preparing personal financial statements.
- Verify that the information is complete and correct.
- Analyze the client's financial statements to ascertain the client's financial capacity.
- Assess the client's investment and risk management strategies.
- Construct a proforma budget by modifying the last income statement to reflect any expected changes in revenues or expenses and the cost of goals as determined by time value analysis.
- Determine whether the client has the resources to achieve the designated goals.
- Seek the client's feedback and preferences to determine which, if any, adjustments need to be made in order to balance finances and goals.

A number of cycles will probably occur before Mr. Fourdraine's goals and financial resources are balanced. An identification of any shortfalls may force the client to reconsider his lifestyle preferences and to redefine his goals. This feedback will determine the future development of the plan. The final solution will be the one that allows the achievement of the client's goals using the institution's products and services, as recommended by the advisor.

1A.6 CONCLUSION

According to a recent survey by the Canadian Securities Administrators, 64% of respondents said it is important to have a formal written financial plan, but only 25% had one (Lamb, 2009). The gap can be explained in large part by either the lack of available financial planners, or people's inability to access the resources that are at hand. At any rate, there is a significant demand that planners have not yet captured. Financial planning is a *win-win* situation in which clients and planners receive mutual benefits. It is hoped that the knowledge and skills presented in this book will inspire advisors to move more into the planning realm for the sake of their clients and their own business.

KEY TERMS

Sequential problem solving.   Mathematically searching for a balance between a client's financial situation and the cost of goals until equilibrium has been found.

CHAPTER 2

THE FINANCIAL ADVISOR'S CHARACTER

2.0 INTRODUCTION

> Forty-seven percent of top executives and 76% of MBA graduates report that they would commit fraud if it would help increase their company's bottom lines. Other research finds that convicts in 11 American minimum security prisons had higher scores on ethical dilemma exams (insurance fraud) than MBAs (Jennings, 2003).

Chapter 1 suggested that character plays a major role in creating value for clients and in gaining their trust and loyalty. The essence of character is a personal moral code and ethical principles that guide behaviour. Any widely-publicized unethical act by an advisor will cast suspicion on all advisors. **The commitment to act ethically benefits customers, the profession, and financial institutions.**

Trust, a key issue for clients, comprises two aspects. First, the client must trust the advisor's technical competency. It is a major event for some clients to seek financial advice. In doing so, clients are asking for help with something of major importance to them: their wealth. Their wealth might represent a family legacy, the fruit of years of hard labour and sacrifice by former generations – a legacy they must guard and pass on. Wealth could also represent years of hard work and sacrifice by clients who, perhaps, have taken business risks to succeed. In asking for help to manage their wealth, clients may feel that they are putting their legacy or the tangible evidence of their business success at risk. Clients want to feel that the advisor is up to the task of helping them manage their wealth and all that it represents.

Second, the client must trust that the advisor will work in the client's best interests. Throughout the relationship, the advisor may learn significant personal facts about the client's life and finances. Clients will be reluctant to reveal personal information if they are unsure how the adviser will use that information. Clients may fear that in revealing personal information they are exposing themselves to the persuasive power of the advisor, who may manipulate them into buying products or services they don't need. The more clients trust that advisors will always act in their best interests, the more they will cooperate and reveal personal information.

The advisor's ethical character must be above reproach and deserving of the client's trust.

2.1 ETHICAL PRINCIPLES

Ethical principles that guide the selling of financial services derive from three sources: a country's legal system, standards prescribed by a profession, and internal institutional regulations. Ethical guidelines may apply to product features, the markets in which securities are traded, or the conduct of those who sell them. Most of the following discussion concerns the third element – the advisor's conduct.

> An advisor, in recalling a client interview, said, *My only concern was to convince the client at all costs to purchase the investment so I could have a financial reward.*

There is something fundamentally wrong with this advisor's attitude. The description of **fiduciary** duty that follows will help us understand the problem.

Much of an advisor's ethical obligations arise from the nature of the relationship between advisors and clients, who seek their help. If the client is dependent upon the advisor for advice or action because the client does not have the same depth of knowledge or access to markets, the advisor owes the client a **fiduciary** duty, that is, the advisor must act at all times in the client's best interests. The greater the client's reliance on the advisor, the greater the advisor's fiduciary duty. In a transaction service, the advisor must respond to the client's requests and execute them responsibly. In a counselling relationship, the advisor must understand the client's concerns, fairly portray the institution's products, and suggest only appropriate products and services. In a planning relationship, advisors must do all the above, plus design plans that fit their clients' circumstances and advance them towards their goals.

Based on this understanding of fiduciary duty, we can see that the advisor who made the statement above was committed to the wrong party's interests – self-interest instead of the client's interest.

> A client was extremely disappointed in the return from a time deposit. The financial advisor recommended the client switch to an investment account with higher returns and only a small increase in risk. The advisor also suggested adding money from the client's current account, which had an even lower rate of interest. The client asked the branch manager – a friend of the client's – for advice. The manager called the advisor and told him not to change the client's account, explaining: *Our client is totally satisfied with the return from the time deposit. The client has a current account in the branch that holds a large sum of money—in the millions—from which the branch makes a good profit.* The advisor got the message: a review of the client's accounts might tempt the client to shift money from the term deposit and current account into an investment account that was less lucrative for the branch.

Whose interests is the branch manager serving?

In addition to having a general fiduciary obligation to always act in clients' best interests, advisors must be aware of specific ethical principles that should direct their actions. These guidelines, when followed, help build the advisor's reputation as trustworthy and lessen the possibility that clients may charge that they have been misled, or their instructions mishandled.

2.1.1 The Advisor Must Exercise a *Duty of Care* and Avoid Negligence.

Advisors owe a **duty of care** to those who rely on their expertise. They must perform their obligations carefully and conscientiously. Advisors must not be careless in carrying out any tasks on behalf of their clients: orders must be executed on time and without error; advice must be based on sound financial principles; and analysis must be accurate, complete, and based on valid data.

This principle does not impose a duty on the advisor to always be right (especially where it cannot be reasonably foreseen that negative outcomes might occur), but it does impose the obligation to always take reasonable care in gathering information, performing analysis, reaching conclusions, making recommendations, and carrying out client instructions.

> Mr. Habash asked an advisor at Wadi International Bank to calculate the yearly amount he could withdraw from his portfolio over 20 years if he were to retire in eight years, at age 55. After doing some calculations, the advisor informed the client that he could withdraw $50,000 per year, if he invested $20,000 a year now, until age 55. Mr. Habash was pleased with the news because it meant that he did not have to save as much for the next eight years as he first thought. Based on this outlook, Mr. Habash resigned from his job and took a short-term job with less pay. Several months after he had resigned, the advisor at Wadi International informed him that he had reviewed the calculation and that an error had been made – the correct amount was $30,000 per year. Mr. Habash was very upset and threatened action against the advisor and the bank. He said that he would not have quit his job if he had known the correct figure was $30,000.

The advisor's calculations were wrong and the advisor should have known that Mr. Habash would base his subsequent action upon them. Furthermore, the advisor had been negligent in taking several months to inform Mr. Habash of the mistake. Mr. Habash suffered an economic loss as a result of the combined negligence.

One financial planner confessed in the author's presence: *the answer to a lot of retirement planning questions has to do with the time value of money and I really don't know anything about that.* With this admission, the planner and institution are heading towards trouble. One can imagine situations in which clients would be given wrong advice because the advisor did not know how to make the proper calculations.

The standard of care that is usually applied to an advisor's actions is that of other professionals of similar background and position. In determining whether an advisor acted negligently, the question will be asked: *What would another advisor with similar experience and training have done?*

In the past few years, the financial weakness of several major North American corporations was exposed while analysts were concurrently recommending the same corporations as strong *buys*. Investors, who were left with large losses, have made claims against the analysts' firms for their employees' negligence. It has become clear that the analysts had not been diligent and had not performed a thorough analysis of the investment quality of these corporations. In many cases, analysts simply passed on the opinions of others, or bowed to pressure from underwriting divisions within the firm.

2.1.2 The Advisor Must Avoid or Disclose Conflicts of Interest.

Two types of conflicts may arise for advisors. The first is the result of an advisor working for two parties, each on the opposite side of a transaction. The second is the result of the interests of the advisor (or the advisor's institution) conflicting with the interests of clients.

> The advisor suggested that the client invest in a gold import business. The client was unaware that the advisor's institution financed the gold importer.

In the above situation, the advisor has a conflict of interest. The advisor and the institution are involved in both sides of the transaction – financing the gold importer and recommending the import business as an investment. If the advisor believed this was a good investment for the client, the advisor should inform the client of the conflict, leaving the client free to decide about the investment on its own merits. Fully disclosing such information avoids the conflict.

> The client told the advisor that she was going to retire and sell her business. She also revealed her lowest acceptable selling price, which she was using for planning purposes. The advisor told a cousin about the conversation and encouraged the cousin to make an offer based on the advisor's knowledge of the client's *bottom line*.

The advisor is in a conflict of interest and has chosen to put personal and family loyalties ahead of loyalty to the client. The conflict could have been avoided by keeping the client's business valuation confidential.

Commissioned financial advisers have an inherent conflict of interest because the products that are best for the client are not always those that pay the highest commission. Revealing the fact that the advisor receives a commission is enough to avoid the problem.

> An advisor friend of mine says that when he recommends two possible funds as suitable investments, he always tells his clients that his commission on one is higher.

With this knowledge, the client can factor cost into the purchase decision. Incidentally, the advisor who reveals all reports that in the majority of cases, clients choose the higher-fee product because they think the advisor should *make something out of it too*. This anecdote coincides with the result of laboratory studies that indicate that clients follow the advice of advisers, who reveal their fees, to nearly the same extent as they would if they did not know about the amount of fees (quoted in Redhead, 2009).

It is a standard practice in North America for financial publications and broadcasts to require all investment commentators to reveal their positions in the securities they discus, in print or *on the air*. Such revelations allow audiences to better assess the quality of the information and the motivation behind its presentation.

2.1.3 The Advisor must not Misrepresent Product Features or Performance.
In brief, the advisor must not make false statements about products and services.

> An advisor received money from clients on the premise that he was investing their money in safe, fixed-income securities. In reality, he was putting their money in stock believing that he had the ability to make an excess return above the fixed rate. His strategy was to use his client's money to make a profit, pay his clients a portion of the profits to match the promised return, and keep the excess. His dishonesty came to light when a market *slump* rendered him unable to reimburse his clients.

Some misrepresentations may result from unintentional or careless acts. But when misrepresentation is a deliberate attempt to mislead, it is unethical. Some misrepresentations are more direct than the example above and are simply the making of false statements, for example: describing a fund as low risk, when it is high risk; portraying a service as costless, when there is a fee; promising a return based on the advisor's expectations rather than any guarantee; and describing a locked-in fund as liquid.

It is difficult to caution clients with unrealistic expectations. When competition is strong or the market has been bullish, clients may have high expectations about future performance, and advisors might succumb to the temptation to over-promise for fear of losing business. But over-promising – misleading – runs the significant risk of producing angry clients when actual results turn out to be less than indicated.

2.1.4 The Advisor Must Fully Inform Clients of all Relevant Facts.
This principle is closely related to the previous one. Clients must be free to decide to purchase financial products and services aware of all relevant information. If the advisor fails to mention significant information that might have influenced the client to have made different choices, the advisor has violated this principle. It is not enough to give a client an investment prospectus; the advisor must draw the client's attention to important details.

> The advisor always informs clients of the past returns of the institution's bond fund. But the advisor does not usually discuss the currency risk in the fund. The advisor's justification is this: *I don't want to confuse my clients, especially older clients, with this highly technical information.*

The advisor must inform clients about the total risk involved in all investments, including currency risk. The excuse that the technicalities might confuse clients is troublesome. The advisor must find a way to make clients understand and if they are not capable of understanding, then the advisor should question whether the investment is appropriate.

> **Mr. Montcrif:** *I want to be able to send my son to college when he grows up. So, I am looking for a good, safe investment for the long-term.*
> **Advisor**: *You should invest your money in the stock market and in technology stock in particular. Over the long-term they will outperform everything else. .*
> **Mr. Montcrif:** *Ok, take $100,000 and invest it for me.*
> Two years later, Mr. Montcrif discovered that he had lost 30% of his capital. Angrily, he called his advisor.
> **Mr. Montcrif:** *Why did you not tell me that these kinds of investments are risky and that I could lose my capital?*
> **Advisor**: *I am sure I did warn you about that.*
> (On reflection, the advisor is not as confident about what he said and even remembers assuming that Mr. Montcrif would know these things.)

This incident is unfortunate and could lead to difficulty for the advisor. There are a number of factors that created this situation. First, there was a problem with terminology: the advisor did not ask the client to clarify what he meant by a *good, safe* investment for the *long-term*. Secondly, the advisor did not fully inform the client about the risk – as the advisor admitted. And thirdly, the advisor raised unrealistic expectations by not fully informing the client about the fluctuating nature of equity returns, especially technology returns. The client was not fully informed of the risks when he invested.

2.1.5 The Advisor Must Maintain Confidentiality.

In the course of gathering information from clients, advisors become aware of highly personal facts. Advisors have the duty to maintain confidentiality about clients' personal and financial affairs and should not reveal that information to any third party without their clients' expressed consent. There is no surer way to erode trust than to betray confidentiality.

> The client owns a highly successful medical supply company. He asked an advisor how he should invest the proceeds if he decided to sell his business. The client informed the advisor that secrecy was very important because he did not want his employees to learn of his plans prematurely and seek other employment before he exited the business. To help with the investment side of the client's concerns, the advisor asked an investment specialist to accompany him on a visit to the client's business. The advisor introduced the client to the investment specialist, who quickly expressed his admiration for the client's skills in building up his business and wished him well on his retirement. The client immediately asked the advisor how the specialist knew about his retirement. The advisor confessed that he had told him. The client was upset and sternly reminded the advisor that he had shared his plans with him in confidence.

Keeping confidence includes not revealing client information to co-workers. In general, no personal information should be shared with others, outside or inside the institution without the client's consent. There is no faster way to erode a client's trust in an advisor than to divulge personal and confidential information to others. The strength of the bond of trust between advisors and clients is forged on the confidence of clients that all information they share will be kept secret. If that confidence is betrayed, advisors will cease to be honourable in the eyes of clients and relationships will be strained and broken.

2.1.6 The Advisor must not Exploit Client Weaknesses.

Advisors may have clients with less knowledge or bargaining power than they do. In these situations, the advisor may be tempted to take advantage of their clients' lesser positions to exert undue influence over their purchase decisions.

> The client, a retired shopkeeper, asked an investment advisor to recommend a portfolio of securities that would fund his retirement. He admitted that he did not know anything about investments and would follow the advisor's advice. The advisor offered to put together a *safe* and *secure* portfolio that would pay the client a fixed income and provide for growth. After a year, the client asked his nephew, who held an M.B.A., to review his portfolio. The nephew was alarmed and asked his uncle if he was familiar with the holdings in his portfolio. His uncle said he was not even though he had been concerned about its decreasing value.
>
> Using past statements, the nephew discovered that the advisor had put twenty-five percent of the portfolio in a low-interest account from which the client's regular income was paid. The rest of the money had been invested in a precious metal fund. The nephew concluded that the advisor had assumed that the risky investment in metals would grow substantially and its profits could be used to *top-up* the low-income account from which the monthly payments were made. It was obvious that the advisor earned a higher commission on the precious metal fund. The client was sure none of this had been explained to him.

It appears that the advisor had exploited the client's lack of knowledge and investment experience to sell him an unsuitable service – for the advisor's benefit. The strategy was far from *safe and secure*. The advisor used his position of influence to sell a product that clearly put his own interests ahead of his client's. (In addition, the principles of misrepresentation and full information were violated.)

When there is a difference of power between two parties and the party in the superior position uses that position to exploit the relative weakness of the other, it is said to be an **unconscionable** act. Unconscionable acts occur when there is a difference between the parties as the result of such things as mental capacity, health, education, or bargaining power, and an advisor takes advantage of this inequality to unduly influence the choices and actions of clients for the advisor's benefit.

Today, the structure of complex financial products and services often gives financial institutions and their employees, who understand these products, power over their less knowledgeable clients. The important features and risks of these products must be clearly explained or the products avoided as being unsuitable.

2.1.7 The Advisor Must Recommend Only Products that are Suited to a Client's Situation – The Know-Your-Client Rule.

> The about-to-retire client told the advisor that she needed monthly income to supplement a retirement pension. The advisor recommended a hedge fund.

Hedge funds do not provide monthly income; the advisor has recommended an inappropriate product. It did not fit the client's objectives and income needs.

In most financial advisory professions, a central regulating authority requires the *know-your-client* rule, which stipulates that advisors recommend only those products and services that match their clients' objectives, personal circumstances, risk profiles and levels of knowledge. In order to do this, advisors must have a current knowledge of their clients' financial status, goals, values, constraints, special circumstances, and risk tolerance. Volatile securities are not appropriate for clients who cannot afford to risk or do not have the psychological temperament to withstand the ups and downs of the marketplace. Complicated investments are not appropriate for clients who do not have the background to understand anything more than basic investments. Advisors should make sure that clients do not leave their presence in doubt about the features of the products and services purchased.

2.2 CONCLUSION

It could be argued that advisors should have sufficient integrity to put the interests of their clients above all else, but research has shown that despite good intentions, psychological biases can lead to unethical behaviour (Moore *et al*, 2006). These *self-serving biases* lead people to rationalize unethical behaviour in order to preserve their self-images as ethical people using such self-justifications as: *It is not my fault; it is what management wants* or *Clients make the final decision*. Self-serving biases may also lead advisors to appeal to a higher loyalty, with such justifications as: *I have a family to support*.

It is also possible that colleagues and management can undermine advisors' ethical standards by sending strong subliminal messages that conforming to the values and behaviours of those around them is highly desirable. An institutional culture that strongly emphasizes sales targets could be assumed to imply that sales volume is more important than other factors such as ethics.

These challenges to ethical action should not be taken to mean that acting ethically is an unrealistic goal, but they do warn that advisors need to be diligent and scrutinize their behaviour and motivations and intentionally choose to follow ethical principles.

KEY TERMS

Duty of care. Carrying out all tasks on behalf of clients carefully and conscientiously.

Fiduciary duty. The obligation financial advisors have to always act in the best interests of their clients.

Know your client. All products and services sold to clients must fit their financial and personal situations. Advisors should recommend only those products and services that match the client's objectives, personal circumstances, risk profile and level of knowledge.

Misrepresentation. Making false statements about products or services. Misleading clients so that they have a wrong understanding of the characteristics and features of a product or service

Negligence. Not performing tasks with care and not following clients' instructions or performing duties in a careful and diligent manner.

Unconscionable. An action that occurs when there is a difference of power between two parties and the party in the superior position uses that position to exploit the relative weakness of the other.

MODULE II

EFFECTIVE COMMUNICATION SKILLS

CHAPTER 3

THE COMMUNICATION PROCESS

3.0 INTRODUCTION

> **Advisor:** (Speaking to a client.) *Our bank has a new product that will give you flexibility and safety, and with only a bit more risk. It keeps your options open and makes it possible to take advantage of the market when it starts to go up.*
> **Client:** *Did you say options are safe? I don't want anything to do with them.*

In the above incident there is a *communication problem*. But what is a *communication problem*? What is the exact difficulty? After reading this chapter, you should be able to describe in some detail the component activities of communication between people and the specific problems that hinder it and the skills that improve it.

Here are a few reasons why excellent communication skills are so important for a financial advisor:

- to gain a complete and accurate understanding of clients' situations
- to clearly explain products and services and how they meet clients' needs
- to negotiate satisfactory financial plans with clients
- to deal with client complaints
- to clear up misunderstandings
- to resolve conflicts

There is a strong link between communication skills and effective client relationships. The US Department of Labor Skills Analysis has hundreds of occupations in its database and identifies and rates the relative importance of the basic competencies required for various jobs. For financial advisors, it has rated Oral Comprehension, which it defines as the ability to listen to and understand information and ideas presented through spoken words and sentences, and Oral Expression, which it defines as the ability to communicate information and ideas in speaking so others will understand, as the two most important abilities required of financial advisors (U.S. Department of Labor, 2010a).

On-the-job communication is often cited as the critical ability financial advisors must have to be successful. And research has shown that the greatest degree of customer dissatisfaction with financial institutions is poor communication between clients and financial representatives, especially in the understanding of clients' needs and the clear presentation of product information. The improvement of communication skills is not just a good idea, it is essential for creating customer satisfaction.

Communication comes from the Latin word *communis,* meaning commonness; based on this derivation, we can describe communication as the process of establishing a commonness or oneness of thought between people. Unfortunately, reality is often different from the ideal, and oneness of thought is not always achieved. We begin with an explanation of the dynamics of communication, how it should occur, what can go wrong, and how it can be improved.

3.1 THE COMMUNICATION MODEL

The way communication occurs can be compared to the working of a telephone with a sender, the transmission of a signal, and a receiver. The sender encodes a message, transmits it through a channel, and then the receiver decodes and responds to it. Figure 3.1 depicts the components and shows how they interrelate. Let us work our way through the model.

Figure 3.1
The Communication Model

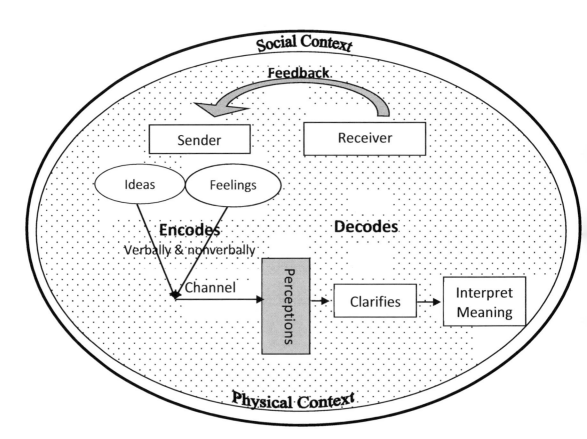

3.1.1 The Sender

The communication process begins when a sender transmits an idea or a feeling, or both, to a receiver. (This transmission may be intentional or unintentional.) Most messages are a blend of ideas and feelings, encoded verbally and non-verbally. For example, if a client says, *I need advice on how to get good investment returns because I don't want to have to worry about money when I retire,* the client is making a request, stating a desire, and expressing feelings of insecurity. If the client says, *I make about $100,000 a year and I want this same yearly income in retirement,* the client is giving information about current income and future goals. If a customer says, *I'm not sure if we can take a vacation and save money to help my disabled granddaughter,* the client is expressing a conflict between two important objectives: travel and a granddaughter's welfare. The client is also expressing anxiety about the difficulty of accomplishing both goals with limited resources. A good listener will pick up both the feeling – worry – and the informational aspects of the message – limited financial resources.

3.1.2 Encoding the Message

In order to communicate a message, the sender must *encode* it or *package* it in symbols. As you read this book, you are looking at the symbols (written words and diagrams) that have been chosen to encode the ideas that were in the author's mind.

Human language is made up of a series of symbols that have evolved over time. Symbols vary from one language to another, and also from one era to another. English is not spoken the way it was 500 years ago, or even twenty years ago. New words appear as a result of technological and societal change. English, as with other languages, is spoken differently in various parts of the world, and even within regions of the same country. For example, a *lift* in North America can mean a car ride, while in England, it is an elevator. The English dramatist George Bernard Shaw is reported to have said, *England and America are two countries separated by the same language.*

At a meeting I attended recently regarding technological changes, the conversation was filled with words such as: *web*, *net*, *notebooks*, *terminals*, and *servers*. All these words have meanings that are different from what they were 20 or even 10 years ago. The conversation was also filled with words that did not even exist twenty years ago: *megabytes*, *ROM*, *download*, and *motherboards*.

Sometimes new words or terms are invented to replace ones that have upsetting overtones or evoke negative perceptions. President George W. Bush asked congress for $25 billion, not to carry on the Iraq war, but for a *Freedom Fund*. In the 1980s, *junk bonds* were common. The term *high yield bond* is now used. *Third world* debt has been replaced by *emerging market* debt. Words have power.

Those who study language describe three particular problems with words that can lead to communication difficulties: **semantics**, **syntax**, and ***pragmatics***.

3.1.2.1 Semantics. *Semantics* is the relationship between objects or ideas, and the symbols used to represent them. Most people call a monitor and a keyboard linked through a processing unit a *computer*, but why isn't it called a *ropart*, for instance? The reason is that the word *computer* has a history and there is agreement that the word will represent the configuration of hardware we are talking about. In any language there is general agreement as to the words that go with particular objects or concepts, and any violation of the rules can result in miscommunication. This is a particular problem for people learning another language.

There are three semantic problems that cause particular difficulty.

1. The use of a *wrong* word. This can happen as the result of a *slip-of-the-tongue* (a mistake) by the speaker or as a result of the speaker's lack of familiarity with the vocabulary, as seen in the following examples.

> As the client left the advisor's office, the advisor said: *Thank you for coming in today. I* **evaluate** *your business.* The client left the office not knowing exactly what the advisor meant. He thought he probably meant *value*.

> The client admitted he did not know much about investments, but he was sure he did not want to invest in any *haj* funds. The advisor thought the client was probably referring to *hedge* funds, which he had just read something about.

2. The use of a correct word, but with a different meaning for each party.

> The client told the advisor he was interested only in *safe* investments.

The word *safe* is a good word and correct in this context, but it could mean something different to the client and to the advisor. To the client, it could mean he does not want to invest in any equities; to the advisor, it could mean that the client is interested in only *blue-chip* equities. Without a discussion of what *safe* means, a serious misunderstanding could occur.

During the BP oil spill crisis in the Gulf of Mexico, BP Chairman, Carl-Henric Svanberg made an unfortunate mistake in June of 2010 when he insisted the company cared about the *small people* affected by the oil spill. In the United States, the phrase *small people* would be taken as a derogatory remark, while to the Swedish Svanberg, it might have been an attempt to be sympathetic to the ordinary person.

3. The use of a correct word that is unfamiliar to the receiver.

> The advisor continued the presentation: *as you can see from this risk-return space, the correlation between the two assets is low to negative.*

The advisor's words may be correctly chosen, but if the client is not familiar with highly technical terms such as *risk-return space,* and *correlation*, the client will not understand. This is a problem with ***jargon***. Financial and investment advisors have particular difficulty with jargon because technical terms are a standard part of their world – as they are for any professional – and most clients are usually not familiar with that world. When advisors use jargon, clients can become lost and lose interest or make incorrect assumptions.

3.1.2.2 Syntax. The order of words in a sentence conveys a particular meaning. If a client says, ***some*** *of my investments are with that institution,* it is different from saying, *my investments are with* ***some*** *institution.* In the first case, only part of the client's investments is under management by that institution. In the second case, all of the client's investments are held by an unnamed institution. By merely changing the order of the words in the sentence, a new meaning is created. The order of words and the rules applying to the order of words in a sentence is called ***syntax***.

Problems with syntax can result in sentences that are vague and difficult to understand.

An advisor told a client: *call me when you leave London at home.*

The advisor's words might have caused the client momentary hesitation. It is certain the advisor meant: *Call me at home, when you leave London.* The meaning of the following newspaper headline is not as easy to interpret: *Complaints of discrimination by the four women...* Who made the complaints – the four women or those who were affected by the four women's behaviour? Miscommunication can occur when the intention of the sender's words are not clear from sentence construction.

3.1.2.3 Pragmatics. Words may have different meanings in different contexts. This situation is called ***pragmatics***. An advisor told a co-worker about difficulty in meeting a target. The advisor also made the same remark to a friend when they were on a rifle practice range. The meaning of *target* depends upon the context, or setting, in which the word is spoken. We know this is also true with words such as *net, web,* and *mouse.* The meaning of these words has been greatly expanded during the last decade. Pragmatics makes doing crossword puzzles interesting – the clue can be interpreted from different contexts. For example, if the clue says *ring,* is it a piece of jewellery, or a boxing arena, or the noise a telephone makes, or...? Or how about the clue *cell wall?* Is that a prison cell, or a biological cell?

The major encoding problems that financial advisors need to be concerned about involve semantics and syntax – pragmatics is less of a problem.

3.1.3 Channels and Media

The sender selects the symbols that will best convey the message (encoding), and then chooses the channel and medium by which to transmit the message. Channels are oral, written and nonverbal, and media are the available options within each channel. For example, the sender may choose a written channel to send a message and then must decide amongst the media options such as a written letter, a fax, or an e-mail. Through channels, feelings and ideas are transmitted to the receiver. Channels and media can be judged by their appropriateness, effectiveness, and information richness.

Some channels and media are too impersonal for highly personal or confidential information. One customer of a financial institution severed his relationship with the institution after receiving notice by e-mail that his loan payment was overdue and the principal was in danger of being called. He felt his long and positive relationship with the bank entitled him to a more direct notification and a personal conversation.

It would be highly ineffective to fax a brochure that includes important coloured charts to a client. Neither is it a good use of time to read a table of numbers over the phone when it could be sent as an e-mail attachment. Huge volumes of data are not communicated by voice-to-voice methods because the high degree of memory required of the receiver.

Oops – Wrong Channel

Dale Talon was demoted from general manager…of the National Hockey League's (NHL) Chicago Blackhawks after an administrative… [error that] cost the team millions of dollars. According to league rules, teams must fax or courier contract offers to certain free agent players before July 1 in order to retain their rights. The Hawks instead mailed their offers to several players and they didn't arrive until after the deadline. The NHL's Players' Association claimed they should be declared free agents, and thus entitled to much larger contracts. The Hawks… [signed the players in question] for over $3 million per season. But if they'd just used their fax machine and met the deadline, the team likely could've signed both players for around $1.7 million combined (Macleans Magazine, 2009).

Daft and Lengel (1984) have rated media in reference to their *information richness*. They suggest that the richest source of transmission is a face-to-face conversation because of audio and visual activity, nonverbal and verbal languages occurring simultaneously, and immediate and on-going feedback to the sender. An informational-rich channel allows for the transmission of emotions as well as ideas. If a person likes to judge another person's state of mind and feelings by reading nonverbal cues, then a face-to-face conversation is the best. Electronic means are not as *rich* and are best for communicating ideas. A public address system set to *low* during *a* presentation, sitting at a distance from a speaker with a quiet voice, a fax machine low on toner, and a telephone line plagued by interference are all potential barriers to effective communication. Choosing the proper channel and medium to convey a message is an important component of successful communication.

3.1.4 Perceptual Filters

In Figure 3.1 the *perceptions* box intermediates between the encoding and decoding process. Perceptions have the potential to filter and distort the intended message, or even block it.

(Chapter 4 discusses perceptions more thoroughly.) Have you ever reacted too strongly to a person's message, only to have the sender tell you that what you thought you heard was not what was meant? Something got in the way of your understanding the message. The problem may have been with perceptual filters.

Messages that contain disturbing news, contradictory opinions, or distressing emotions may be blocked or re-worked by the receiver's perceptual system. I recently observed two of my friends talking to each other. Unfortunately, one of them does not like the other. To me, his negative attitude was obvious in his tone and body language. But it was not obvious to the other person. For some reason, he blocked out the sender's negativity.

3.1.5 The Receiver – Decoding the Message

The receiver must work to *decode* the message. Decoding involves two processes:

1. Making sure the message is understood
2. Determining the message's meaning and importance to the receiver

Before reacting to a message, the receiver must first understand it. Understanding involves assessing the message's **clarity** and **completeness**. If a client says to an advisor, *I am interested in the arrangement we talked about last time,* the advisor will not necessarily understand what the client is referring to – the client's statement is vague. The advisor should ask for clarification: *Which arrangement is that?* If another client says, *I came in to talk about…* and before he finishes his sentence, he begins to cough; the advisor will likely ask him to repeat what he said. Problems created for receivers may originate with senders who speak too softly, too fast, or violate semantic or syntactic rules. As the aging process affects my hearing and rate of comprehension, one of my frustrations is being served over the telephone by fast-talking service representatives whom I cannot understand. My usual coping strategy is to respond with an equally fast, or faster, rate of speech. My tactic usually results in slowing down the representative.

If a message is not understood, the receiver can send the message *back* for clarification. Sometimes, however, the receiver might decide to carry on and act as if the message were understood, hoping it will not matter and that its meaning will become clear as the conversation proceeds, or to make **inferences** and guess what was said. These are dangerous strategies and can result in misunderstanding or embarrassment. The possibilities are pictured in Figure 3.2.

Figure 3.2
Is the Message Understood?

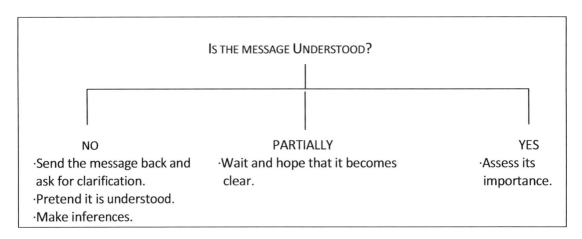

A former student telephoned me and asked for a letter of reference He introduced himself at the beginning of the conversation, but I didn't hear his name, even though I remembered him. I hoped he would repeat his name as we talked or that the conversation would prompt my recall. Unfortunately, by the time I agreed to write the letter, I still could not remember his name. Eventually, I had to admit, with some embarrassment, that I had not fully heard his name.

After having placed a hotel wake-up call, the operator phoned me back and asked, *Was that 6-1-5 for the wake-up call?* I was grateful that the operator asked for clarification and did not guess.

Making inferences can be troublesome. When the complete message has not been received, the receiver may be tempted to fill in the missing parts. The advisor should be aware that when making inferences and *filling in gaps,* the message intended and the message received may be very different. A client who expresses the need for income may be understood to mean income from *fixed* investments rather than what was really intended - *monthly* income.

Once the message is understood, the receiver can decide on its meaning and importance. The possibilities are presented in Figure 3.3. ***FIRE*** – a clear message to those in a crowded room – will be judged as highly important and acted upon immediately. A negative return in my latest investment report is highly relevant to me and will get my immediate attention, whereas my computer desk-top service that notifies me that it is *Monday*, especially if I already know, is inconsequential.

Figure 3.3
Is the Message Important?

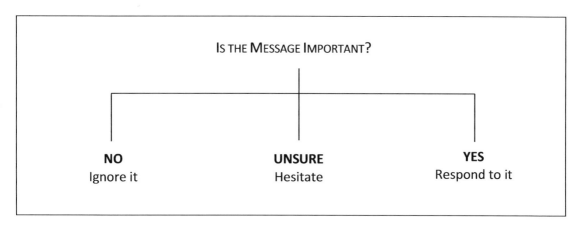

A message may be judged as highly important because of its implications for such things as finances, social standing, vocation, or security. A receiver is likely to respond to messages that are perceived to be highly relevant and important. This is why the financial advisor in presenting a financial offer to a client, should express it in terms that the client is likely to find relevant and important. If the advisor says to the client, *I know a way for you to have the vacation and help your granddaughter*, the advisor will have the client's attention. Simple, short directives are effective: *I would like you to sit down and consider this suggestion. It could help you achieve your goals.*

On the other hand, the message will be ignored if the receiver decides the message is unimportant. If the message's importance is not certain, the receiver may hesitate and wait for further information to judge its relevance.

Once the message is understood and the receiver judges its meaning, the receiver may respond. The arrow going back from receiver to sender in Figure 3.1 indicates the *feedback loop* and that the communication process is not just one-directional. In a discussion, the sender and the receiver alternate roles.

3.1.6 Feedback
The message intended by the sender is not always received in pristine form by the receiver for reasons we have already considered, therefore, securing feedback is critical to good communication.

During a jetliner hijacking in New York City, the head of the negotiation team for the New York Police Department said the key to starting negotiations with the hijacker was obtaining an agreement that the hijacker would let the negotiator know if he said anything that the hijacker disagreed with or upset him.

Knowing how the receiver responds to the sender's message is critical for the sender who can then, if necessary, make adjustments to assure that there are no misunderstandings. If the receiver does not offer feedback, the sender will have to encourage the receiver to indicate whether the message was clear. Soliciting feedback is vital for giving the advisor confidence that the client has understood. The relationship between the client and the advisor is best pictured as two people walking down a road, side-by-side, towards a common objective: achievement of the client's goals. The advisor does not want to be too far ahead, or too far behind, the client. Feedback is critical for letting the advisor know just where they are in relation to one another and whether to adjust the pace.

3.1.7 Physical Context

Face-to-face communication takes place in a physical setting, as indicated in the inner oval in Figure 3.1. This setting can either facilitate or hinder communication. In a financial institution, the physical context could be a private office with comfortable seating or it could be in a larger open area with little privacy. The attributes of the physical context including its physical comfort and the number of distractions, affect the quality of the conversation.

Noise is anything that distorts or interferes with the transmission and reception of a message in the physical context. (Some definitions of noise expand the meaning to include internal distractions.) In Figure 3.1 noise is depicted by the dotted field surrounding the communication process. Noise includes disruptive near-by conversations, ringing telephones, and street traffic. Noise can degrade the quality of the message to the point where it loses its clarity, distracts the receiver's attention, or interferes with the receiver's understanding. By neglecting to control for noise, the advisor may become distracted, only partially hear the client's words, or appear uninterested. When the advisor's telephone is not set to take messages, there is the risk of a major irritant disrupting the flow of the conversation, and when the advisor answers the telephone, a strong message is communicated to the client that the person on the other end of the conversation is more important than the client sitting in front of the advisor, who made the effort to visit the advisor's office.

When there is a choice, advisors may prefer to meet clients in their homes or at their places of business, or in the advisor's own office. Such things as freedom from distraction, control over the environment, control of the agenda, a desire to see clients in their own *habitat*, convenience, and proximity to support resources will influence the advisor's preference.

In the physical context, personal space has a significant influence on communication. We have our **comfort zones**, or appropriate distances for interaction. Anthropologist, Edward T. Hall (1966), identified four distance zones regulating interpersonal interactions. The zones and accompanying distance for Northern North Americans are:

- **Intimate** distance, used for giving comfort and protection – 0 to 18 inches (0 to 45 centimetres)

- **Personal** distance, used for interactions with friends or acquaintances – 18 inches to 4 feet (45 centimetres to 1.25 metres)
- **Social** distance, the zone used for business and casual social interactions – 4 feet to 11.5 feet (1.25 to 3.5 metres)
- **Public** distance, used for impersonal and formal interactions – more than 11.5 feet (3.5 metres)

Canadians and citizens of the United States do not like to have their space and comfort zones invaded. It would not be appropriate for the advisor to intrude into the client's intimate zone, or even into the personal zone, unless the advisor and client are close friends. Experts in **proxemics** (the study of social distances and communication) say that when a sales person gets closer than a metre, the customer will feel crowded. A distance of 1.2 to 1.5 metres is appropriate for most client-advisor conversations and close enough for an advisor to indicate interest without intruding into the client's personal zone. Advisors may feel it is appropriate at times to move closer to clients, such as when they want to reduce the status differentials or when the advisor wants to convey empathy about a client's personal circumstances. To simply come out from behind a desk and sit in a near-by chair may convey more than words are able.

The advisor has to be sensitive to the different norms of other cultures. While North Americans prize their individual space; Latin Americans tend to be more comfortable conversing within a closer proximity. It is imperative for financial services professionals who work in multicultural contexts to be sensitive to such differences.

3.1.8 Social Context
The outer oval of Figure 3.1 indicates that communication occurs in a social setting or within a web of relationships. The relationship between the sender and receiver and the social context influence the degree of formality in the vocabulary and casualness of the conversation. We don't use the same vocabulary when we talk to our neighbour as we do when we talk to the president of a large corporation. The way we relate to a superior during a game of golf may be more relaxed and informal than it would be in an office environment. The nature of the relationship and the setting affects the choice of words and the flow of the conversation.

When we talk with others, we tend to make judgements about our relative status. We are much more comfortable talking to our peers than those we judge to be our superiors. Cues to how formal a social context should be are often given by **status differentials** and the parties' reaction to them. Status differentials are indicators of social position and rank exhibited by such things as titles, attire, degrees, experience, and wealth. These status differentials may influence how formal or informal a conversation will be.

Some people who enter a financial institution are intimidated and anxious. Clients hope for something important from the advisor such as advice, credit, or good investment returns, but they may feel unsure about the advisor's willingness or ability to provide these. Clients may also feel inadequate and unsure about their knowledge in relation to the perceived expertise of the advisor. Although clients like to feel they are talking to knowledgeable advisors, anything that reinforces status differentials has the possibility of hindering the conversation. Advisors should recognize the signs that clients may feel uncomfortable. Differences can be minimized as the advisor moves out from behind the desk, and sets a warm and congenial atmosphere.

> When a client entered a financial institution to purchase an investment fund, the service representative directed the client to the manager. The representative made it clear that the manager was very busy and implied that if the client were lucky, the manager might have some time. Upon entering the manager's office, the client felt anxious and unsure about being there.

On the other hand, some customers value the presence of status differentials, such as a large office, a huge desk, wood panelling, or fine clothing, because these make them feel confident they are talking to an authority. However, status will not compensate for any service deficiencies. A wealthy gentleman told me that his advisor was a very important man with lots of experience and an impressive client list, but he still did not like the fact that he sent him a proposed restructured portfolio with a *take-it-or-leave-it* attitude and did not offer to discuss it with him.

3.2 Effective Communication

Good relationships are built upon excellent communication skills; therefore, it is critical that advisors understand the basics of effective communication.

> An elderly client told the financial advisor that the advisor had made a remark during their last conversation that had upset him greatly. The advisor felt embarrassed and asked the client for details. The elderly gentleman said he did not appreciate being told that he was a *miser* (tight with money). The advisor was stunned. He did not remember calling the client a *miser*, nor would he ever do something like that. He told the client that he was sorry for the misunderstanding, but he remembered that during the conversation he had complimented the client on a decision the advisor thought was a *wiser* thing to do than most clients would have done. The client was convinced he had heard the word *miser* and was still offended.

How did this miscommunication occur? Was the problem with the sender? Did he make a slip and say *miser*? Did he not pronounce the word *wiser* clearly? Or was the problem with the receiver? Does the client have a hearing problem? Or was he distracted by internal thoughts at that time and not fully concentrating? Or did noise interfere with the message? Actually, the advisor recalled construction work outside the office during their last meeting. Messages are encoded not only with words, but also with gestures, tones, eye movements, and other nonverbal expressions. If the receiver is not tuned-in to reading nonverbal language, important parts of a message may be missed. (Chapter 5 discusses nonverbal communication.)

There are many places where miscommunication can be created. It is a wonder that most messages are successfully transmitted and received. The following are offered as some guidelines for effective communication.

3.2.1 The Sender - Sending Clear Messages

There are several things the sender can do to help ensure that the message is received as intended.

- Use an appropriate channel.
- Speak clearly and avoid jargon.
- Send simple messages. Break complex ideas into simple ones that the receiver has time to digest.
- Clearly pronounce words. As my grandmother continually reminded me: it is not the volume that counts, but the clarity of the words.
- Adopt an un-hurried pace in explaining technical matters, especially to those with little or no knowledge of the subject. If it becomes apparent that the client has a greater capacity to understand than first assumed, the pace of the discussion can be increased.
- With clients whose native language is not English, choose basic words, use short sentences, and pause frequently.
- Ask for feedback. Frequently ask clients if they have understood or have any questions about what has been said.

> The investment advisor thought he heard the client say: *Buy one thousand shares of IBM for my account*. What the client actually said was: *Buy one thousand shares of IB**N***. The Client lost several thousands of dollars on the transaction.

In critical matters such as order taking, make sure the message has been accurately understood.

3.2.2 The Receiver – Listen Carefully

- Concentrate on the message.
- Put aside internal distractions that compete for your attention.
- Offer feedback and indicate when the message has not been clearly understood.
- Listen for the meaning not only in the words, but also in the nonverbal parts of the message. A good listener looks for and tries to interpret the meaning of the sender's facial expressions, eye movements, gestures, and posture (more on this in Chapter 5).
- Look for both the content and feeling components of messages. Both strands are woven together and skill is required to identify each. For complete communication, the receiver must be aware of and acknowledge the emotion as well as the content of the message. By doing so, a strong indication is given that the advisor is interested in understanding the client's complete concerns. Chapter 6 reveals how this action is an integral part of the important activity of active listening.

3.3 CONCLUSION

Clear communication, as has been indicated in several places is critical for good client relationships and client satisfaction. This chapter has presented the basics of the communication process with the hope that it will be used to gain insight into any current problems you may face and provide more tools for your *kit bag* to utilize at the opportune time. In subsequent chapters, we will delve deeper into the competencies advisors require to effectively send and receive messages.

Bob Elliott and Ray Goulding comprised the much-loved radio comedy team of *Bob and Ray* that broadcast over United States' radio stations from the 1950s to the 1980s. One of their classic routines – the *Komodo Dragon* – in which the interviewer's dreadful listening skills are displayed, can be found at the following Internet site (as of August, 2010): http://www.youtube.com/watch?v=uM86QCvPDHE.

KEY TERMS

Comfort zones. Appropriate distances for senders and receivers to be apart when communicating. The distance depends on the nature of the event and the relationship between the sender and the receiver.

Communication channel. The means by which a message is sent – oral, written, or nonverbal.

Communication media. The method within a channel chosen to send a message.

Encoding. The translation of a message into symbols (written, spoken, nonverbal) so that it can be transmitted to a receiver.

Decoding. The job of the receiver to understand and decide upon the meaning of a message.

Inference. Filling in parts of a message with guesses when the receiver has not heard the complete message.

Information-rich channel. Communication channels that allow for the passing of more than words. Nonverbal messages and visual activity can be communicated, and feedback to the sender is immediate and on-going.

Noise. Anything that distorts or interferes with the transmission and reception of a message in the physical context.

Physical context. The physical setting in which a face-to-face conversation occurs.

Pragmatics. The different meaning words take on depending on the context.

Proxemics. The study of physical distances between people while they are communicating.

Semantics. The relationship between symbols and what they represent.

Social context. The social setting or web of relationships within which a conversation occurs. It is one factor that influences the degree of formality in the vocabulary and casualness of the conversation.

Status differentials. Indicators of social position and rank exhibited by such things as titles, attire, experience, and wealth. They influence the conversation's degree of formality.

Syntax. The order of words in a sentence and the rules applying to the order.

CHAPTER 4

PERCEPTIONS

4.0 PERCEPTIONS AND THE PERCEPTUAL PROCESS

> A delicatessen operator performed an experiment with some cheese. He cut two large wedges from the same block and placed them in his showcase. One wedge he labelled *Imported English Cheddar*, and the other, *Smelly Cheese*. The *Imported English*, at twice the price, far outsold the *Smelly* cheese.

Figure 3.1 in Chapter 3 indicated that perceptions influence how messages are understood. The example above indicates that our perceptions also influence our judgements. The formation of perceptions and the injection of layers of perceptions between the message that was intended and the one that was received is a complex cognitive process, but one that is necessary to understand in order to deepen our knowledge of the communication process and the formation of relationships. In this chapter, we will discuss the origins of perceptions, their interaction with information, their potential to damage relationships, and how they can be managed.

Perception is not reality. Some philosophers and psychologists believe that the real, objective world cannot be known. They argue that all we ever know is our *perception* of reality. This explains why the same situation is sometimes understood differently by different people. For example, to some, classical music is dull and boring, while for others it is a delight with its resonating tones, lofty themes, and the virtuosity of its performers. Who is right? It is a matter of perception. A customer may not be interested in a particular investment because it is too *risky*. But to the advisor who recommended it, it is *safe* because it adds diversification to the client's portfolio. Two friends conduct business with the same financial advisor, but one finds the advisor friendly and accommodating while the other finds the advisor abrupt and unsympathetic. Is the advisor really two different people, or is this a matter of two people having different perceptions?

4.1 FUNCTIONS OF THE PERCEPTUAL PROCESS

In general, perceptions are the way we make sense of our experiences of the world. Humans are *sense-making* beings. Perceptions are the result of our minds interpreting the messages our senses receive to provide order and meaning. We do not like ambiguity or mental disorder. We want to understand what our senses hear, see, and experience. To feel in control, we want to categorize and give meaning to our experiences. Bombarded constantly by large quantities of information and sensory stimuli, our perceptual system keeps us from being overwhelmed by selecting and formulating pieces of information into patterns to which we give meaning. But perceptions can also interfere with our understanding of what is *real*. Perceptions, therefore, both help and hinder our communication and relationships.

Our perceptual system helps us deal with information by **selecting**, **organizing** and **labelling** it. Figure 4.1 illustrates the relationship amongst these functions.

Figure 4.1
Functions of the Perceptual System

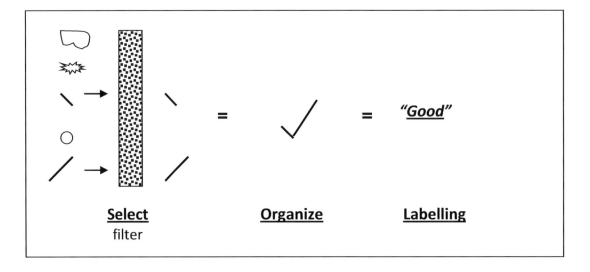

4.1.1 Selecting
In Figure 4.1 only the "╱" and "╲" figures are selected and allowed to pass into awareness. The other information is filtered out.

Much of the information presented to us is screened out because we cannot deal with everything our senses pick up. It is said that the eye can receive about 5 billion bits of information per second, but the brain can process only about 500 bits per second. Fortunately, when our perceptual system is working well, it screens out a lot of irrelevant information. Imagine trying to read and understand this book while listening to the news on TV, or to your spouse who has some important news to share. (It is interesting how young people seem to be more able to *multi-task* their attention.) Not all information gets through to us. Some will move to the *foreground* of our consciousness, while other information will be assigned to the *background*. (The field of Gestalt psychology has much to say about this.) Depending on our needs, our attention continually cycles between information in the foreground and information in the background. A call to dinner will certainly come to the foreground as more important than anything we are reading, which will then be relocated to the background of our awareness.

Journalist Thomas Friedman, reporting on the work of the American psychologist Richard Day who taught at the American University in Beirut, says that Day discovered that amongst his students those who best withstood the 1982 Israeli invasion of Beirut were in the best physical and mental health and thus able to view their environment *selectively*. They learned how to block out anything going on around them that was not under their own control and to focus instead on their immediate environment and the things they could control. This prevented *system overload* (Friedman, 1990, p.38).

Just like e-mail filters, our perceptual system does a wonderful job of blocking out extraneous information so that we can concentrate on relevant information, but why do we select some stimuli and not others?

We select information that relates to our **interests**. After a hard day at work, you sit in your favourite chair in front of the television just before you go to bed. While dozing, a financial news report comments on the erratic movement of shares of a company you bought that day for a major client's account. It is certain that your attention will be fully awakened.

We pay attention to stimuli that relate to our physical and psychological needs. Most people entering a bank would not notice the size of doorways, the presence of raised thresholds, the width of aisles, and the height of counter tops, but if you are in a wheelchair you will notice because these things are barriers that must be navigated over, through, and around.

Other internal factors affect the screening process. Physical and cognitive impairments and ingested chemicals can affect our receptivity to stimuli. Psychological moods can alter our perceptions. External characteristics of the stimuli also influence our attention. Advertisers buy large ads in publications and use colour or shading purposely to ensure they attract readers' attentions. (The use of colour will not get my attention because my physical capacity limits my perception of colour – I am *colour-blind*.)

There is a downside to the selection process: we have a tendency to screen out information or stimuli that do not fit with what we already know and believe. If a client is convinced that hedge funds are risky, the client may block out any information that presents the other side of the case. This saves the client from having to adjust any beliefs. We like stability in our beliefs. We don't like to change them and we resist other people's attempts to change them. Unfortunately, this can make us rigid when we need to be open-minded.

4.1.2 Organizing
In Figure 4.1 the "/" and the " \" symbols were organized to form "✓", a checkmark. The information that we do not screen out, we attempt to organize in a meaningful way so that we can make use of it. We like mental order. Despite our various domestic housekeeping abilities, we all want to be neat mental housekeepers and keep all thoughts, ideas, and perceptual fragments tidy in our minds. We want to organize our experiences and understand them. Author Nissam Taleb (2007), in commenting on brain processes that use information to reach conclusions, says, *Even from an anatomical perspective, it is impossible for our brain to see anything in raw form without some interpretation*. He goes on to say, *There appears to be a sense-making organ in us (p.65).*

If you explain the symptoms of your ailment to your doctor, your doctor will listen and then suggest what it all indicates. A rash on your arms, upset stomach, and dryness of the mouth – this may all indicate an allergic reaction to a prescribed medication. While listening to you, your doctor was organizing your symptoms into a diagnosis.

As advisors listen to clients and organize information into conclusions about their concerns, opportunities may result. For example, after listening to a client talk about his family's situation and his business, the advisor might conclude that a main concern for the client is succession planning and the future of his business. This conclusion, if verified, could be the basis for future planning discussions. But problems can occur when we organize information incorrectly and draw the wrong conclusions.

> After having talked to the client for a long time, the advisor concluded that the client was not interested in equities and it would be a formidable challenge to open the client's mind to the ability of equities to reduce risk in the client's overall portfolio. Fortunately, the advisor verified this perception with the client, and the client strongly denied that equities were a problem and affirmed openness to their use. The advisor realized that for some reason the client's true beliefs had been missed.

4.1.2.1 Inferences. Figure 3.2 revealed that when a message is not clearly understood, the receiver may pretend it is clear. Without all the relevant facts, the wrong conclusions may be drawn. Rather than seek the missing information, the receiver might simply fill in the missing parts and make inferences and assumptions about the complete message. This tendency to fill in the gaps allows us to read half-lit signs at night, but it can create problems if we fill the gaps with the wrong information.

> After an advisor presented an investment to a client, the advisor asked the client for a reaction. The client said, *yes, that looks like a good product.* The advisor assumed the client was ready to invest in the product and reached for the appropriate forms. However, when the advisor asked the client to sign the papers, the client drew back, held up a hand, and said, *What are you doing? I said it was a good product, but not that it is right for me. I have no interest in it. You bankers are all the same and can't wait to close the deal.*

In the above example, the advisor had eagerly filled in the missing thoughts of the client and had prematurely inferred that just because the client thought the product was good, he wanted to invest in it. The advisor had gotten too far ahead of the client and had provoked the client's annoyance and a particular stereotype of bankers.

4.1.3 Labelling

In Figure 4.1, the ✓ checkmark was interpreted as a *good* thing. When you receive a report back from a superior or instructor, your eyes quickly scan the document to see if there are "✓s" or "Xs" scribbled on it. The prevalence of one over the other will cause you either comfort or distress. Based on your experience, you probably have labelled, "✓s" as *good* and "Xs" as *bad*. Some public school systems have adopted a policy that prohibits teachers from using red ink when they mark student assignments. Apparently, some students (and their parents) find red marks on their assignments distressful and suggestive of inadequacy.

After we have screened out irrelevant information and organized the most important information into a meaningful pattern, we make judgements about its meaning and assign a label. After your doctor has made a diagnosis, you will want to know the doctor's judgement – is it *serious* or *minor*, *terminal* or *treatable*? How did the doctor *label* your condition?

When we meet someone we knew previously, we have a tendency to search our memory banks for the label we tagged on them. Was the person a *friend*, *a good friend* or was the person someone we *disliked*? Was the person a *troublemaker*, the *smartest* student in the class, or the *class clown*? Such re-acquaintances can be awkward as we sort through our memory banks to find the previously assigned labels.

After watching a television documentary on polar bears living around Churchill, Manitoba, Canada, I labelled Churchill, Manitoba a *dangerous* place. In the future, when someone asks me for my opinion of Churchill, Manitoba, I do not need to review the facts; I will recall my label and simply say, *It is a dangerous place*. If I am exposed to new facts or experiences, and if I open my mind to consider them, I might reassess my label.

A financial advisor using information from the client's balance sheet and cash flow statement calculated the client's Debt Service Ratio (TDSR) to be 60%. (The advisor had previously selected the relevant information and had organized it by making calculations.) The number by itself means nothing. Is 60% *good* or *bad*? It needs to be labelled. A TDSR of 60% is actually *bad* and may indicate over-indebtedness or a lack of debt capacity. As the mind selects and organizes, it completes its perception by labelling information, and assigning a meaning to it.

Our labels are *labour-saving* devices; they save us from having to reinterpret our experiences. Once we assign a label, we tend to cling to that label – it is a lot less work than going through the selecting-organizing-assessment process all over again. For example, an advisor may have gathered information about the ABC fund and decided that it has potential for above average returns. Any time the ABC fund is mentioned, the advisor will think *above average returns*. The analysis does not have to be re-done. However, when we cling to our labels in the face of contradictory information, we have a problem and unless advisors are open to updating their perceptions with new information, they may give wrong advice.

4.1.3.1 Frames. A Canadian national newspaper did some research over a series of years to determine the adequacy of investment advice given by banks. Each year, the newspaper sent reporters acting as investors to visit various Canadian banks with a story about their investment needs. The newspaper reported on the most recent research in a story introduced by the headline: ***BANKS DO LITTLE TO AID FUND BUYERS***. The newspaper reported that the ability of the banks to provide good advice had not improved. Another newspaper picked up the same story and provided this headline: ***BANKS IMPROVE MARKS***

ON ADVICE. The second newspaper reported that the banks were doing better. The first headline presented a negative view of the bank's service while the second story was more positive. Each newspaper used the same data, but presented a different perspective. The senders of the message – the newspaper journalists, in this case – passed on their perspective with the *facts* giving readers a way to view the story. When this occurs, we say that the sender is attempting to *frame* a situation with a certain perspective and give the receiver (the reader) a way to view it. A frame is a perspective embedded in a message that gives the receiver a ready-made opinion or viewpoint on the information. The sender labels the information and hopes the receiver will accept the label.

In the early years of commercial aviation, a stewardess warned passengers: *We are flying through a* **storm**. *Fasten your* **safety** *belts; it will be less* **dangerous.** Today, flight attendants are trained to avoid raising anxiety by relaying less alarming messages: *We are flying through some* **turbulence**; *please fasten your* **seat** *belts – you will be more* **comfortable.**

In the above situation, frames were used to shift passengers' attitudes so they would view dangerous situations as simply uncomfortable. There is power in selecting the *right* language to convey the *right* message to prevent the hearer from straying too far from the intended message or adopting unwanted associations. (As is the replacement of the term *stewardess* with *flight attendant* to demonstrate gender equality.)

I often wonder what would happen if the owner of a business close to my home met my dog and I during one of our early morning walks around his property. He might be angry and accuse me of trespassing. If he does, I am ready with my defence as I attempt to frame the situation in a positive light. I will suggest that the way he should look at the situation is that he is getting free security service from my German Shepherd on our morning *patrols*. I hope he accepts my frame and doesn't charge me with trespassing.

> Because of past experience, Mr. Sequira will not accept financial advice from anyone younger than forty. He told the youthful advisor, *I don't think advisors under 40 have the knowledge or commitment to serve older customers.* The young advisor listened respectfully and suggested that one advantage of having a younger advisor was that younger advisors have the latest education and information on product and market innovations. The advisor also assured Mr. Sequira that as part of an inter-generational team, Mr. Sequira was free to talk to any members of the team. The advisor also assured Mr. Sequira that he would work twice as hard to gain his confidence. With this reassurance, Mr. Sequira decided to deal with the young advisor.

The advisor was able to *reframe* the situation and give Mr. Sequira a new way to view it.

Psychologists Daniel Kahneman and Amos Tversky pioneered research in the area of perception and frames in relation to risk, and financial losses and gains. (In 2002, subsequent to Tversky's death in 1986, Kahneman won a Nobel prize in Economics for their research.) Kahneman and Tversky's work demonstrated that people's attitudes toward risk depends on whether a situation is framed as a *gain* or a *loss*. Consider the following decision choices. [Percent of respondents choosing an alternative are in brackets.]

Decision (1) choose between
A. a sure gain of $100 [72%]
B. 50% chance to gain $200 and 50% chance to gain nothing [28%]
Subjects predominantly choose A, the certain alternative.

Decision (2) choose between
C. a sure loss of $100 [36%]
D. 50% chance to lose nothing and 50% chance to lose $200 [64%]
Subjects predominantly choose D, the riskier alternative.

These basic choices were reformulated in various ways, but subjects overwhelmingly chose riskier behaviour when losses were involved. Kahneman and Tversky produced substantial evidence that framing options in terms of gains or losses yielded different preferences. Kahneman and Tversky proved that our perspectives often drive our decisions and behaviour.

In the world of financial services, an advisor may suggest to a client that a fund's yearly management fee is an *investment* and not a *cost* or that the institution's international fund is the *best* in the industry. Using these frames, the sender hopes the receiver will label or perceive these situations the same way.

Frames have great power to influence people's decision-making activity. Advisors, realizing the power of frames, must be mindful that in fulfilling their fiduciary duties they must fully disclose all facts without embedding their own prejudices and preferences. However, as seen in the following example, framing could be of benefit to clients.

A client with a yearly income of more than $250,000 never seems to have money to support his two sons at university. The boys have borrowed money from family members to stay enrolled. The client is aware of, and embarrassed by, the situation, but he says he never has the funds to support his sons after *necessities*. His latest necessity is renovating the front of his house to change the slope of the roof to give it more of a *Mediterranean* look — no one else in the neighbourhood has this feature and he wants to be the first.

At the root of the problem is budgeting, but it is difficult to suggest that the client should make a *budget* because he believes budgets are only for poor people. Instead of suggesting a *budget*, the advisor might frame the situation suggesting that in order to make sure his money goes where he wants it to go, he should keep track of it. In doing this, the advisor has described the budgeting process without actually using the word *budget*.

When a sender frames a message, the receiver should try to *un-pack it,* that is, separate the facts from the sender's perception of the facts. For example, a client may tell the advisor that he can't afford to invest any more money in his retirement fund. Is this the truth or the way the client sees it? The advisor can accept his client's statement as a fact or explore the matter and separate the facts from the client's feelings. In reality, the client may have the money, but feels that he would rather invest in something he can see the results of now, rather than in 15 years.

4.2 STEREOTYPES AND BIASES

Our perceptions help us, but as we have seen, they can also create problems, such as screening out relevant information, organizing information incorrectly, or reinforcing out-dated labels. A client may judge all persons of a particular gender inadequate to offer financial advice. What will it take to change the client's perception? When our perceptions are particularly rigid and detrimental, we call them **biases** and **stereotypes**. They are prejudgements about people before having the necessary information to reach conclusions about them.

Stereotypes are common characteristics we apply to all members of the **same group:** *All Canadians like ice hockey; all professors are absent-minded.* A stereotype is a shortcut. It is a ready-made packaged opinion that acts as a frame of reference in dealing with others. It provides a way to view others without having to get to know them directly. Stereotypes are one of the greatest barriers to communication and the understanding of others.

> The elderly mother of a friend of mine asked him to accompany her to a meeting with her financial advisor. The mother had reviewed her portfolio and had a few suggestions to make based on her considerable experience and knowledge. The son noticed during the interview that the advisor's attention was focused entirely on him while ignoring his mother. Finally, the mother attempted to gain the advisor's attention with a comment. The advisor, in response, turned towards her and said: *My, don't you look nice today, my dear.* Feeling insulted, she stood and told her son that they were leaving. She felt the advisor's comment reflected the opinion that as a woman she would not be interested in, or knowledgeable about, financial matters, but would respond to flattery.

Biases are opinions we have about individuals based on our knowledge of them in limited areas. I once taught a course on personal investing to a group of non-experts in which the son of a famous Canadian financier was a student. After each class, the student would question me about very elementary financial concepts. I was surprised. I had assumed that he had inherited his father's financial acumen. I let my knowledge of his father influence my opinion of him.

If advisors let their experience of one aspect of a client's life colour their opinion of the client's total character, they are taking a perceptual short-cut, using biases instead of direct information to understand the client. Biases have the same potential danger as stereotypes: they give us an opinion of others that is not necessarily based on fact. At the root of stereotypes and biases are inaccurate perceptions and a failure to discern differences among people of the same group or distinguish among various positive and negative characteristics of the same person. Labels cannot adequately describe anyone.

Biases and stereotypes plague us all. The advisor may judge young people as irresponsible in handling money, older people as incapable of understanding complex situations, certain professions as knowledgeable in all areas, particular ethnic groups as being difficult to deal with, and women as being less interested in finances. When cultural and nationality differences are added in, difficulties increase.

The overall negative effect of perceptions and filters is that they prevent the advisor from getting to know and understand the unique characteristics and needs of clients, something which has to be done before the advisor can make appropriate recommendations.

4.3 Managing Perceptions

The first important principle in dealing with perceptions is to be aware that they exist and that they tempt us to make quick and general judgements. The second principle is to be committed to identifying them in ourselves as well as in others. In summary, here are a few key points with regard to perceptions.

- Our perceptual system and the forming of perceptions help us function amidst a sea of information by selecting, organizing, and labelling that information.
- Our perceptual system and perceptions can interfere with our communication and damage our relationships.
  - We may block critical information from our awareness if it does not coincide with our beliefs.
  - We may come to the wrong conclusions by combining the wrong data and making connections that are not true.
  - We may supply missing information so we can reach conclusions, but we may supply the wrong information.
  - We may cling to our old labels and relate to people through them.
- Frames or perspectives embedded by senders in their messages have the power to influence receivers' attitudes. When using frames, advisors must balance their attempts with their fiduciary duties. Advisors should be prepared to separate clients' perspectives from the facts to get a better understanding of their clients' *real* situations.
- Stereotypes and biases can damage relationships and the advising process. Advisors must be vigilant and reject them and get to know clients directly without any prejudgements.
- Throughout the advising process, the greatest protection against the negative influence of perceptions is for advisors to seek verification of their understanding of their clients' situations.

4.4 CONCLUSION

Our perceptual systems are an important part of our cognitive makeup. They assure that we are not overwhelmed by all the sensory data to which we are exposed. They help us organize information so we can reach conclusions. They help us label our experiences for later reference. But perceptions can lead to misperceptions of people and situations, interfere with communication, and damage relationships. A client-centred approach with its commitment to gaining an accurate and complete understanding of each client's unique situation will help to avoid these problems.

KEY TERMS

Biases. Opinions about specific individuals based on knowledge of them in limited areas.

Frames. A perspective embedded in a message designed to give the receiver a ready-made opinion or way to view a situation without having to go through the labelling process.

Inferences. The supplying of missing information from a message by making assumptions about what is missing so that the message can be understood.

Labelling. Assigning meaning to information after it has been organized into a pattern.

Organizing. Forming information that enters a person's awareness into a pattern that can be interpreted and used.

Perceptions. Perceptions are the result of our minds interpreting the messages our senses receive to provide order and meaning to the environment.

Selecting. The work of the perceptual system in allowing some information to enter a person's awareness while other information is blocked.

Stereotypes. A ready-made packaged opinion that acts as a frame of reference in dealing with others.

CHAPTER 5

NONVERBAL COMMUNICATION

5.0 THE POWER OF NONVERBAL COMMUNICATION

> *So*, the advisor continued, *if you buy more shares of Albotech, which has gone down in price, you will lower your average price, and in that way you really haven't lost anything.* The client, folded his arms across his chest, leaned back, and responded, *ah…yes…, right*. Much to the advisor's surprise, the client never followed through on the advice or asked for any more suggestions.

There are nonverbal signs here that the client is not sold on the advisor's recommendation: his posture – folded arms, and his **paralanguage** – the *ah*. If the advisor had been able to identify and verify the nonverbal language, he might have prevented the client from slipping away.

While visiting the Bargello Museum in Florence, Italy, I made a quick tour while my wife lingered and admired the statues. Having finished my perambulations, and to fill in time, I joined a tour group in front of the statue of St. George the Dragon-Slayer. (See St.

George to the left.) St. George was caught in a moment just before a dragon-confronting expedition. The guide pointed out many things I had missed in my whirl-wind tour and drew the group's attention to the way the artist, Donatello, had managed to convey both fear and determination in the marble statue: in St. George's stance – feet apart, but hiding behind his shield; in the placement of his hands – one half-curled like a fist, the other covering, perhaps, his fluttering stomach; and in his eyes and mouth – appearing at the same time determined, but fearful. By the end of the guide's talk, I had great admiration for the artist and a renewed appreciation for the ability to convey deep feelings nonverbally.

Nonverbal language often constitutes a large part of a message, especially concerning the sender's emotions and attitudes. Mehrabian believed that as much as 93 percent of a message is communicated nonverbally, but recent surveys suggest that 65 percent is more accurate (in Tubbs, 2000, p.101). Nevertheless, this is enough of a significant proportion to recommend that advisors have an understanding of the different forms of nonverbal communication.

Nonverbal language is a rich source of information because it is less under the sender's control than the sender's words. Sigmund Freud (1963) observed: *He that has eyes to see and ears to hear may convince himself that no mortal can keep a secret. If his lips are silent, he chatters with his fingertips; betrayal oozes out of him in every pore* (p.96). Nonverbal messages are predominantly involuntary and unconscious. For example, when people are in an embarrassing or stressful situation, they may exhibit reactions that are not entirely under their control, such as a red face, sweaty hands and occasional stuttering, all which indicate much about their emotional states. This uncontrollable physiological reaction is the foundation of the workings of the polygraph (*lie detector*). Nonverbal messages are valuable insights into the sender's emotions because they usually emerge unfiltered and spontaneous.

The ability to *read* nonverbal communication is an important skill that financial advisors must master. But there is a warning that goes with this – see below.

5.1 *Reading* Nonverbal Language

Some people are better *readers* of nonverbal language than others. Customs and immigration officials are notoriously perceptive at identifying would-be smugglers and others with illegal intentions from a reading of their posture, the tone of their voices, or their eye movements. An awareness of nonverbal communication is an important skill advisors need to *read* their clients' complete messages and, in turn, to convey important messages to them.

The first step in reading nonverbal language is to be aware of it. There are several good books, some referenced at the end of this book, which can help develop powers of observation and interpretation. To be aware of the nonverbal components of communication requires listening with eyes as well as ears. But, we need to begin with a warning: even though a lot is known about nonverbal language, **we cannot construct a dictionary that defines specific nonverbal behaviour**. Specific *nonverbals* do not always translate into exact meanings. Scratching your head does not always mean you are confused (you may have an itchy head). A flushed red face does not always indicate repressed anger (high blood pressure or physical exertion can produce the same effect). Cultural differences add to the interpretation problem. For example, the acceptability of eye contact varies from culture to culture. In general, it is suggested that Northern Europeans and North Americans maintain less eye contact than Arabs, Latin Americans and Southern Europeans. The latter groups are known as *contact cultures* and tend to stand closer, touch more, and exchange more eye contact. On the other hand, Japanese do not appreciate public touching, even a pat on the back, and direct eye contact is often unwelcome. In Tibet, unlike most of the rest of the world, sticking out one's tongue at guests is considered good manners.

Nonverbal language offers *cues* that *might* indicate certain thoughts and feelings of the sender, but they need to be verified. Because the same nonverbals can convey different messages, we cannot provide exact interpretations of all facial expressions, postures, and gestures. **There are no rules of grammar or agreed-upon theory of how particular feelings translate into specific nonverbal signs.** Nonverbal expressions are often individualized and the same expression could have a different meaning depending on the person, the circumstance, or the culture. This does not mean we should not attempt to decode nonverbal messages, but rather, we should proceed with caution. **We must treat** nonverbal behaviour as cues to verify through follow-up questions or in combination with other information.

5.2 FORMS OF NONVERBAL COMMUNICATION

Nonverbal language can be broadly classified as involving either body movements or voice. Body movements include facial cues, eye movements, posture, hand gestures, and touch. Voice elements of nonverbal communication include the ways the voice is used to convey words and sounds made with the voice.

5.2.1 Facial Cues

The human face is so pliable that it can easily register a range of emotions, such as boredom, surprise, approval, and disapproval – in quick succession if required. **Facial cues such as the shape of the mouth, lips and eyebrows, wrinkling of the forehead, and tenseness or relaxation of the facial muscles are the single most important source of nonverbal communications.** Researchers have found that there are at least eight distinguishable positions of the eyebrows and forehead, eight more of the eyes and lids, and ten for the lower face. The study of facial cues as expressions of specific emotions has a long history. The famous biologist Charles Darwin was interested in finding out whether the facial expressions associated with particular emotions were universal. Paul Ekman at the University of California at San Francisco found in his research that, despite cultural differences, facial expressions for four primary emotions (fear, anger, sadness, enjoyment) are recognized by people in cultures around the world (cited in Goleman, 2005).

5.2.2 EYE MOVEMENTS.

The face and eyes are the most noticed parts of the body, and may be the main channel through which nonverbal messages are sent and the first place they are scrutinized by the receiver. **Eye contact is perhaps the single most important facial cue used in communication.** Cues given through eye contact seem to reveal a great deal about the thoughts and feelings of the sender and receiver. Hess's research (1965 and 1975) found that the sizes of eye pupils were indexes of the subject's interest in a topic. He showed that Chinese jade dealers watch the eyes of their prospective customers for interest in a particular stone because pupils enlarge with increased interest. Similarly, magicians are able to tell the card a person is thinking of by studying the card-selector's eyes. Successful poker players are adept at masking their facial clues and eye movements.

When I was a psychology student, a classmate of mine gave a seminar on behavioural psychology and included an effective experiment. He purposefully looked at students only on one side of the classroom. He avoided eye contact with the other half of the class, which included the professor. When the professor's side of the classroom asked a question, my classmate either ignored the question or gave a short, off-handed reply. When someone from the other side of the room asked a question, he was lavish in his praise and showered the inquirer with concentrated attention. When the class was over, he asked everyone how they felt about his presentation. The professor immediately erupted and said he felt that the presenter had ignored some very good questions, especially his. After the student revealed his experiment, the professor admitted that he was becoming annoyed and had felt rejected throughout his presentation because of the presenter's lack of eye contact and responsiveness.

Southwest Airlines maintains an open-seating policy in which specific seats cannot be booked or assigned before travel. Passengers who board first often take an aisle or window seat, and then lay articles on the middle seat to discourage other passengers from occupying their *comfort zone*. During one boarding procedure, a frustrated flight attendant who was having difficulty securing the cooperation of passengers in aisle seats to let boarding passengers get around them, announced: *Those of you who have seats on the aisle, look up and make eye contact with on-coming passengers.* It worked – aisle passengers let others pass – but why? The answer is clear: it is harder to remain indifferent or unhelpful to someone if you are looking at them – the power of eye contact.

Researchers at Dalhousie University, Halifax, Canada, found that people's emotions are expressed mostly through the upper face (eyes, brows, and forehead) and most people miss these cues because they usually focus on the lower part of the face (nose, lips, and cheeks). Dalhousie researchers say that the upper part of the face is most apt to *leak* one's true emotions (Science News, 2008).

5.2.3 Posture
Another way we communicate nonverbally is through our posture or the way we carry our body. The English language is full of expressions that link emotional states with body postures:

- o   *I won't take this lying down.*
- o   *Sit down and take a load off your feet.*
- o   *He can stand on his own two feet.*

Sometimes these cues are subtle and are hard to detect, such as slumping in a chair or slightly lowered shoulders; at other times, the cues are dramatic, such as a client abruptly walking out of your office. Psychologist Albert Mehrabian (1981) found that the degree of tension or relaxation exhibited in body posture is a good indication of a person's mental state.

5.2.4 Hand Gestures
Those who study communication say that hand gestures rank second in importance to facial cues. We know from our experience that much is said with hand gestures – from a sign of approval and acceptance to a rude signal of rejection and disdain. How are you feeling when you tap your fingers on the desk while you are talking with someone? Are your fingers giving emphasis to your words or are they saying something in addition to what your words are conveying? Researchers have identified more than one hundred different hand gestures that convey a message. The *OK* sign formed by the thumb and finger is a sign of acceptability in Western cultures, but it is impolite in Greece and Russia, and in Brazil it is an obscene gesture.

As perhaps in no other aspect of nonverbal communication, hand gestures are culturally conditioned. Thus, as Morris (1979) points out, the same gestures can convey different things to members of different cultures, and over time gestures can change within the same culture.

Many people with speech and hearing impairments rely on hand gestures to communicate. Whole systems of semantics and syntax have developed as part of various versions of sign language. Long before my grandchildren's speech was developed their parents taught them hand gestures to communicate simple concepts such as *finished, more, cookie, please, and thank you.*

5.2.5 Touch

Touch is one of our most important means of nonverbal communication. The study of **haptics –** the role of touch in communication – has made several important discoveries. A gentle touch can convey warmth, acceptance, and caring while a forceful and unwelcome grab can convey hostility and aggression. The degree and form of touching is highly determined by cultural norms and social relationships. A handshake may be an appropriate way for a western man to greet a western woman and signal that he accepts her as an equal, while it may be a totally inappropriate and unacceptable gesture in an eastern culture. A handshake between two close friends may be inappropriate; a hug or embrace may better express the nature of their relationship.

5.2.6 Voice and Paralanguage

Along with what is said, the manner in which it is said conveys a message. Have you ever heard anyone say, *it is not so much what you say, but how you say it?* The words *Hello, nice to meet you,* can sound cold and mechanical, or they can convey warmth and enthusiasm. The term **paralanguage** describes the nonverbal element of a verbal message. Technically, it means something beyond or in addition to language itself. Paralanguage has two components: *voice qualities,* such as pitch, range, rate of speech, and volume; and *vocalizations* or noises, such as crying, laughing, and groaning. Silence might also be added to the list. The voice, apart from words, can convey a range of feelings such as resistance, agreement, and disagreement. Research by Soskin and Kauffman (1961) concluded that *voice sounds alone, independent of …vocal messages, carry important clues to the emotional state of a speaker* (p.78). One team of researchers identified four categories of emotions conveyed by paralanguage: positive feelings, dislike, sadness, and fear. Research has found that desired vocal qualities may vary by culture. Buller and Aune (1992) found that listeners feel more positive about people who seem to talk at a similar rate as their own. (Some sales training programs emphasize *mirroring* as an important skill.) While some cultures place an emphasis on loudness and forcefulness of speech others value softness.

Communication through paralanguage isn't always intentional. Sometimes our voice may indicate our true feelings when we're trying to create an impression different from our feelings. You may have had experiences of trying to sound calm and in control when you actually felt very anxious. You were able to mask your true feelings until your voice *cracked* or quivered.

5.3 INTERPRETING NONVERBAL COMMUNICATION

Now that we know something about nonverbal communication, let us consider three particular situations in which awareness of nonverbal language can add to an advisor's understanding of a client's state of mind and feelings.

5.3.1 A Difference between Words and Feelings

Nonverbal language may indicate incongruence between what the client says and actually feels. Arms folded tightly across the chest *might* indicate that the client is not as open to the advisor's recommendation as verbalized. This cue should lead the advisor to seek verification: *Are you sure that this proposal is acceptable?* This might give the client permission to voice any reservations. Having the client's honest reaction is important for avoiding future misunderstandings and false expectations, or loss of the client's business. The advisor, committed to understanding the client's reality, should continually wonder: *Does the client's tone of voice, emphasis, facial expressions, gestures, and posture match the content of the message?*

5.3.2 An Indication of the Nonverbalized

Nonverbal language can indicate that the client has latent feelings that have not been expressed. A repetitive tapping of the foot accompanied by a shifting forward and backward in a chair *might* indicate that the client is impatient. This can be verified by asking, *Are you happy with the pace of our coverage of the issues?* When no feedback is verbalized, advisors should look for it in nonverbal language, as the following example shows.

The advisor arranged to meet with a wealthy real estate trader who had expressed interest in investing in a real estate fund.

Client: *What do you think of this stock?* (Waving a piece of paper.) *My friend told me it will double in value within the next month.*
Advisor: *Most analysts think it is undervalued because its P/E is lower than the sector's.*
Client: *Ah...so do you think it will double in value?*
Advisor: *Well, I do think, as I said, that it is undervalued and it is trading above the 200 day moving average and all indictors look good. Our view is that it is a good buy for the long term.*
Client: (Shakes his head and half closes his eyes.)
Advisor: *So, let's go ahead and open an account and buy the shares.*
(The advisor explained the risks involved in equities, the importance of adopting a long- term horizon, and the charges associated with the transaction. It was clear to the advisor that the client's investment knowledge was low. The client signed the document. A few days later the client called to check his account and was pleased to find it had increased in value. A few days later, the client visited the advisor to express his strong disappointment that his investment had dropped in value.
Client: *What about my profits?*

> **Advisor**: *I am sorry to tell you that your account has lost all that it had gained. As you may have heard, the company was adversely effected by the death of the CEO.*
> **Client**: *WHAT!!! (Shouting and pounding his hand on the advisor's desk.)*
> **Client**: *What about my profits you told me about last week; where did they go?*
> **Advisor**: *The profits were unrealized.*
> **Client**: *What do you mean by realized and unrealized? Where did my money go? Who took it from my account?*
> **Advisor**: *Sir, we did not take any money from your account. You lost money in the account due to price depreciation.*
> **Client**: *I am going to call the branch manager and complain.*

This is a strange conversation because of the client's lack of understanding of the workings of the markets. But what is more significant is that in the early part of the first conversation, the advisor missed an opportunity to verify the client's lack of understanding when in response to the advisor's mention of moving averages the client shook his head and squinted his eyes – all of which may have communicated confusion. This would have been a good time for the advisor to have stopped and asked, *have I said something that is not clear to you or that made you uncomfortable?* Instead, the advisor initiated action to open an account and trade the shares. The product should not have been sold to the client, who had minimal understanding of investments and markets, without further explanation. Furthermore, the advisor's use of jargon in both conversations probably added to the client's confusion and subsequent outburst.

5.3.3 Reinforcement of the Verbalized

Third, nonverbal language may reinforce the speaker's words. In the incident above, the client shouted (paralanguage) and pounded his hand on the advisor's desk to reinforce his strong displeasure. When words and nonverbal language match, we can say there is **congruence** between the two. People who communicate with congruence tend to be more direct, easier to understand, and effective.

5.4 USING NONVERBAL COMMUNICATION EFFECTIVELY

As well as focusing on clients' nonverbal messages, advisors should be aware of the nonverbal messages they send. Nonverbal language can be an important means of conveying *positive regard* to clients, which is the advisor's attitude that clients are highly valued, their concerns important, and the opportunity to help them is deeply appreciated. Advisors need to convey respect and empathy towards clients, and to create supportive and friendly atmospheres. These things can be accomplished through words and the use of nonverbal messages that reinforce verbal ones – the use of touch, tone of voice, finding the appropriate distance, eye contact, etc.

The following list suggests nonverbal behaviours that communicate positive regard.

Friendliness

- Smile
- Direct eye contact (if appropriate)
- Hand shake (if appropriate)
- Offering hospitality (providing coffee or tea and a comfortable seat)

Respect

- Full focused attention on the client (see the discussion on active listening in Chapter 6)
- Clear enunciation of words

Interest in the Client

- Maintaining a relaxed, yet alert posture
- Minimizing distracting gestures
- Leaning slightly towards the client
- Nodding the head

5.5 Conclusion

The nonverbal components of messages convey important information about a client, especially the client's attitudes and feelings towards the advisor and the advisor's recommendations. Advisors should be aware of this dimension of communication and be attentive to the nonverbal messages they and their clients send. Even though it is impossible to be definitive about the meaning of all nonverbal language, the advisor should treat nonverbal expressions as cues to be verified through follow-up questions. Identifying and verifying nonverbal messages is an important component of the communication process and for assuring that the client and advisor are in-step and developing a shared understanding of the client's concerns.

KEY TERMS

Congruence. When words and nonverbal language match.
Haptics. The study of the role of touch in communication.
Paralanguage. The nonverbal element of a verbal message.
Positive regard. An attitude that other people are highly valued and that their concerns are important.

MODULE III

CONDUCTING THE INTERVIEW

CHAPTER 6

EFFECTIVE RELATIONSHIP SKILLS

6.0 EFFECTIVE INTERVIEWING SKILLS

The most successful advisors get that way not because of their grasp of financial-planning subtleties – although that helps – but because of their mastery of the so-called "soft" skills. In addition to asking the right questions, top advisors are good at listening to clients (McIntyre, 2004, p.B6).

Further testimony to the effectiveness of listening and questioning skills is offered by Dan Richards, president of Strategic Imperatives Ltd., a Toronto financial services industry consultancy and research firm: *The most important set of skills that an advisor has to have is probably the most undervalued – and that is the questioning and listening skills....* (in McIntyre, 2004, B6)

The following incident shows how the lack of good interview skills undermines the development of client relationships.

The Webbs are faced with the possibility of having to sell their recreational vehicle. Mr. and Mrs. Webb each have high-paying jobs and their well-furnished home is in one of the nicest areas of the city. Despite their impressive income and sizeable assets, they never seem to have enough money.

Mrs. Webb: *I don't want to sell the vehicle. We get a lot of pleasure out of it. The trips with my parents are about the only thing we do together.*

Advisor: *You will find other things to do. If you don't sell it now, you will get deeper in debt. It's that simple.*

Mrs. Webb: *Are you sure? I just can't see it.*

Advisor: *You have to realize that the combined income of you and your husband is not great enough to support your expensive lifestyle.* (The advisor lists their expenses.)

Mrs. Webb: *I still don't see what you mean,*

Mr. Webb: (Who had been sitting quietly) *That stupid vehicle! I wanted a summer home. That would have made a lot more sense.*

In this incident, the Webbs and the advisor do not appear to be making much progress in solving the Webb's problem. The recreational vehicle means a great deal to Mrs. Webb because it allows her to spend time with her parents, but no one has understood that, or at least communicated an understanding of that, and this is one reason she has difficulty understanding it as an expense. The advisor had a difficult time explaining the Webb's budgetary problem partly because the advisor missed that Mrs. Webb is a *visual* and not an *auditory* learner and for her listening to a litany of expenses is not as good as seeing them written down. Another looming problem is that the advisor is siding with Mr. Webb.

This chapter discusses critical communication skills, which if they had been practiced in the example above, would have helped the advisor solve the Webb's problem. Ross Cammareri, Senior Vice President and National Advisor of Sales and Product Marketing for AGF Canada, says that when AGF recruits, it looks for

> people with strong communication and social skills who take a 'client-centric' approach.... At AGF, we spend a lot of time listening to our clients and working to understand their needs…so our people must be great at listening and translating what they hear into solutions that fit those needs (Investment Executive's Career Guide, 2008, p.88).

We have been stressing the importance of effective relationship skills during client interviews. Now it is time to be more precise – what do we mean by *effective* relationship skills? Before peeling back the layers, we can generally say that good relationship skills include showing respect, using active listening and empathy, and asking the right kinds of questions at the right time.

6.1 SHOWING RESPECT

From the beginning of client conversations, advisors must show respect for clients and their needs. The advisor must communicate to clients that their needs and goals are of supreme importance. Advisors who show respect for clients will greet them in a friendly manner, assure their comfort, and listen to them with their full attention. Psychologist Carl Rogers (1951) called such respect the showing of *positive regard*. (The concept was introduced in the previous chapter.)

The following incidents show a lack of respect and positive regard.

> While I was talking with a service representative at the financial institution's front counter, another service representative leaned in front of her – in between us – and started talking to her about an irrelevant branch matter.
>
> I made an appointment to see a financial advisor and as soon as I arrived at her office, I checked in with the receptionist. The receptionist phoned the advisor and announced: *Your 10 o'clock is here.*

In both instances I felt unappreciated and that I was just another customer, or even worse – a time slot. Showing clients' that they are valued strengthens client relationships.

6.2 ACTIVE LISTENING

> ***Building trust isn't about talking, it's about listening*** (Callahan, 2008, p.35).

George Williams, president of KARAT Consulting International, says the key to relationship building is using the 80-20 principle: *we should listen 80% of the time and talk 20% of the time* (Williams, 2000, p.B16).

The United States Bureau of Labor Statistics publishes an analysis of the skills and knowledge critical for competency in a wide range of jobs (amongst employed 24 to 44 year-olds). For financial advisors, the skill of ***active listening*** received a score of 75 out of 100 as to its importance (third only to critical thinking and speaking). For financial services salespeople, active listening is tied with critical thinking for first place as a necessary skill. The study defines active listening as *giving full attention to what other people are saying, taking time to understand the points being made, asking questions as appropriate, and not interrupting at inappropriate times* (U.S. Department of Labor, 2010b).

Active listening is more than hearing; it is a more complex and intentional activity. Active listening involves **hearing**, **paying attention**, **understanding**, **analyzing**, and **remembering**. Every study of listening shows that, on average, we are bad listeners. Factors that contribute to this weakness are a lack of practice, discomfort in holding back our own opinions, inattention to the other's concerns, and preoccupation with our own concerns.

The ability of the average listener to understand is four times greater than the rate at which the average person speaks, so three-fourths of the listener's time is spare time. Consequently, listeners sometimes *park* their attention, when they become bored, especially when the other person talks for a long uninterrupted period. During such times, when these ***thought gaps*** exist, the listener will have to concentrate especially hard to overcome them by doing the following:

- listening for and analyzing the speaker's main ideas and central themes – not the details
- focusing on the speaker's meaning – not the words
- thinking ahead and speculating about what the speaker might say next, and why
- comparing what the speaker is saying with what you already know about the speaker or the subject – do they coincide?
- analyzing how the speaker reaches conclusions – what assumptions are made?
- looking for nonverbal behaviour – does it agree with or contradict the speaker's words?

The following guidelines can be added.

- Identify both the feeling and content of the message. One without the other is an incomplete message. The feeling level is picked up largely through a reading of nonverbal cues. The way the client hesitates, the inflection of the voice, what is stressed and what is mumbled, facial expressions, body posture, hand movements, eye movements and breathing - all of these convey important parts of a message.

- Use pauses effectively to give the other person a chance to respond freely and move the conversation to issues of concern.
- Control the temptation to interrupt and add your comments.
- Get feedback from the client and verify your understanding of the client's feelings, ideas, and concerns.

The objective of active listening is to understand what is important to others and to try to see the world from their perspective. To listen actively requires an inquisitive mind and this guiding question: *what is it like to be the other person?* Figure 6.1 below is the multi-faceted Chinese character for listening. The left section denotes the *ear*. The right section, starting at the top, denotes *you,* the next *eyes*, the next *undivided attention*, and the last *heart*.

Figure 6.1
The Chinese Character for Listening

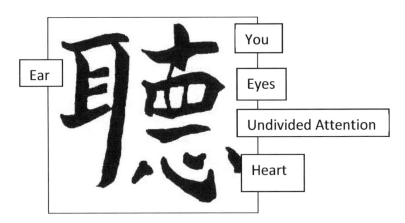

As the Chinese character implies, when we actively listen we invest our full energy in to understanding the other person with our ears, eyes, and heart – a total involvement.

In the following example, is the advisor really listening to the client?

> **Client:** *I don't know what to do.*
> **Advisor:** *What seems to be the problem?*
> **Client:** *I want to buy a new house, but I don't know whether I can afford it. Also, my daughter is ready to enter college and that will be a major expense. I don't know what to do.*
> **Advisor:** *You really want that house.*
> **Client:** *Well…I want to pay for my daughter's schooling, too, and I can't afford both.*
> **Advisor:** *Let's look at some ways you can finance the house.*

The advisor was not listening. The client had more than one concern; two equally important goals were in competition and it was frustrating not to be able to afford both: the house and the daughter's education. The feeling of frustration is what the advisor should have acknowledged and discussed with the client as a starting point. After this, the advisor could have helped adjust the client's goals, establish priorities in the light of the client's financial resources, and develop possible solutions to try to accommodate both goals.

Active listening goes a long way towards creating an atmosphere of trust in which clients have confidence that the advisor understands and is concerned about their best interests.

We have already discussed some of the ingredients of active listening: setting aside biases and stereotypes, ignoring distractions, reading nonverbal language, and being aware of the sender's entire message – content and feeling. To these, we would add the use of **restating**, **paraphrasing** and **summarizing**, which concentrate the listener's attention and let the other person know that the listener understands.

6.2.1 Restating
Restating is repeating what the other person has said, using the other person's words. Nothing new is added. The restatement may sound a bit mechanical, but it has power to convey an understanding of the other's concerns. If a client says: *I need bigger returns from my investments, but I really don't want to take any extra risks*, a restatement would be: *You need bigger returns from your investments, but you don't want to take any extra risks*. Restating does not add any new information; its role is to open the door to deeper discussion and understanding.

6.2.2 Paraphrasing
Paraphrasing is a restatement of what has been said, in the **hearer's** words. It is a restatement of the other person's perceived meaning behind the words. Like restating, it adds no new information. Paraphrasing is useful for clarifying and acknowledging the sender's feelings. Paraphrasing requires intense listening. It requires that the listener not judge what has been said, but appreciate its worth. Before a paraphrase can be made, the receiver must have a clear understanding of the complete message – content and feeling. For example, when the client says, *I need bigger returns from my investments, but I really don't want to take any extra risks.* An accurate paraphrase would be: *You feel caught between two things: getting an extra return and not wanting to take any chances.*

6.2.3 Summarizing
Summarizing is similar to paraphrasing and restating, but it relates not to a particular part of a conversation but to an extended or entire conversation. It is particularly useful after a client's lengthy monologue. It allows the advisor to focus on the *business at hand* and to give direction to the rest of the conversation. When the client is overly talkative and often introduces irrelevancies, summaries can provide boundaries and focus the discussion on issues related to the advisor's expertise, while conveying respect. Summarizing allows the advisor to tie together a number of ideas and to regain control of the conversation. This provides the client with an opportunity to hear what has been said and to correct any misunderstandings.

Summarizing is also helpful for opening and closing meetings, and for indicating what needs to be accomplished next. It gives the advisor and the client an opportunity to verify that they have a shared understanding of the client's concerns.

Summarizing at the beginning of a session provides a review of previous discussions and sets an agenda for the current meeting. It also conveys that the advisor listened carefully to the client the last time they met. The advisor might open an interview by saying: *The last time we talked we were looking at a number of options for providing for your children's education. Since then, I have obtained more information and I suggest we review it today.* Advisors should keep brief summaries of each session so their memories can be refreshed prior to future meetings.

A meeting might conclude this way: *We have discussed a number of things, but your biggest concern seems to be providing for your children's education. You feel you have most other things under control, but you are concerned about the escalating costs of university education. I will prepare some material on educational savings plans and the next time we meet, we can consider how these could help you.* The summary moves discussions towards decisions and closure.

Paraphrasing, restating, and summarizing provide valuable feedback and promote the development of further communication.

6.2.4 Feedback and Verification

Throughout a conversation securing feedback and verification are critical for assuring that the advisor accurately understands the client's concerns. Not to do this is to run the risk of losing the client. There is a slight difference between **verification** and **feedback**. Feedback is asking for another person's reaction to what you have said. Verification is checking out your understanding of what the other person has said to determine if your understanding is correct. Both are important components of active listening. The following examples illustrate the difference.

> **Advisor:** *In summary, that is why I think this investment would fit your situation.*
> **Client:** (Silence. Shifting around as though uncomfortable with what the advisor is saying.)
> **Advisor:** *Let me stop here and ask what your reaction is to what I have proposed.*

In this situation, the advisor asked for feedback. The advisor does not know what the client thinks, but wants to know – and should want to know. This is a simple but often neglected process. Many advisor-client relationships have deteriorated when the advisor has not obtained feedback to determine the client's response. Working with a client is like walking a path together side-by-side. If the advisor gets too far ahead, clients will lag behind and stray off the path. If the advisor is too far behind, clients will wonder if the advisor is able to add any value. Asking for feedback gives clients a chance to catch up and re-establish the mutual conversation. At many points in an interview where feedback should have been sought and was not, it can be predicted that the client will not make any commitment to the advisor's recommendations.

As stated, verification is slightly different from feedback.

> **Advisor:** *In summary, that is why I think this investment product would fit your situation.*
> **Client:** (Silence, moving around in his chair as though he wants to say something.)
> **Advisor:** *It seems as though you might be uncomfortable with this recommendation.*

The difference between asking for feedback and verifying is subtle. Technically, the difference is that feedback is open-ended and asks for a response. Seeking verification checks the sender's perception of the receiver's reaction. In the example above, the advisor wants to know if the perceptions formed from a reading of the client's nonverbal cues are correct.

When an advisor seeks verification, it should give the client some comfort to know that the advisor is not going to suggest a solution until the advisor understands the client's situation. Verification communicates respect and a desire to understand. It also builds rapport, and minimizes misperceptions and misunderstandings. Verification can be sought by using such phrases as

o *What I hear you saying is…*
o *So you think…*
o *Let me see if I understand what you have said.*
o *Did I understand you to say…..?*
o *What you are saying is…Do I have that right?*
o *Let me rephrase what you have said so I can be sure I understand exactly what you mean.*
o *What I heard you say was….is that right?*

Verification is important after the client has provided personal information and the advisor needs to know if it has been recorded correctly. It is also important for making sure the advisor has understood any transaction instructions the client has given. In the following incident, there is a problem lurking because of a lack of verification.

> An advisor suggested to the client that it was time to sell certain shares in the client's portfolio. The client responded, *right.* The advisor assumed the client meant *right – sell them* and sold the shares, but the client actually meant *right – I will think about it.*

If the advisor had sought verification, the misinterpretation of *right* could have been avoided.

6.3 EMPATHY

A skill related to active listening is the ability to *empathize*. Empathy is often confused with sympathy, but sympathy means experiencing the same feelings as another, while empathy is understanding how another feels without having the same feelings. If a person has never experienced the loss of someone close to them, it is impossible to sympathize with another's grief, but it is possible to empathize. To empathize, one must be able to enter other people's worlds and understand their thoughts and feelings.

Expressing empathy is a simple concept but difficult to practice. Our tendency is to evaluate what we hear, or to be in a hurry to offer our own opinion rather than let the other person tell his or her own story. Ashenbrenner and Snalling (1988) suggest that some of the difficulties we have in being empathetic arise from the following:

- a readiness to be judgmental and to criticize what we hear
- preoccupation with our own concerns
- excessive talking with the belief that only when we are talking do we add value

To this, we could add a concern that financial professionals should concentrate on dispensing advice and presenting products. There is, of course, time for these things, but only after a shared understanding of the client's situation has been created.

Stephen Covey (1990) says we have difficulty listening empathetically because

> Most people do not listen with the intent to understand; they listen with the intent to reply.... When I say empathetic listening, I mean listening with intent to understand. I mean seeking first to understand, to really understand (p.239f.).

Egan (1994) expresses it this way: *empathy involves translating your understanding of the client's experiences...into a response through which you share that understanding with the client* (p.110). Note the two aspects of empathy: understanding the other person's thought process and emotions (or content and feeling of the message as we have described it previously); and conveying to the sender that the receiver understands. This may be done by paraphrasing or restating the client's words. As a general rule, in being empathetic, one should never say directly to another, *I understand*. No two people's situations are alike. For example, I may tell you that I have been at home sick all week and was not able to attend an important work meeting. Having been in a similar situation and wanting to show your support, you might say, *I understand*. But the truth is that I was much happier sick at home avoiding a contentious meeting; the experience you had, which you assumed I shared, was one of regret.

Of all the activities that have been identified and researched in the field of counselling, empathy emerges as the key ingredient of success.

The importance of empathy can be seen by its absence in the following negative example.

A client made an appointment with the manager of the bank where he had been a customer for fifteen years. One of the bank's policies had upset him. As a long-time customer, he felt he deserved better treatment. He considered moving his business to another bank, but before he did, he decided to give the manager some feedback.

At the meeting with the manager, the customer was initially impressed when the manager sat upright at his desk, placed a pad of paper in front of himself, and with pen poised, asked, *What can I do for you?* The manager appeared eager to help and ready to listen actively. After listening to the complaint, the manager responded: *That is the policy of our institution and I can do nothing to change it.*

They discussed the situation further while the manager continued to justify the bank's policy. The customer finished the conversation by saying, *I just wanted you to know that I am upset and I am considering taking my business elsewhere.*

The manager made no other comments. The customer left frustrated and immediately cancelled a majority of his business with the institution.

For the customer, the money involved was not the issue – he simply hoped for some understanding of his point of view. He wanted the manager to acknowledge his feelings. He really didn't want to go to the effort of relocating his business and was open to staying if the manager had shown some empathy. Even if the manager had said: *I'm sorry, I know you are upset and I can see why, but I'm afraid I can't do anything about it,* it would have gone a long way to making the customer feel better and he probably would have remained a good customer of the bank.

The preceding incident displayed the manager's lack of empathy and failure to view the situation from the client's perspective. What a difference an empathetic response would have made – instead of a defensive one. Incidents like this reinforce perceptions that financial service representatives are more concerned about corporate policies and procedures than clients' needs. Financial service representatives can't do much about the wider perceptions, but they can meet people with empathy and understanding. Advisors don't always have to agree with their clients, or agree to things that are not in their institution's best interest, but they should try to understand their clients' points of view and feelings.

Empathy is important because clients are more likely to do business with an advisor they believe has a feel for their concerns. The attitude of many customers is: **I don't care how much you know, until I know how much you care.** Advising follows understanding. **Financial representatives earn the right to give advice by first listening.** The client's needs and goals must be understood before any financial products and services are proposed.

I learned this lesson from my eldest daughter when she was three years-old. She was playing with toys in the family room when I called her to come for lunch. She ignored me. Her mother asked me to call her again; I did, but this time I raised my voice – she still did not come. I was about to call even louder when I decided to try a new strategy. I went to the family room where she was playing; I sat down beside her on the floor and for less than a minute played with her and her toys; I then stood up and told her we should go for lunch – she followed me!

I had taken the time and made the effort to enter her world, and then she followed me into my world of the household routine. I was empathetic to her situation. I tried this approach a few years later when the issues were a little more important. My daughter would sometimes come home unhappy from school; she would throw her books on the floor and refuse my requests for her help with some household chores. Remembering the toy-lunch incident, the next time this happened, I said to her, *It looks like you have had a bad day at school; come and help me and tell me about it.* I wish I could claim that as a parent I was always empathetic, but when I tried, it usually brought positive results.

6.3.1 KINDS OF EMPATHY

Hammond *et al.* (1977) suggest that there are three kinds of empathetic responses: **subtractive**, **reciprocal**, and **additive**. The difference is the extent to which the advisor understands the client's feelings and responds in a helpful manner.

Subtractive or non-empathetic responses convey no understanding of the client's concerns and feelings. It really is the opposite of empathy and is destructive to relationships. Subtractive responses include premature advice-giving, arguing, changing the subject, ridiculing, criticizing, making light of the client's situation, and diverting attention away from the client's feelings. A friend said he visited his doctor to discuss a breathing problem. He knew the doctor was frustrated with trying to find a solution, but he was shocked when the doctor made an off-handed suggestion that he should get an electric drill and drill out his nasal passages. (The doctor later apologized.)

Reciprocal responses accurately reflect the client's feelings. They do not add to, or go beyond, what the client has expressed, nor do they minimize or ignore what the client has said. Restating and paraphrasing are good ways to express reciprocal empathy. A client told the advisor that he was interested only in ethical investments because they were in line with his basic beliefs and values. The advisor responded: *You want your investments to be ethical ones because of your beliefs and values.* On the surface, this may look like a useless re-statement of the obvious, or even, depending on the tone, a mocking of the client. However, in practice, it gives the client a strong signal that the advisor is listening and is taking the client's preferences seriously. It is amazing how this simple technique is so difficult for some people to perform, but yet how powerful it is in developing relationships.

Additive responses accurately reflect the client's feelings and move the client to focus on business issues. An additive response is a reciprocal response with an offer to help added. For example, the client expressed how upset he was over the loss of personal belongings in a fire. The advisor responded by saying: *This was obviously a very upsetting experience, losing things that have been part of your life and history. There are probably some financial aspects of this as well; what can I do to help at this time?*

Additive responses are the most important kind of empathy for financial advisors to express.

The nature of additive empathy can be seen in an experience with the lost baggage department of large international airlines company. A family member (actually, my eldest daughter again) lost her luggage – or more accurately, the airlines lost it for her on a trip home from Japan. She had it packed with gifts and valuable mementos of her three-year stay in Japan. On arriving home, she phoned the *800* number to follow up the lost luggage form that she had submitted at the airport. It was like phoning a suicide prevention hot-line. The airline representative was very empathetic: *This must be very upsetting to you; you lost some things that are very precious to you. I want you to know how important it is to us to find your luggage. If you have any questions about how we are doing, please call us any time, night or day.*

Fortunately, the airline found the luggage. Because of the airline's technical and relational competency in handling my daughter's problem, they have become our airline of choice.

To be clear, we should make the distinction between a response that sounds like additive empathy, but is not.

The client complained that the return from a time deposit was less than that on other fixed-income investments, or what other institutions were offering.

Client: *I am really disappointed in this investment. If I had invested this money in real estate, I would have obtained a much better return.*
Advisor: *I am really sorry about this rate; let us see how we can come up with the best investment for your situation.*

The advisor reflected a feeling, but it was the **advisor's** and not the client's. In saying *I am really sorry*, the focus is on the advisor's feeling. A better response would adjust the first part of the statement to reflect the client's feelings: *It sounds as if you are really disappointed with the return from this investment and wish you had invested in something else: let us see how we can come up with the best investment for your situation.*

Figure 6.2 illustrates the difference in the three kinds of empathy by giving an example of a client's statement and three types of empathetic responses.

Figure 6.2
Kinds of Empathy

Client Statement:
I have been working hard and even though things have been going well, I might lose my job.

Subtractive Response:
Why don't you look for another job; they can't be that difficult to find?
Comment: This response exhibits no understanding of the client's problem. The advice is inappropriate and will probably discourage the client from expressing further feelings.

Reciprocal Response:
That sounds discouraging; in spite of your hard work, you may be laid off anyway.
Comment: This statement reflects the client's feelings and indicates that the client's concern has been heard and respected. Reciprocal empathy does not ignore, nor subtract from what has been said, but neither does it add anything new.

Additive Response:
That sounds worrisome; in spite of your hard work, you still may be laid off. That probably has some financial implications for you that we should examine.
Comment: This statement, again, communicates that the client has been heard, but it also guides the discussion towards the financial implications of the situation. There are probably a number of financial aspects that must be considered including the impact on the family budget, and possible liquidation of investments to provide emergency funds.

Advisors should strive to respond in an additive manner to help move the conversation towards problems they can help solve. At the minimum, advisors should respond in a reciprocal manner. Subtractive comments are unacceptable.

6.4 EFFECTIVE USE OF QUESTIONS

It is unlikely that clients will remember or volunteer all the information the advisor requires. Clients may not be fully aware of what information is important and relevant. To assure the collection of significant information, advisors must be skilful listeners and questioners. Information can be solicited in a number of ways: restatement of a portion of what the client has said (*You think you may not be able to afford to educate your children at a first-rate university*); directing the client to give more information (*Tell me more about the kind of service you are looking for*); and asking effective questions. An over-use of questions can turn the interview into an interrogation and put the client on the defensive, but appropriate questions asked in the right manner can solicit critical information and advance relationships. Advisors need to understand the types of questions that can be asked, and how and when to ask them. This section highlights four types of questions: **open-ended**, **closed-ended**, **indirect**, and **loaded**.

6.4.1 Open-Ended Questions

Open-ended questions ask for a client's response to general questions about specific topics. Clients are free to answer as they desire. They are asked to give their opinions or experiences in as much detail as they wish, as seen in the following examples.

- o   *What are your feelings about taking some risk with your investments?*
- o   *What are your goals?*
- o   *What is your investment experience?*
- o   *How would you describe your investment objectives?*
- o   *Where do you see yourself personally and financially in 10 years?*

As the advisor listens to the client's answers, the client's goals, values, preferences, needs, and personal situation become clearer. The advisor is free to follow up the answer and gather more information by directing the questioning to more specific issues.

Open-ended questions are most beneficial early in an interview in order to relax clients and to encourage them to talk about their concerns. Open-ended questions are also less threatening to resistant clients. The chief disadvantage of open-ended questions is that they may take a great deal of time to answer, and in the process, the advisor may lose control of the interview and not get the particular information needed. Open-ended questions require the use of active and empathetic listening and sometimes summarization.

6.4.2 Closed-Ended Questions

Closed-ended questions ask directly for specific information. Here are examples of closed-ended questions.

   o *Have you invested in equities before?*
   o *When do you plan to retire?*
   o *Do you want to start an education fund for your children?*
   o *Are all your investments with our institution?*

Closed-ended questions, like the ones above, can be answered in a few words. They can be used to focus the interview and to acquire specific pieces of vital information at critical points. Contrast the first two closed-ended questions above with these two open-ended questions that ask for the same information: *What experience have you had with investing in equities?* and *What are your retirement plans?* Recast as open questions, the two original closed-ended questions should elicit more in-depth answers. A response to the first open-ended question might describe past and current investments and the client's success and satisfaction with the advice received. A response to the second question might disclose how long the client has worked and if any employer retirement plans or retirement savings are in place. An answer to the closed-ended equivalent would have revealed none of this information. The type of question that is appropriate to use depends on the kind of information required and the stage of the relationship.

6.4.3 Indirect Questions

Indirect questions are *round-about* ways of obtaining information without directly asking for it. This approach can be particularly useful when the advisor perceives that the client is somewhat secretive. There are two types of indirect questions. The first type is really not a question at all – it does not end with a question mark. It is a statement that explains why the advisor needs certain information. Here are some examples:

   o *I would be interested in knowing about your investment experience; it will guide my suggestions.*
   o *I will need to have an understanding of your income and expenses to analyze your financial situation.*

The second type of indirect question is a question that asks for permission to ask a direct question. For example: *Do you mind if I ask you about your other investments, the ones you don't have with us?* (Structurally, this is a closed-ended question because it can be answered with one or two words, but its intent is to be indirect.)

Such indirect questions are useful when the client is resistant to sharing personal information and defensive about any attempts to solicit it. The indirect question: *In order to make a recommendation, I will have to know how much you have available each month to invest,* will probably be perceived as less threatening than the closed-ended question: *How much do you make?* The same can be said for this indirect question, *Do you mind if I ask you about your monthly saving and investing?*

The response to both types of indirect questions will either be that the client grants the advisor permission to proceed or indicates that the topic is *off-limits.* Setting the question up this way avoids making the client feel put on-the-spot.

6.4.4. Loaded Questions
One kind of question that can be troublesome is the **loaded** question – also called a *leading* question. It directs the responder to give an answer the questioner wants to hear. It is sometimes used to *nudge* the client to answer in a way that is clearly to the benefit of the advisor, but not necessarily to the client, as seen in the following examples.

    o   *Don't you think my suggestions are good and our products are what you need?*
    o   *Do you see that this program fits your goals and needs?*

It is clear that the advisor would prefer the client to answer *yes* to both questions. Loaded questions show a lack of respect. They are counterproductive if the client feels pressured or manipulated by them and they may erode any trust that has been established. If prior discussions with clients have been managed correctly, clients should naturally come to the conclusion that the product solutions are appropriate without being forced into a position of having to agree – probably with reservations.

6.5 GUIDELINES FOR ASKING QUESTIONS
To acquire the information needed to gain an accurate and complete understanding of the client's situation, the advisor must be skilful in formulating and asking questions. The following guidelines should be kept in mind.

- Do not rely on questions to gather information. Use a combination of restatements, paraphrases, direct requests, and questions.
- Use a **variety** of closed-ended and open-ended questions.
- Use the ***funnelling*** approach that starts with open-ended questions and moves to closed-ended questions as rapport is established, and as specific details are required. Like a funnel, the opening questions are very broad and general, but as the interview

proceeds, the advisor asks more specific questions, narrowing down the exact information sought.

- When seeking information that might be perceived by the client as highly personal, the advisor should ask indirect questions. Of course, if the relationship between the client and advisor has been established, questions might be asked more directly and not phrased in such diplomatic language. When in doubt about the client's reaction, advisors should err on the side of caution and diplomacy.

- Do not fire a barrage of questions at clients; give clients time to formulate thoughtful responses. Interviews should be dialogues, not interrogations.

- A question's usefulness lasts after an answer has been provided. Be ready to follow up answers to questions with other questions to learn more: *So, based on what you have said, it seems that one of your major concerns is currency fluctuations. Is this correct?* (This follow-up question was prompted by the client's answer to a question about risk tolerance.)

6.6 INADEQUATE ANSWERS

Despite the advisor's ability to ask appropriate questions, clients will not always respond in useful ways. Tubbs and Moss (2000) call these *inadequate* responses. Listed below are some types of inadequate answers and suggestions for dealing with them.

- **No response** requires the advisor to determine if the topic is sensitive, if the client did not hear the question, or if the question should be phrased in another way and repeated to make it more understandable or acceptable.

- **A partial answer** gives part of the answer the advisor expected. For example, in answering the advisor's question about the client's place of employment, the client responded: *I have been working there 15 years.* The place of employment was not indicated. The advisor may restate the part of the question that was not answered – *and where do you work?* In determining the communication problem, the advisor should assess whether the fault lies with the advisor and whether the questions are too complicated or there are too many asked at one time.

- **Irrelevant answers** miss the question all together. In response to the advisor's question about the client's employment, the client responded: *My next purchase will be a new car."* An irrelevant answer may be a sign that the client is reluctant to divulge personal information. Irrelevant answers are sometimes a polite way of saying *no* to the request for information. The advisor should take irrelevant answers as cues that the client either misunderstands or that the questions were unwelcome.

- **Inaccurate answers** are clearly wrong. The client's answer: *I have been working there 55 years*, asked of someone in their 40s cannot be correct. The client may be reluctant to divulge the facts because the question is felt to be too personal or that the answer will create a negative perception of the client. If the advisor senses that the client is giving a number of inaccurate answers, the advisor needs to think about how to create a more open and trusting relationship in which the client feels more comfortable to give open and honest answers.

- The **over-verbalized answer** is opposite to the other types of inadequate answers. The client is overly eager to give too much detail and to provide more information than the advisor needs. The challenge for the advisor is to limit the client's talkativeness. To manage this type of response, the advisor should make use of frequent summary statements each time leading the client back to the topic at hand. The advisor should also consider asking more closed questions.

6.7 CONCLUSION

One of the advisor's main objectives is to work with clients to build a shared understanding of their situations and financial concerns. This requires more than soliciting key information; it also requires building relationships in which clients feel understood and are willing to provide the information the advisor needs in order to create value for them. The concepts and strategies in this chapter are aimed at helping advisors come to an understanding of their clients' needs and goals by being active listeners, using empathy, asking the right kinds of questions at the appropriate times, and dealing skilfully with inadequate answers.

In Chapter 3, we introduced the comedy team of Bob and Ray to help illustrate some important communication skills (or lack of them). In the Internet clip (as of August, 2010), whose address follows (with a brief introduction), Bob and Ray demonstrate the importance of patience in listening:

http://www.npr.org/templates/player/mediaPlayer.html?action=1&t=1&islist=false&id= 88761223&m=88770981

KEY TERMS

Active listening. Giving full attention to the speaker. It requires hearing, paying attention, understanding, analyzing, and remembering.

Additive empathy. Responses that accurately reflect the other person's feelings and move the other person to focus on business issues.

Closed-ended questions. Questions that ask for direct, specific information.

Empathy. Understanding how another person feels without having the same feelings.

Feedback. The speaker asks the listener to respond to what the speaker has said.

Funnel approach. Questioning that starts with open-ended questions and moves to closed-ended questions as rapport is established, and as specific details are required.

Inaccurate answers. Answers that are clearly wrong.

Indirect questions. Indirect or roundabout ways of obtaining information without actually asking for it directly.

Irrelevant answers. Giving an answer that does not relate to the question that was asked.

Loaded questions. Questions that direct the responder to answer in a way the questioner wishes.

Open-ended questions. Questions that ask for a client's response to a general question about a particular topic.

Over-verbalized answers. Answers that provide too much detail and more information than the questioner needs or asked for.

Paraphrasing. A restatement of what has been said, in the hearer's words.

Partial answers. Supplying part of an answer to a question.

Reciprocal empathy. Responses that accurately reflect the other person's feelings.

Restating. Repeating what the other person has said, in the other person's words.

Subtractive empathy. Responses that convey no understanding of the other person's concerns and feelings.

Summarizing. Similar to paraphrasing and restating, but it relates not to a particular part of a conversation but to an extended or entire conversation.

Sympathy. Having the same feelings as someone else.

Thought gaps. Times when the listener is inattentive and not listening.

Verification. A person checks out his or her understanding of what the other person has said to determine if that understanding is correct.

CHAPTER 7

THE INTERVIEW AGENDA

7.0 THE SEMI-STRUCTURED INTERVIEW

> Mr. Abbas expressed an interest in investing in an equity fund. The advisor presented a technology fund as a potential candidate. During the presentation, the advisor noticed the client leaning back, at first, and then, near the conclusion of the presentation, moving forward, as if getting more interested. By the conclusion of the presentation, the advisor was sure Mr. Abbas was ready to invest in the fund.
>
> **Advisor:** *I am sure you want to sign now. Don't you?*
> **Mr. Abbas:** *Do you know that I am retiring soon?*
> **Advisor:** *By-the-way, how much do you want to invest?*
> **Mr. Abbas**: *I am interested in investing a certain amount.*
> **Advisor:** *Everybody wants to retire including myself.*
> **Mr. Abbas:** *Do you have any other investment products?*
> **Advisor:** *You can trust me; there is nothing better than this fund.*
> **Mr. Abbas:** (Standing up.) *I will think about it.* (Mr. Abbass left and the advisor never heard from him again.)

In the above incident, there are some glaring weaknesses in the advisor's approach: the reliance on assumptions; the use of loaded questions; a failure to listen actively; and a lack of verification and feedback. Any one of these mistakes could explain the client's failure to continue the relationship. But the problem that this chapter focuses on is the interview's lack of structure – it wandered and led nowhere.

In order to create value, the advisor will have to guide the interview in such a way that all relevant information is gathered and the process led to a conclusion. One approach is to ask a standardized set of questions, in a rigid, established order, but this does not encourage an open, casual conversation. An opposite extreme is to conduct a non-structured interview in which the advisor has no particular questions in mind and lets the conversation ramble past and through various topics until the advisor decides all the relevant information has been gathered. A middle approach – the one advocated here – has a flexible agenda. It is a ***semi-structured*** approach. Using this approach, the advisor has an agenda, a general idea of how to proceed, and a destination in mind, but the advisor is ready to adjust the agenda when other issues appear more important to the client.

A semi-structured approach allows the advisor to gather information and to guide the conversation without appearing too rigid and controlling, or too casual and unfocused. The semi-structured approach has several other advantages.

- It allows the advisor to acquire needed information in a conversational manner.
- It allows the advisor to guide the direction of the conversation.
- It allows the advisor to develop the relationship while drawing out information in a non-threatening manner.

This semi-structured approach is semi-formal and allows for the natural development of a personal relationship as information is collected. The advisor as an interviewer must be able to shift attention between two arenas. At times, the advisor will be concerned with managing the dynamics of the relationship so that it develops in a positive way, and at other times, the advisor will concentrate on the actual questions and content of the answers.

Using a semi-structured approach, the advisor will probe, follow cues, ask open and closed questions, make indirect statements, and seek clarification. The advisor will have questions in mind, but will ask them in the context of the conversation and at the appropriate time. The advisor does not bombard the client with a series of inquiries.

7.1 Attending to the Client's Immediate Concerns and Discussing Goals

Typically, clients will approach financial services representatives with specific concerns. If the advisor is product-centred, a selling strategy will be undertaken. However, an advisor with a client-centred approach will view the client's initial concerns as a doorway through which to gain access to the client's wider range of concerns and goals wherein lay greater opportunities to provide product solutions. The following example illustrates this point.

> A client asked to speak to a financial representative about his account.
>
> **Advisor:** (Inviting the client into his office.) *I hope I can help you sir; you said you were worried about your account. What is the problem?*
> **Client:** *I have a considerable amount of cash in my account and I am worried about its safety. I would feel better if I knew precisely how safe it is.*
> **Advisor:** *Yes. May I see your bank statement?*
> **Client:** *Most certainly.* (The client handed the advisor his statement.) *As you see there is slightly more than one hundred thousand in my account.*
> **Advisor:** *Yes.* (The advisor examined the entries.) *All deposits were made in the last month.*
> **Client:** *That's correct. I have not been in this country long. This is money I brought with me from my home country.*
> **Advisor:** *Well, we are glad to welcome you to this country, and to our institution. As far as your account goes, there is one concern.*
> **Client:** *Oh, really?*

> **Advisor:** *Yes, your money is safe but it is earning a very low rate of return. There are other things you can do with that money to get a better return.*
> **Client:** *I understand. What would you recommend?*
> **Advisor:** *I would suggest we might do the following….*
>
> The advisor explained the various options in detail and helped the client assess them in light of the client's preferences. The client selected one option, thanked the advisor, and left the branch.

Would you say this interview was a success? The answer is: *it depends.*

The advisor certainly offered valuable counselling assistance to the client, but failed to expand the conversation beyond the client's initial concern. The conversation focused only on one issue – rates of return – and the advisor did not try to discover the client's range of financial needs and goals. One obvious question is what are the client's plans for the money in the account. What do the client's savings represent? Are they parked in a convenient place until the client decides what to do with them, or does the client already have a strategy in mind? The savings account is the visible part of the client's financial situation. It is the *tip of the iceberg*; a host of concerns and plans lie beneath the surface. The amount in the account is linked to the client's lifestyle and goals that, in this conversation, remained unexplored. The advisor tried to be helpful in suggesting ways to increase the rate of return, but still the client's goals went undiscovered. Without knowledge of the client's goals, the advisor is limited in what can be done for the client. Following a client-centred approach, the advisor might have said: *Your money is safe and I think there is a way to earn a better return from it, but first, I should know what plans you have for your money.*

A discussion of this issue could lead to a disclosure of the client's financial goals and a discussion of strategies for accomplishing them. In the process, a good working alliance could have been built between the client and advisor; in the long run, a number of the institution's products and services might have been offered as solutions.

It is not uncommon for advisors to have difficulty breaking through the boundaries of routine conversations to initiate a discussion of broader issues and goals. For the sake of their business, and their clients' financial needs, advisors must learn to penetrate this barrier and get beyond a product orientation to initiate a conversation about goals. There are a number of reasons this barrier exists: training in a product orientation; an eagerness to be helpful in a familiar way; uncertainty associated with entering new territory; and a concern that such an interest in their client's goals might be rejected by the client as too personal.

Figure 7.1 depicts the transition the advisor will have to make from routine, product-centred conversations to goal discussions. The solid block in the figure depicts the internal barriers (as mentioned above) that the advisor will have to overcome in order to discuss goals with clients. Figure 7.1 also points out that a discussion of goals eventually leads to the matching of products with goals. By contrast, the product-centred conversation leads to a less effective and short-sighted attempt to *sell* products.

Figure 7.1
Expanding the Discussion

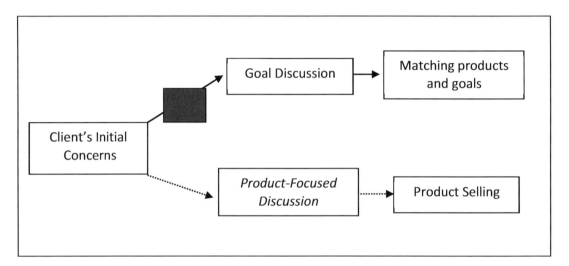

The following are helpful statements or questions to introduce the topic of goals.

- *How do these objectives fit with your other goals?*
- *Before I can give you my suggestions, it would be helpful to know how this investment fits with your goals.*
- *Before we talk about the construction of your portfolio, we should discuss your goals and what you want your investments to accomplish for you.*

Even though the objective is to encourage clients to verbalize their goals, it is supremely important that the advisor first attend to clients' initial questions, or requests. In order to lead clients, the advisor must start from where clients are. **The objective is to attend to clients' initial concerns and then to lead them into a discussion of goals.** To uncover clients' goals advisors will find it helpful to follow cues.

7.1.1 Following Cues

Cues are indicators that certain matters are of concern to a client. For example, when a client says, *My brother is in good financial shape;* **he** [with emphasis] *will be able to retire early,* the client is giving a cue that retirement planning is a strongly felt concern. Picking up cues allows the advisor to focus the conversation on concerns that are often linked to client goals. Active listening facilitates the identification and pursuit of cues, as seen in the advisor's response.

> **Client:** *My brother is in good financial shape; **he** will be able to retire early,*
> **Advisor:** *Retirement planning would seem to be a concern of yours, especially your ability to retire when you want to. How are you coming along with that goal?*

Reacting to cues allows the advisor to raise issues, which were only mentioned briefly or in passing, to the level of intentional conversation. To pick up cues, the advisor's ear must be tuned to listen for concerns that have been stated indirectly, or as asides, and are probably more important than the client has indicated. The advisor's mind should act like a filing cabinet. As the client mentions various issues, the advisor should open mental *files* on them and store new information as more is learned. Once a file reaches the *tipping point*, the advisor can bring the issue to the client's attention for a more thorough and focused discussion of the topic.

The advisor pursues cues by probing and asking more questions about an issue to determine the issues' importance to the client. The pursuit of cues can lead to a discussion of goals, as seen in the following incident.

> Mrs. Zingaro is a lab technologist at a local hospital. Her husband is a manufacturer's agent for a chemical company. They are both in their mid-forties with no children. Mrs. Zingaro and the advisor have talked several times before, usually about mutual funds.
>
> **Mrs. Zingaro**: *My husband had a close call the other day on the road.*
> **Advisor**: *Oh? What do you mean?*
> **Mrs. Zingaro**: *Another car came across the centre line and drove right at him. Fortunately, it veered back at the last moment.*
> **Advisor**: *That must have been scary. I am glad he is alright.*
> **Mrs. Zingaro**: *Me too, of course. It started us thinking about what would happen if he did get hurt on the road, or even worse. You know he travels for a living.*
> **Advisor**: *You have mentioned your concern before. You told me the other day that he does have some disability insurance, but you are worried that you don't have enough saved to provide additional income.*
> **Mrs. Zingaro**: *Yes. It's just...well, if he had to stop working we would have a difficult time. We need to save more.*
> **Advisor**: *It sounds like we should be talking about how to build up a fund along with any insurance that could provide for you in the event of an unfortunate event.*

The advisor remembered that the client had made similar comments before about the couple's financial vulnerability in the face of an accident or sickness, so the advisor thought it would be useful to focus the client's attention and discuss the situation.

Pursuing cues concentrates the conversation on specific topics that fall within the advisor's expertise. Exploring cues can be helped with such phrases as:

    o   *You mentioned this several times before. Is this a concern we should discuss?*

    o   *This seems to be a particular concern of yours. You said before that…*

    o   *We have talked about this, I wonder if we should now consider…*

    o   *Thinking about what you said concerning…maybe we should now think of…*

Recognizing and following cues requires active listening and makes use of our perceptual system which selects and organizes information, in this case tuned to latent client concerns. In following cues, the advisor communicates a more than casual interest in the client's financial concerns and a willingness to take the discussion to a deeper level.

7.1.2 Making Goals Specific

Advisors may have to be very basic with some clients and help them identify and articulate their goals. With other clients, who have given their goals more thought, advisors will arrive more quickly at a discussion of strategies and options for achieving their goals. A critical aspect of discussing goals is making them specific.

Only specific goals have power. Clients with articulated goals are energized to work to achieve them. Vague, ill-defined goals have no power. For example, the goal to retire *early* is too vague to adopt as a workable target, or to be an important motivating force. A general desire must be turned into a concrete objective with a time frame and a cost. The task in making goals specific is to identify their **timing** and **cost**. By what date does the client want to retire and how much will be needed? The client's objective may be three million dollars in 18 years, for example. From here, the advisor will calculate (using time value of money techniques) the on-going cost of making regular contributions to a retirement fund to accumulate the target amount of three million dollars over the next 18 years. (The actual problem will probably be somewhat *messier* with lump sums and employer or government-sponsored retirement benefits involved, which require the advisor to be technically competent in making these kinds of calculations.)

A discussion of goals and the development of strategies to achieve them adds great value to clients' situations and have significant potential for the advisor's short and long-term business prospects.

7.2 PHASES OF THE INTERVIEW

It is helpful to think of an interview as passing through three distinct stages or phases: the Opening, the Body, and the Conclusion. Each phase has its own characteristics and tasks to accomplish. It is important that the advisor understands the objectives of each phase and is able to move the interview along to the conclusion.

7.2.1 The Interview Opening

The opening sets the tone of an interview, and here the advisor has an opportunity to lay the foundation for good relationships. During the opening, the advisor greets the client in a respectful and friendly manner. Using appropriate verbal and nonverbal means, such as a handshake, the offering of a beverage, eye contact, and a smile, the advisor begins to communicate positive regard to clients and that their presence is important and their business is valued. The Japanese word for customer, *okyakusama* – *honourable guest*, or *lord* – is the proper orientation for the financial advisor.

The greeting is usually followed by casual conversation to build rapport and to set a relaxed atmosphere. Some clients may want to get right to business while others may want to socialize. The advisor will use the appropriate skills, such as summarization, to make the transition to business issues when it is time.

In the opening, the purpose and nature of the interview is explained. The advisor should ask the client how much time can be devoted to the meeting as well as to indicate any time constraints of the advisor. If it is a first meeting, the advisor should take time to share relevant personal information, such as experience, training, professional designations, values, members of the team, and the institution's philosophy and strengths. In subsequent meetings, the advisor should summarize the highlights of previous discussions. In the opening phase, the advisor's interest in the client's situation and objectives should be established.

Following is an account, from an advisor's perspective, of the opening phase of the advisor's first meeting with Mr. Hubbard and his wife.

> *The conversation was very fluid. I found out that Mr. Hubbard had worked for the same railway line as my father and we realized that we knew several people in common. After five or ten minutes of casual conversation, I proceeded to explain my role and proposed an agenda for our meeting. They agreed. My agenda had three parts: to ask a few questions around their current investment strategy, review the investment management service they were receiving from their current institution, and to gather information about their personal goals and current financial situation.*

7.2.2 The Interview Body

As the conversation moves into the body, and if it is an initial meeting, the advisor will listen to the client's immediate concerns and then attempt to broaden the conversation to include the client's range of needs and goals.

The checklist in Figure 7.2 is a good guide for picking up cues and identifying the range of client goals and needs at various life stages.

Figure 7.2
Client Concerns

SINGLE/YOUNG AND MARRIED
Goals
- Vehicle/Home purchase
- Further education
- Funds for marriage

Primary Needs
- Budget control
- Paying off accumulated debt
- Establishing a savings program

GROWING FAMILIES
Goals
- Future education for children
- Larger house

Primary Needs
- Budget control
- Establishing an emergency fund
- Protecting family's security

ESTABLISHED FAMILIES
Goals
- Higher education for children
- Replacing major assets
- Retirement planning
- Estate planning

Primary Needs
- Managing cash flow
- Building net worth
- Investing excess savings

RETIRED AND ACTIVE
Goals
- Recreation/Travel
- Personal care

Primary Needs
- Managing cash flow
- Wealth preservation
- Update estate plan

Depending on the content of previous meetings, the advisor will do any of the following in the body of the interview: gather relevant qualitative (non-financial) and quantitative (financial) information; analyze and discuss various strategies and products; present recommendations and product solutions; or sign the proper documents and execute the strategy.

The advisor should use a variety of questioning techniques, a semi-structured style, and a funnelling approach to conduct the interview. To ensure all relevant information has been discussed, the list below contains relevant qualitative and quantitative information that will need to be gathered.

Qualitative Information
- Age of household members
- Special health circumstances
- Extended family obligations
- Occupation
- Investment experience
- Investment knowledge
- Investment risk tolerance
- Goals

Quantitative Information
- Household income
- Household expenses
- Investment assets – financial and real
- Risk management strategies

Returning to the previous conversation with the Hubbards, here is the way the advisor conducted the body of the interview.

> *I went through the agenda with the clients and gathered a great deal of information about their personal and financial goals. I confirmed Mrs. Hubbard's fears about being left with the responsibility of managing a large portfolio, given that Mr. Hubbard had recently suffered a stroke. I was able to determine that the Hubbards had over $750,000 in assets in different financial institutions scattered around the city. I explained the benefits of our Investment Management service, the fees, and basic investment philosophy.*

7.2.3 The Interview Conclusion
After all relevant matters have been discussed in the available time, the advisor will conclude the interview. The conclusion should begin with a summary of what was discussed and the outstanding matters that remain. The advisor should then indicate the next step in the process and gain the client's commitment to it.

Both verbal and nonverbal messages are used to indicate the end of a meeting. The advisor might ask whether the client has further questions, summarize the discussion, indicate the next step, set the time for the next meeting, or if time is short, explain why the meeting must end. If the advisor is having difficulty communicating that the interview is ending, the advisor might use nonverbal language to enforce the verbal message: straightening up, closing a writing pad, tidying up the desk, standing up, breaking eye contact, offering to shake hands, or walking towards the door. Nonverbal language has power to communicate that the meeting is over without having to tell clients directly.

The advisor concluded the interview with the Hubbards this way:

> *I explained the next step would be for me to prepare a proposal and then we would meet to review it. We agreed on a time.*

Table 7.1 below summarizes the advisor's objectives during each phase of the interview.

Table 7.1
Interview Phases

	Objectives
Opening	·To make the client feel welcome and valued ·To summarize previous discussions ·To explain the purpose of the meeting
Body (depending on previous discussions)	·To acquire relevant personal and financial information ·To discuss strategies ·To present a recommendation ·To execute the strategy
Conclusion	·To summarize the discussion ·To indicate the next step ·To gain the client's commitment to the next step

Here is an account of an interview an advisor had with Mr. Saad. During a previous meeting, Mr. Saad had expressed an interest in investment products and the advisor visited him at his office to make a product presentation. The interview is presented in the left-hand column and comments are in the opposite column. The setting of the meeting is Middle Eastern, but the dynamics are typical of most cultures. The incident is instructional for its strengths as well as its weaknesses.

Dialogue	Comments
Mr. Saad: *Good afternoon. It is nice to meet you. Please come into my office.*	
Advisor: *Good afternoon. Thank you. It is hard to park your car here.*	
Mr. Saad: *Yes. I hope you have a good product for me today.*	This ends the opening phase. Many things have been left out including a summary of their last conversation and the purpose of this meeting.
Advisor: *Yes, I have a great low-risk fund that invests mainly in the US and Europe, in companies with BBB and above ratings.* (The client wanders around his office and looks out the window.)	As will be explained in the next chapter, the advisor is not using effective presentation techniques. There are signs that the client's interest has not been engaged. The advisor is treating this as a transaction event and makes no attempt to get to know Mr. Saad or his objectives.
Mr. Saad: *I have been working with this group of companies for 50 years. My experience began when Riyadh was nothing but mud houses.* (He talked about the early years and his part in the city's development.) *Through my life I saw all kinds of bankers and, let us say, thieves. Before they were in suits, but now they are in Saudi thobes.* (The client looks angry.) *Banks deal with us as if we are only targets.*	Mr. Saad has a lot of experience and it appears he would like to share it and have the advisor appreciate it. Chapter 12 explains how we might describe him as coming to the point in life where he is developing some integrity about his life and its purpose. He has definite stereotypes and anger about bankers based upon past experience.
Advisor: *I understand.*	There is no way he could understand. He has not had the same experiences.
Mr. Saad: *No, you don't understand. I was advised to invest in the US market and my company lost lots of money. I don't want to repeat that experience.*	The client sets the advisor straight and is angry about his past losses.
Advisor: *That was a bad decision. Thank you for your time and I hope that we will meet in the future.*	The advisor uses subtractive empathy, which does not enhance the relationship. The advisor leaves abruptly. Apparently, the advisor feels the interview is over even though nothing has been accomplished and there has been no concrete conclusion.

Based on the concepts and techniques in the text, there are many things the advisor could have said and done to develop a relationship and create value for the client, but it appears the advisor felt threatened and did not know how to reach past Mr. Saad's verbal blows in order to begin to appreciate his feelings, experiences, and values. The lack of structure in the interview accounts for a lot of its failure – it does not lead anywhere.

Let us replay the interview and apply the skills we have discussed.

Dialogue	Comments
Mr. Saad: *Good afternoon. It is nice to see you again. Please come into my office.*	Such pleasantries are part of a good **opening**.
Advisor: *Good afternoon. Thank you. It is nice to meet you again. Since we last met and talked about your interest in low-risk investment products, I have been doing a lot of thinking about your needs.*	The advisor continues the opening by summarizing the previous discussion.
Mr. Saad: *I hope you have a good product for me today.*	
Advisor: *Well, I hope so too, but just to review what we were talking about the last time we met. You are interested in low-risk products and you would like to invest in this country or region to help provide capital to others.*	The advisor has verified his understanding of the client's needs.
Mr. Saad: *Yes that is true. What do you have?*	
Advisor: *In order for me to suggest an appropriate investment from the many we have, I would like to know a bit more about your objectives for this money and what it means to you.* (The client resisted the questioning at first and then in response to some open-ended and indirect questions shared a long story about his part in the history of the development of Riyadh.)	We are now in the **body** of the interview and the advisor is using good technique to learn about the client's objectives and values.
Advisor: *I would like to recommend a low-risk fund that invests mainly in the US and Europe, in companies with BBB and above ratings.* (The advisor gave more technical details and the client wandered around his office looking out the window.) *Sir, is this something you think you might be interested in?*	The client gives some indication that he is impatient with the presentation. He must have something else on his mind. The advisor asks for feedback based upon the client's nonverbal actions.
Mr. Saad: *I have been working with this group of companies for 50 years. My experience began in Riyadh when it was just mud houses. Through my life I saw all kinds of bankers and, let us say, "thieves." Before they were in suits, but now they are in Saudi thobes.* (The client looked angry.) *Banks deal with us as if we are only targets.*	It would be normal for most advisors to feel defensive at this point.

Advisor: *Sir, It is clear you are very disappointed by your past banking experiences.*	The advisor is empathetic.
Mr. Saad: *I was advised to invest in the US market and my company lost lots of money.*	
Advisor: *Sir, it sounds as if you were really hurt by that experience. I would like to try and change your perception of banks, especially the one I represent. How could we work together so that these sorts of things would not happen again?*	The advisor is empathetic and, at the same time, leads the client towards business issues – additive empathy.
Mr. Saad: *That is a good question.*	
Advisor: *Could I begin by getting to know your needs and objectives better to make sure that what I recommend is exactly what you need and that you fully understand how it works?* (Pause.)	The pause is important here to give the client a chance to react and let the advisor know if he is ready to proceed.
The advisor and client discussed the client's needs and some possible solutions. The client also made it clear what he expected in terms of full disclosure and updates.	
Advisor: *Mr. Saad, I know you have another appointment soon, so I would like to suggest that we both think carefully about what we have discussed and that when we meet again I can present you with some specific ideas for you to consider. Would next week at this same time be fine with you?*	In the **conclusion** the advisor summarizes the discussion and suggests the next step while securing a commitment to it.

This version of the meeting between the advisor and Mr. Saad has the needed structure – an opening, body, and conclusion. The advisor has also applied active listening skills to bring the client more into the relationship. The chances of the advisor creating value for the client have been greatly enhanced.

7.3 CONCLUSION

The advisor should not rigidly adhere to an agenda, but guide the conversation to cover the client's concerns including a discussion of the client's goals. Using a semi-structured approach, the advisor should guide the discussion through its opening, body, and concluding phases. The advisor should emerge from the meeting with a good understanding of the client's goals, a start on securing the client's trust, and an idea of how best to present the most appropriate products for the client – the topic of the next chapter.

KEY TERMS

Cues. Indicators that certain matters are of concern to the client even when the concern has not been stated directly.

Interview body. The main part of the interview during which the advisor acquires relevant personal and financial information about the client, discusses strategies to solve the client's problems, presents recommendations, or executes agreed-upon strategies.

Interview conclusion. The closing of the interview during which the discussion is summarized, the next step is indicated, and the client's commitment to the next step is gained.

Interview opening. The beginning of the interview in which the client is made to feel valued, the substance of previous discussions is summarized, and the purpose of the meeting is explained.

Semi-structured approach. A flexible approach to conducting an interview with an agenda and conclusion in mind, but a readiness to adjust the agenda when other issues appear more important to the client.

CHAPTER 8

DESIGNING AND PRESENTING A PROPOSAL

8.0 A BALANCING ACT

In the financial planning process, the advisor gathers relevant information about the client's financial situation and personal goals, and then mathematically assesses whether finances and goals can be balanced within the constraints of the client's personal preferences. If achievement of all of the client's financial goals is not feasible, there are five basic options: (1) find additional financial resources through additional income or reduced expenses; (2) make adjustments to the cost and timing of goals; (3) prioritize goals; (4) liquidate assets; or (5) borrow. Several attempts, or iterations, may be needed to bring goals and finances into balance. This requires that the advisor is competent in working with projected financial statements and time value of money calculations. Throughout this balancing process, which may require several attempts and trade-offs, it is important that the advisor secures client feedback and incorporates it into subsequent attempts. Once equilibrium between goals and resources has been obtained, the advisor is ready to present the finished plan which incorporates the use of the advisor's institution's products and services.

8.1 TESTS OF A GOOD STRATEGY

The successful conclusion of the advising process is the construction of a strategy that creates value for clients and uses the institution's services and products. **Products must be presented as solutions and not pushed on clients simply to meet the advisor's sales targets**. A strategy must meet certain tests before it is acceptable: (1) it must satisfy the financial needs and goals of the client; (2) it must consider the client's values and beliefs; and (3) it must be cost efficient.

8.1.1 The Proposal Must Meet the Client's Financial Needs and Goals

> Mr. Ruzi owns a medium-sized construction business. As a self-employed owner, he has no company pension plan and in retirement he will have to rely on investment income. During the course of the year, he accumulates about two million dollars in cash. Near the end of the year, he uses half of this to pay his suppliers. He invests the rest. Currently, most of his investments are in fairly safe securities. Mr. Ruzi and his wife have a disabled son, who is dependent on them.

Mr. Ruzi has a range of financial and personal needs that must all be recognized in designing a strategy. One of his goals is to build an investment portfolio to provide for his retirement. Another goal is to accumulate enough money to provide for his son's care after he and his wife are deceased. One of his needs is for ready cash at the end of each year to pay his suppliers. A viable strategy must keep all of these requirements in mind. Before a proposal is made, the advisor will have to actively listen to gain a thorough understanding of Mr. Ruzi's financial and personal situation including assets and liabilities, the timing of cash flows, his risk tolerance, his plans for retirement, and the nature of his son's disability.

One inappropriate solution to Mr. Ruzi's situation would be a heavy investment in common equity. This would disregard his need for liquidity; however, some equity will have to be considered to provide for the long-term care of his son. Considerable discussion between the advisor and Mr. Ruzi will have to occur before a suitable strategy and portfolio can be designed.

Asa Adler's (1995) research on wealthy consumers of financial services concluded that the majority had questions about the ability of their financial plans to meet their needs. Adler says that many wealthy clients wonder if their financial plans are meeting their financial objectives.

8.1.2 The Proposal Must Fit the Client's Values and Beliefs

As well as meeting financial objectives, a plan must be compatible with clients' risk tolerance, investment knowledge, beliefs, and values. For example, because of religious or philosophical reasons, some investors prefer ethical funds or *Shariah*-compliant investments. These clients do not want to benefit or support gambling, the armaments industries, the sale of liquor, or any other industry that does not reflect their values. It would not be acceptable to suggest investments in these sectors. Likewise, a risk-averse client may shun equity investments. The client's beliefs and values must be honoured.

Mr. Ruzi strongly believes that a family should look after its own members. It would be unthinkable to devise a plan that would rely on government assistance or an institution to care for their son after he and his wife are gone. A suitable plan will incorporate the Ruzis' view of how their son should live after their deaths. Money serves three main functions for the Ruzis: it pays the bills, allows the family to do things they enjoy, and it gives expression to their values. A proposal must acknowledge and incorporate these considerations.

8.1.3 The Proposal must be Cost Efficient

There are usually several possible strategies that can achieve clients' goals and meet their needs. But those that minimize cost, without sacrificing effectiveness, are the most desirable. This is where the advisor must be totally committed to securing the client's best interests. Cost efficient strategies may mean using products that are less lucrative for the advisor or the advisor's institution. For example, the advisor may suggest that Mr. Ruzi should invest excess funds in a long-term security and rely on a credit facility to pay his trade accounts at the end of the year. Another option is to put a certain percentage of surplus cash each month in a liquid account that can be drawn on at year-end. In both cases, funds will be available when needed. However, a final assessment requires a comparison of the cost of the credit facility with expected gains from a long-term investment.

8.2 EFFECTIVE PRESENTATION OF A PROPOSAL

Once a strategy or product solution has been designed, it must be presented in an effective manner for the client's final approval. The following are some guidelines for presenting plans and strategies. (Where the process is not a full planning one, but more of a short-term counseling one, the same guidelines apply to the presentation of products.)

8.2.1 Appeal to Different Learning Styles

The next module discusses the different ways in which people prefer to receive information. The three main ways are **auditory**, **visual**, and **kinesthetic**. In brief, an auditory person prefers to hear the information, a visual person prefers to view the information, and a kinesthetic person prefers to be physically involved with the information by making calculations, drawing diagrams, or being made the subject of examples. The descriptions of these modes are, for now, aimed at simply making the point that the presenter must identify and appeal to the favoured learning style of the receiver. (Your appreciation of this point will be much keener after reading Chapter 9.)

Nonverbal reactions can help the presenter determine the learning style to which the client is most responsive. If one approach does not seem effective, the presenter can switch to another mode. In the following example, the presenter is able to gauge the client's reaction to the presentation and is flexible enough to change styles to find one that is more effective.

> **Advsior:** *Good afternoon Mrs. Hamadan. I hope things have been well with you and your family since we last met.*
>
> **Mrs. Hamadan:** *Yes, very well. Thank you for asking.*
>
> **Advisor:** *Today, I would like to discuss a suggestion I have for your portfolio. As you remember, the last time we met, we discussed your objectives and you asked me to think about an investment that would fit your needs.*
>
> **Mrs. Hamadan:** *Yes, I remember. What do you have for me?*
>
> **Advisor:** *If you would allow me, I have a PowerPoint presentation here on my computer that outlines it very well.*
>
> **Mrs. Hamadan:** *Ah, yes...fine.*
>
> **Advisor:** (The advisor activated the presentation and positioned the laptop screen to face the client. The advisor ran through the presentation and made comments on each slide. As the presentation went on, the advisor noticed that the client frequently turned her head away from the screen. The advisor wondered if the reason, other than the content, was that the client was not visual and did not find the presentation helpful, so the advisor paused the slide show and talked for the rest of the presentation. The client did not seem to miss the slides, but still was not as interested as the advisor hoped she would be.)
>
> *Maybe I will stop here for a while and ask if you have any questions about anything I have presented.*
>
> **Mrs. Hamadan:** *Well, I think the product may be just what I need, but I have some difficulty "getting a feel" for it. In particular, I am not quite sure how I get my money back from it and how the return is calculated.*
>
> **Advisor:** *Perhaps it would help if I gave you an example.*
>
> **Mrs. Hamadan:** *Yes, that would be good.*
>
> **Advisor:** (The advisor provided several examples of how the client could redeem the investment and how the return was calculated under different circumstances.)
>
> **Mrs. Hamadan:** *Ah, yes, now I get it.*

The advisor began with a visual and auditory approach, but the client did not appear to understand until the advisor took a kinesthetic approach and constructed examples using calculations. The advisor was aware of the client's nonverbal reactions, asked for feedback, and was able to switch to different learning styles, and so was ultimately successful in making the presentation.

8.2.2 Use Appropriate Language – Avoid Jargon

A client may have difficulty comprehending the presentation because of the presenter's choice of words. The client may find the advisor's terminology too technical and filled with jargon. Advisors should avoid jargon and use simple, non-technical language until they are sure of their clients' levels of understanding. Problems with *semantics* and *syntax* (see Chapter 3) can also hamper a presentation.

In the following example, the advisor's use of jargon plays a major role in losing the client.

Advisor: *Since we last met, I have created a plan that will help you achieve your goals.*

Client: *Good! I am looking forward to your recommendations.*

Advisor: *I think it is time you started investing in hedge funds. Personally, I like the event-driven strategies. There are several...* (the client interrupts)...

Client: *Are those risky?*

Advisor: *Not as bad as distressed debt. There are several opportunities in the market now. I think the time is past for "M and A's", but there are other plays to be made. For instance, the arbitrage sector looks good. Whatever fund we go into, I recommend one with a high water mark, just to cut the downside risk.*

Client: (Scratching his head.) *Ah, yes. I suppose. How risky are these?*

Advisor: *The main thing is we don't want to get caught looking for the highest Sharpe ratio. It is an entirely inappropriate measurement with hedge funds.*

Client: *Hmmm. How does this all help my situation? Do you have any literature I can look at?*

Advisor: *No, but we had some. I really think this is the way you should go.*

This conversation is full of jargon. One wonders where the client's attention is during the thought gaps. One thing is certain: the advisor and client are not communicating and the client feels ostracized from the conversation. Compounding the problem in the above example is the advisor's unwillingness to entertain the client's questions. Stopping to deal with these could have put the conversation back on track.

The use of jargon and technical language is an inherent problem for financial professionals for whom it is part of every-day conversation. In order to avoid jargon, advisors must be empathetic and experience the conversation from the client's perspective.

8.2.3 Seek Feedback

In all situations where the advisor is uncertain of the client's ability to understand, the approach is the same: obtain the client's feedback. Ask whether the client understands or has any questions. Even a simple pause sometimes gives a confused client time to catch up. This is a major benefit of the semi-structured interview style which allows room for, and encourages, client feedback. Both examples we have looked at show the importance of feedback when it has been asked for and when it has been ignored.

8.2.4 Be Ready to Adjust Pace and Direction

When feedback indicates that the client does not understand the presentation, the advisor should be ready to modify the ***pace*** and ***direction*** of the presentation. Pace refers to the speed of the presentation, and direction refers to the range of topics that are discussed and the depth of detail. It is a good idea for the advisor to pause periodically to give the client a chance to direct the discussion towards items of interest and concern. A pause is similar to waiting for a traffic signal. It is the advisor's way of saying: *Do you want me to stop, wait, or proceed? And if you want me to go on, in which direction?*

If verbal or nonverbal clues indicate that the client is not following the presentation, the advisor must yield and find another way to express the same idea. The advisor should be ready to change the direction of the conversation to topics related to the client's immediate questions and concerns.

8.2.5 Move from the Simple to the Complex

One of the key principals in presentations is to start with general, basic explanations and then move to more complexity as the depth of the client's knowledge becomes clearer. Beginning with complex and detailed explanations is an assured way to lose clients. Here is an example of this point.

Dr. Matwawana: *I am concerned about my investments. I just inherited a sizeable sum from my late uncle and I am not sure what to do with it.*

Advisor: *I would be glad to help. Where should we begin?*

Dr. Matwawana: *Well, I have been reading a lot lately and it seems that one important thing is asset allocation.*

Advisor: *Yes, I agree. That is a very important concern. Second to that is diversification within asset categories.*

Dr. Matwawana: *Yes, pardon me for asking, but what does that mean?*

Advisor: *What I mean is that we should not only talk about diversification across asset categories, but within them as well.*

Dr. Matwawana: *Yes, of course.* (Scratching his head.)

Advisor: *We have a range of appropriate investments available through our institution. We could look at fixed income securities as well as equity, and of course, there are the hybrids. Actually, convertible, fixed-income securities are not a bad option at this time with the yield curve moving down. I would suggest that the speculative premium on convertibles is rather favourable right now and a drop in real rates will have a buoyant effect on price appreciation. And of course there is the embedded option these contain.*

Dr. Matwawana: *Thank you. You have been very helpful; you have given me a lot to think about. Goodbye.*

Will Doctor Matwawana return? The problem is not only the degree of complexity in the advisor's explanation, but the over-use of jargon. These two seem to go together.

When Dr. Matwawana approached the advisor, he had a problem: he did not know how to invest his new-found wealth. He was looking for someone to help him solve his problem. Instead, he received a barrage of details and very complex explanations. He became lost and confused, and appeared to give up.

Let us replay the scene and replace the first advisor with one who has much better presentation skills, one who is more able to move from the simple to the complex, and to adjust the pace and direction of the conversation in line with the client's questions and knowledge.

> **Dr. Matwawana:** *I am concerned about my investments. I just inherited a sizeable sum from my late uncle and I am not sure what to do with it.*
> **Advisor:** *I would be glad to help. Where should we begin?*
> **Dr. Matwawana:** *Well, I have been reading a lot lately and it seems that one important thing is asset allocation.*
> **Advisor:** *Yes, I agree. That is a very important concern. How familiar are you with the concept?*
> **Dr. Matwawana:** *Somewhat, but not entirely.*
> **Advisor:** *Let me begin, and please feel free to ask questions at any time. There are basically two types of investments: fixed income and equity, as you probably know. Fixed income pays a regular rate of interest or dividends. Equity is basically stock and it may also pay dividends, but the usual reason people invest in equity is in the hope that its value will increase.* (Pause.)
> **Dr. Matwawana:** *Aren't there two kinds of stock?*
> **Advisor:** *Yes, common and preferred.* (Pause.) *All asset allocation refers to is how much you invest in each type of asset. There are a number of general guidelines to follow. Should we talk about those?*

The second advisor has a much higher chance of satisfying Dr. Matwawana's needs and gaining his trust and loyalty. He began at a slow pace with simple explanations and looked for feedback; receiving it, he proceeded to go into more complexity and detail. The advisor also welcomed and encouraged questions. For the advisor, the answers were signposts pointing to the direction in which he should proceed. He often paused to give Dr. Matwawana opportunity to think through what he had heard and to ask questions. This approach assured that the advisor and the client were walking together in the same direction and at the same speed. In the second example, Dr. Matwawana is much more likely to feel value has been created.

8.3 MAKING A DECISION AND GAINING COMMITMENT

After the advisor and client have discussed the client's concerns and the advisor has a good understanding of the client's needs and goals, the conversation approaches closure, that is, the point at which discussion is finished and implementation of the plan follows. In order for this to happen, the client must make a commitment to act and purchase the institution's products and services that the advisor has suggested. The incident below is one advisor's attempt to reach closure and to get the client to make a commitment.

> **Advisor:** *As I have said, I highly recommend you buy these shares, now. You have to act now or the opportunity to gain from their price appreciation will be lost. If you don't act now, you will lose a big profit.*
> **Client:** *As I said, let me think about it! OK?*

In the incident above, the client reacted negatively to the pressure exerted to *close the deal*. No wonder the client did not commit. It probably was apparent to the client that a decision was in the best interests of the **advisor**, but not necessarily in her best interests. Pressure to get clients to *do business* is not part of a value creation model. In the client-centred, value-creation mode, commitment to action is important because without it, clients will not take care of their financial needs and reach their goals. Gaining client commitment is one of the hardest parts of the advising process. If, up to this point, the advisor has competently managed interactions with the client, the client's commitment should follow naturally. If at this point, the client resists, it is because something has been missed: an accurate and complete understanding of the client's needs and goals; sufficient use of feedback and verification; encouragement of the client to raise questions; or appreciation of the client's reluctance to commit to something perceived as risky. These deficiencies in the process may be the result of the advisor's preoccupation with products rather than the client's needs.

How then in a value creation mode can an advisor encourage clients to commit to action and purchase the products and services that will enact the agreed-upon strategy?

8.3.1 FACING CLIENTS WITH A CHOICE

Surveys in sales management indicate that many buyers fail to make a decision because the salesperson has not asked for one. After a plan or product has been presented, explained, discussed, and all objections processed, clients need to be faced with a decision. In moving from talking about achieving objectives to initiating action, clients must make a conscious decision to proceed. There must be a point in the conversation where clients are confronted with a choice. In English parliamentary language, *the question must be put.*

The following are suggestions for calling for a decision.

- *Do you want us to get started on this now?*
- *Are you ready to go ahead with this?*
- *If we have addressed all of your questions and concerns, the next step is to take action.*
- *We have made a lot of progress and identified solutions to meet your needs. It is now time to take action.*
- *In planning for your future, we have agreed upon a plan. The next step is to put it into action.*

The question should be put in a way that brings the issue to a focus and clearly indicates that the next step is the client's agreement. The advisor does not do the client a favour by dropping the matter. Many clients' good intentions never become conscious decisions that are implemented because clients were not faced with the necessity of committing to action. As a result, both clients and the advisor's institution lose.

Research on goal commitment indicates that people are more likely to pursue goals if they have made them public and told others what they are going to do (Hollenbeck *et. al.*, 1989). The public pronouncement of the intention to pursue specific goals is a crucial component of sustained effort. If individuals tell someone that they are going to work towards a certain goal, it is more likely that they will make an all-out effort to achieve it. That someone can be the advisor.

8.3.2 ADOPTING CHALLENGING GOALS

Research into goal setting has established that commitment to achieving goals varies directly with the degree of difficulty associated with them. More challenging goals appear to lead to greater effort and accomplishment. Locke et al. (1981) stated that, *the major finding in goal-setting research is that difficult goals lead to higher levels of performance than do easy or vague goals (p.125)*. Easy goals do not arouse as high levels of energy and sustained effort as more challenging goals do. However, this is true only up to a point: goals need to be balanced with feasibility. Goals that are too high and have a low probability of being achieved are de-motivating.

The source of the following story is difficult to verify. It has assumed the status of an *urban myth* in the management realm, but it makes an important point.

> An employer needed a new salesperson. He interviewed several individuals using a standard set of questions, but with no positive results. He decided to devise a new approach. He placed a dartboard and darts prominently at one end of the waiting room, and installed a two-way mirror so he could observe the waiting candidates from his office. All the applicants picked up the darts but they varied in how closely they stood to the dartboard when they threw the darts. The employer noticed that some stood so close that they would never miss the bulls-eye; others stood at the opposite end of the room and had little chance of even hitting the board; and the remainder stood half-way between, not too close and not too far away. He invited those who stood halfway for a final interview. He reasoned that those who stood too close liked to play it too safe; those who stood too far away were taking on impossible challenges; and those who stood close enough to hit the board, but far enough away to make it a challenge, would be more likely to take on reasonable challenges and not give up.

An important part of motivating clients to commit to action is to encourage them to take on challenging, but realistic, goals. Realistic challenges are more motivating and have a greater chance of being achieved.

If the phases of the interview have been managed correctly, making a decision should be a logical next step and should not have to be forced by the advisor. If the client is reluctant, the advisor needs to understand the reasons for the hesitation. One of the most frustrating, and often puzzling, aspects of dealing with clients is the contradiction between their apparent agreement with the advisor's suggestions and lack of commitment to action. It is even more puzzling when clients break off further contact with the advisor.

> The advisor spent considerable time getting to know the client and presented a detailed portfolio designed to meet the client's needs. The advisor sought the client's feedback throughout the process. The advisor decided it was time to call for a commitment.

> **Advisor:** *This looks like a portfolio that would meet your needs.*
> **Client:** *If you think so. Leave me your proposal so I can study it during my next business trip, and I will get back to you.*
> **Advisor:** *I would like some more information about your liquidity needs and your risk tolerance.*
> **Client:** *Actually I'm too busy right now. I will discuss these points with you at our next meeting.*

The next meeting never happened – why should it? It is obvious that the client became disinterested. Perhaps it was the fact that after the presentation, the advisor asked for more information. If the advisor felt the proposal was good, why would critical aspects such as liquidity and risk tolerance not have been included already? It is fairly certain that the client was unimpressed with this incomplete proposal. In this light, the advisor's call for a commitment was premature. When clients are left feeling that their complete needs have not been understood, any proposal is simply a package of assets and/or liabilities, which any institution can offer.

8.4 CONCLUSION

In the value-creation, client-centred process, products and services are means of achieving clients' needs and goals. They must be presented in an effective manner so that clients understand their benefits. Effective presentation must be followed with strategies for encouraging client commitment.

KEY TERMS

Direction of presentation. The range of topics that are discussed and the depth of detail with which they are discussed.
Pace of presentation. The speed of a presentation.

MODULE IV

UNDERSTANDING THE CLIENT

CHAPTER 9

PERSONALITY DIMENSIONS

9.0 PERSONAL DIMENSIONS

> *You can't be older than 25. I am not interested in being advised by someone younger than my grandchildren. How, with your lack of experience, can you hope to advise me? I am sorry, but I will request the manager to assign me an older advisor.*

If you were the advisor in this incident, how would you react to the client? Would you be defensive? Would you argue and attempt to change the client's mind? Or would you simply agree that the best thing for the client is to have an older advisor? In this brief incident, some very important and complicated issues are involved.

If we look beneath the surface of the incident, we will find that personal factors, such as the client's beliefs, values, and needs are involved. Although these dimensions are at the core of our personalities, they are difficult to define – philosophers and academics have tried for centuries. It is much easier to simply acknowledge that they exist and influence our lives, relationships, and choices. This chapter offers some basic definitions of these dimensions and describes how they influence the kinds of relationships clients want with advisors, the degree of their openness, the kinds of services and products they seek and will accept, and their likelihood of making a commitment to a recommendation. The chapter then describes other individual processes that explain the differences people have with regard to information: the way they like to receive information, the form of information they prefer, and the methods they use to make decisions based on that information. To be client-centred and to create customized value for clients, advisors must understand and work with these personal individualized dimensions.

9.1 BELIEFS, VALUES, NEEDS, AND ATTITUDES

In the opening incident, the client is unhappy about being advised by someone perceived as immature and inexperienced. What accounts for the client's attitude? Some or all of the following could explain it.

- The client's **belief** that young people (under 25, in this case) do not have the wisdom or experience to advise older people.
- The client **values** receiving advice from someone with maturity and experience.
- The client **needs** advice he can rely on.
- The client had a bad **experience** with a young advisor.

We can see from above that clients' beliefs, values, needs, and experiences condition their attitudes toward advisors and their institutions' practices, products, and services.

The relationship between beliefs and other personal dimensions is depicted in Figure 9.1. Although Figure 9.1 is not an accurate representation of these complex relationships, it can help us understand their significant roles and interaction. Even though these dimensions are shown as discrete processes, in reality, they overlay, weave through, and wrap around each other, often without any defining boundary. The dimensions contained in text boxes are not directly observable but the behaviour they influence can be seen. The factors contained in the oval shapes are visible to others. The patterned background of the diagram represents the all-pervasive influence of culture that affects these dimensions.

Figure 9.1
Personal Dimensions

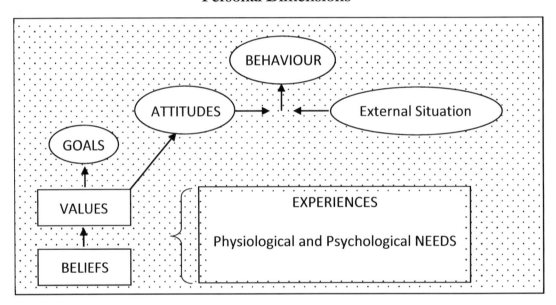

As depicted in Figure 9.1, beliefs lead to values, which affect our goals. Advisors should realize the deep processes that generate goals. Beliefs and values shape attitudes, which when brought in contact with an external situation, result in a predisposition, or readiness, to behave in a certain way, as the client in our incident did. Beliefs and values are influenced by past experiences, and physiological and psychological needs. Let us explore these concepts further.

9.1.1 Beliefs

During a presentation to a wealthy client, the advisor encouraged the client to take more risk to gain a higher return. The client responded: *My wealth is my family heritage. If getting more returns means that I have to risk capital, it will not be appealing to me because it is against all my beliefs. I want to pass this wealth to my children. I don't want to risk losing any of their security.*

At the core of our personalities are a set of fixed truths we hold as foundational to who we are. These **beliefs** are strongly held propositions about the way things are or should be. They are related to a wide range of subjects – from the best make of car to the existence of God. Beliefs produce opinions on a wide range of topics: *young people cannot provide advice to older people, equities will always outperform bonds, it is bad to take a risk, the greatest good is to help other people, etc.* Beliefs exert influence over clients' choices of financial products and services. For example, the client in the above incident will presumably reject any proposal that includes equity or any other perceived risky investment because of the strong belief that risk will jeopardize the family's legacy and will interfere with his duty to pass this legacy on to succeeding generations.

Beliefs originate as people think and reflect on life's experiences, make judgments, and form conclusions. They may also be adopted uncritically because of the influence of an authoritative person, group, culture, or set of precepts. Some individuals hold their beliefs dogmatically even in the face of contradictory experience or evidence, while others hold their beliefs tentatively as working hypotheses that could change as they encounter new experience and ideas.

One client may believe that it is a parent's duty to provide for a child's education, while another may believe just as strongly that it is the child's responsibility. Who is right? Objectively, there is no right answer. Advisors should understand that people's belief systems must be respected, even though the advisor may not agree with them. In the incident above, if the advisor thought it important to encourage the client to be more open to risk, the advisor should realize this is a difficult task and the topic must be approached with respect, skill, diplomacy and patience, and with the readiness to ultimately accept the client's beliefs as a given constraint on the portfolio.

The following vignette by the American author Carl Sandburg effectively illustrates the point that our beliefs – in this case about the nature of people – are influenced by past experiences.

What kind of people live in these parts?
Well, stranger, what kind of people lived in your country?
They were for the most part selfish, lying gossips who denigrated others.
Well, stranger, you will find the same type of people in these parts.
The stranger, bewildered, sat down when a second stranger arrived.
What kind of people live in these parts? asked the second stranger.
Well, stranger, what kind of people lived in your country?
Most were honest, hard-working, God-fearing and likable people.
This is the type of people you'll find around here.

- Carl Sandburg (1936)

9.1.2 Values

Our **values** arise from our beliefs and they influence our preferences for certain behaviours, or outcomes. Examples of values are fairness, honesty, integrity, respect for others, financial security, a lavish lifestyle, and self-respect. Here is how these abstract concepts fit together. If I believe it is good to be rich, I will value industriousness, ambition, and shrewdness that will help me attain my goal of wealth. A good question is why I believe it is good to be rich. The answer could come from several sources: my thinking and reasoning, my experiences (maybe I suffered poverty in the past and vowed, never again), advice from a respected authority, my parent's expectations, or a combination of these.

The way in which beliefs, values, and goals inter-relate is seen in the following example:

> Mr. Khaldun believes a family should share good times before the children grow up and leave home. He believes this will create a family bond that will last throughout life. Based on his belief, he values family time together. His goal is to save enough money to take his family to *Disney World*.

In talking to customers about their financial goals, advisors need to know that goals are related to beliefs and values. The re-thinking of goals may necessitate a reconsideration of values and beliefs, especially when clients' financial resources are limited and prioritizing may be necessary.

Our beliefs and values are also inherited from our families and cultures. Eastern cultures, more than Western cultures, uphold the duty of children to care for elderly family members. As a result, those in the East may elevate financial care of elderly family members to a higher status than Westerners. However, beliefs and values are so highly individualized that they may differ markedly even among individuals within the same culture.

Milton Rokeach (1973), a leading values scholar, suggested that an individual only holds a few values and that everybody shares a limited number of values even across cultures. He identified two types of values: ***instrumental values*** and ***terminal values***. Instrumental values are ways we desire people to treat one another, or qualities we admire, such as honesty, ambition, compassion, courage, and intelligence. Terminal values concern ends or goals we desire for ourselves or society, such as health, social justice, excitement, family security, equality, and happiness.

Personal values influence the kind of financial help people seek.

> Mr. Forrester values honesty, responsibility, and respect of others. With this value system, it is easy to understand why he wants to deal only with financial institutions that have not been involved in any unethical practices. He also seeks out financial advice from those who treat him with respect and whose ethics are above criticism.

9.1.3 Needs

Needs are the tension we feel as a result of the gaps between the way things are and the way we would like them to be. Our needs motivate us because we want to overcome that gap and rid ourselves of the tension. Psychologists speak of two general types of needs: **physiological** (related to biological functions) and **psychological** (related to emotional/intellectual functions). When we are hungry (a physiological need), we seek food. When we feel inadequate, we want assurance and acceptance (psychological needs). In both cases, we experience discomfort and our aim is to find relief and satisfaction in the form of food or affirmation. Our needs influence many aspects of our relationships and personalities, including our perceptions, values, and goals. For example, the financial advisor who has not met a monthly funds sales target may welcome any sign of interest in mutual funds by a client. The client becomes a way for the adviser to meet sales targets. Mark Twain, the American humourist, is purported to have said, *when you have a hammer, everything looks like a nail.*

Abraham Maslow (1954) suggested that everyone is motivated to satisfy five innate needs. He arranged these in a hierarchy that represents ascendency from basic to complex needs. In Figure 9.2, the bottom two he considered *lower-level* needs and the top three, he labelled *higher-level needs*.

Figure 9.2
Maslow's Hierarchy of Needs

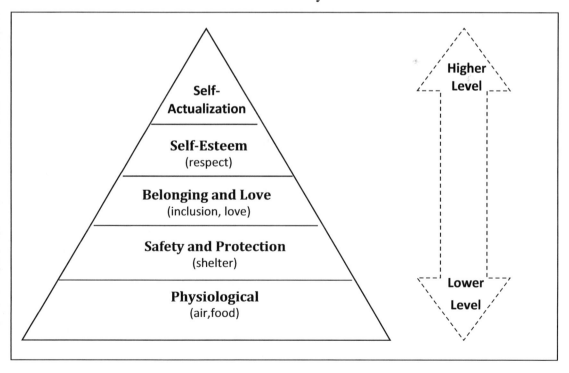

The satisfaction of lower-level physiological needs produces a general state of well-being and contentment. The *higher-level* psycho-social needs drive individuals to go beyond the satisfaction of physiological appetites to reach their full human potential. Maslow's view is that a person is not completely whole until the satisfaction of lower-order needs has given way to the achievement of higher-order needs. Only when the lower-order needs are at least minimally satisfied will the individual seek to fulfill higher needs. While Maslow acknowledged that several needs may motivate behaviour simultaneously, he proposed that unsatisfied needs are the main motivators.

> Mr. Burden likes sailing; it is his passion and gives him a sense of freedom. He has been taking sailing lessons for the past two years and hopes to soon own a small sailboat. Within the next three years, he would like to be able to move up to a thirty-foot boat. But before he can accomplish this goal, he wants to build up a retirement fund. After he purchases the boat, he would like to finish the college degree he started ten years ago. His employer does not require the degree, but it is important to him.

Mr. Burden's needs can be arranged in order of importance. His post-retirement security is his first priority. Owning a sailboat and the sense of freedom that goes with is next, followed by finishing his college degree, which would give him a sense of great achievement because not having a college degree has always made him feel that he has not reached his full potential. These needs – lower-level and higher-level – translate into specific goals with financial implications and will have a lot to do with what he values, the kind of financial issues he will be interested in discussing, and the types of financial products and services he will be interested in purchasing.

9.1.4 Attitudes

> Mr. Tubbs is an elderly gentleman who became wealthy operating his own import business. The company was begun by his grandfather, passed down to his father, and then given to him. Mr. Tubbs works hard and spends long hours in the business. His family complains that they do not see much of him. Mr. Tubbs recently approached a financial advisor about some personal investment issues. Despite the advisor's interest shown to him, Mr. Tubbs was reluctant to reveal much about himself or to engage in extensive conversations. He feels the information the advisor asked for was highly personal. He was also reluctant to ask the advisor for help because he feels he cannot trust anyone else to be as concerned about his situation as he is; after all, his wealth is a legacy and a trust from his family. Consequently, Mr. Tubbs appears short-tempered, resistant, and secretive. The advisor does not know how to relate to him.

On the surface, the advisor finds Mr. Tubbs a bit difficult to deal with. He resists the advisor's attempts to get to know him. What is the source of Mr. Tubbs' suspicious and secretive attitude? Does the advisor have any chance of changing his attitude and engaging him in an open conversation? The answers to these questions lie in understanding deeper aspects of Mr. Tubbs' personality: his beliefs, values, and needs. It is clear that Mr. Tubbs believes that he is guarding a family legacy and that no one else can fully appreciate his sense of duty. Consequently, he values hard work and self-reliance. He feels that he needs investment security and certainty in order to fulfill his destiny and carry out the responsibility laid upon him. The advisor will not make much progress with Mr. Tubbs until he recognizes the factors that influence Mr. Tubb's attitudes and finds a way to open a discussion with him about some of these personal issues.

Attitudes are the personality characteristics that are *nearest the surface* or closest to action. They are predispositions to act in certain ways. Attitudes in combination with particular situations will trigger a fairly consistent reaction. Johns (1996) describes an attitude as *a fairly stable emotional tendency to respond consistently to some specific object, situation, person, or category of people (p.132).* Popular wisdom says that we know people best when we can predict their reaction to various situations, that is, when we know their attitudes. I know if I ask my four-year old grandson if he is ready to go to bed, his immediate reaction will be *no.* One manager I worked for had the same reaction to any new idea: *no.* Eventually, I gave up proposing new ideas because I knew they would be rejected. Advisors will judge the likely reaction of familiar customers to various kinds of conversation before they initiate it. For example, before advisors use humour with clients, it is best to know their attitudes and likely reactions in order to avoid misunderstandings and any unintended offence.

As Figure 9.1 indicated, attitudes result from the convergence of beliefs, values, experiences, and needs. For example, if a client believes the advisor has her best interests at heart and she values the kind of service the advisor offers, then the client will likely be open to the advisor's advice. On the other hand, a client who is resistant to investing in anything but fixed-income securities may be influenced by a belief about the superiority of riskless (as the client sees them) fixed-income securities. Given this background, the client will have a negative attitude towards any other investment alternatives.

Attitudes are relatively endurable and hard to influence. Looking again at Figure 9.1, we can see that attitudes are hard to change because of their link with many other personal dimensions: beliefs, values, experiences, and needs. Attempts at influencing a person's attitudes should focus on understanding the person's underlying dimensions. In the case of the client committed to fixed-income securities, the advisor might point out the *risks* of investing in only fixed-income securities with their inflation and credit risk, and the diversifying effect of equity. Johns (1996) points out that seeking moderate change of attitudes is the most realistic objective.

Based on this background, let us focus on another set of individual dimensions that have an impact on an important part of the advising process: clients' information processing preferences.

9.2 INFORMATION PROCESSING
Would you rather read a book or listen to a talk on the same subject? If you were considering buying a big-screen television, would you gather technical specifications on all

makes and models or ask friends how they like their brand of TV? When it comes time to decide about investing in mutual funds, some people carefully analyze the options and weigh their individual strengths and weaknesses, while others base their selection on subjective feelings. These are all differences in the ways people gather and process information. There are three dimensions to consider.

1. The way individuals like to **receive** information – their **learning style.**
2. The **kind** of information individuals prefer.
3. The way individuals **reach conclusions** with collected information.

9.2.1 Learning Styles

George Hartman, in the introduction to his book, *Risk is a Four Letter Word,* stated that he did not include many graphs or *number crunching* because they tend to lose people (Hartman, 1998). We will soon see the shortcomings of this pedagogical belief. On the other hand, the following excerpt from the *CFA Conference Proceedings Quarterly* (December, 2009) shows one presenter was aware of different learning styles: *This definition is the classic thumbnail sketch of a CDO. It is helpful, however, for many to visualize what is happening in a risk-return diagram…In Figure 1…* (P.46). The author then presents a diagram.

As we discussed briefly in Chapter 8, people like to receive information in different ways. There are three natural modes, often referred to as learning styles: *visual, auditory*, and *kinesthetic*. People seldom have only one learning style, but one usually predominates. Knowledge of different styles can be useful for building client relationships, and for making effective presentations. Research shows that counsellors who present information in a manner consistent with their clients' learning styles are perceived in more positive terms than those who do not (Cormier & Cormier, 1985).

Auditory learners make up 25% of the population. They like to **hear** information. They learn best by listening. Pictures, diagrams, and brochures tend to distract them. Students who learn by listening to lectures without taking notes and remember what they hear are, undoubtedly, auditory learners. (And are sometimes a source of irritation to fellow classmates who must take copious notes and review them diligently.) Careful verbal explanations are most effective with this type of person.

Visual learners make up approximately 35% of the population. They like to **see** information and learn best by reading words or looking at diagrams. With visual learners, the advisor should make full use of printed material: brochures, pamphlets, diagrams, charts, and PowerPoint presentations.

Kinesthetic learners represent about 40% of the population, and are action and sensory oriented. They like to be involved and interact with information. They need to relate to it physically, or kinesthetically. They learn best by hands-on experiences. Rather than listening to instructions about the installation of a new piece of electronic equipment, or reading the manual, they prefer to *jump in* and try to assemble it. Showing them a diagram is not as good as drawing one in their presence and accompanying it with an example. Examples are important for kinesthetic learners, especially examples that apply to them. To explain how a stripped bond works, it would be best to demonstrate physically, using a sheet of paper, how an interest-bearing bond has its coupons and face *ripped apart* and sold separately, by actually ripping the paper. (Despite many *brilliant* explanations, this was the method that finally got through to one of my finance students.)

9.2.1.1   Identifying Learning Styles. There are various tests to determine individual learning styles. (See the Exercise section for this chapter in the Participants' Manual.) It is not appropriate to ask a client to fill out a questionnaire (like the one in the Manual), so the advisor will have to devise other means to determine client learning styles. Perhaps, the best way is to try a number of approaches and note the one to which the client seems to respond the most favourably.

Madonik (1990) claims that different eye movements are linked to different learning styles.

> Eyes looking upward or defocused typically indicate people accessing a visual system, eyes moving side to side or down to the left [from the observer's perspective] are usually seen with people seeking and retrieving auditory data and eyes travelling downward and to the right side most times are tending to indicate people going for kinesthetic information (p.19).

Another indicator is the type of language used by speakers. According to Bandler and Grinder (1975), people's preferred style can be seen in the adjectives, adverbs, and verbs they use. Visual learners will refer to mental pictures. They make many references to visual process such as *seeing, picturing,* and *reflecting – I see now.* People with predominant auditory styles will use language related to hearing, sounds and verbal analysis. This style is typified by words such as *loud, hear, harmony, thinking, knowing, understanding,* and *analyzing – I hear what you say.* A kinesthetic style is action and feeling oriented. This style encompasses visceral feelings, emotions, and tactile and muscular sensations. This modality is represented by words like *sensing, feeling, doing, being,* and *acting - I get it now.*

In the absence of a clear indication of the client's style, the advisor should adopt a universal approach. While presenting information verbally, the advisor can offer brochures and other printed material and at the same time construct examples, draw diagrams, and perform calculations. From this, the advisor should get a sense of the client's preferences. This approach is much better than reverting to the advisor's own preferred style or assuming that everyone is the same.

Knowledge of the three basic ways in which people prefer to receive information gives the advisor access to different *channels.* The channel can be *switched* to another mode when the advisor feels the client is not getting the message. This ability adds to the advisor's flexibility and effectiveness.

9.2.2 Types of Information

I asked someone how the countries of Bahrain and Qatar compared. The person I asked, in turn asked me, *Do you want details or general impressions?* There is a difference.

Psychologist Carl Jung, in his study of personalities, identified factors that categorized people according to the kinds of information they prefer and the way they like to use information to reach conclusions. According to Jung, each activity occurs along a continuum anchored by two dominant modes. Figure 9.3 shows the preferences for **kinds of information** and Figure 9.4 shows the variations in ways people **make up their minds and come to conclusions.** These preferences should not be confused with the **ways people like to *receive* information,** which are learning styles.

Figure 9.3
Preferences for Types of Information

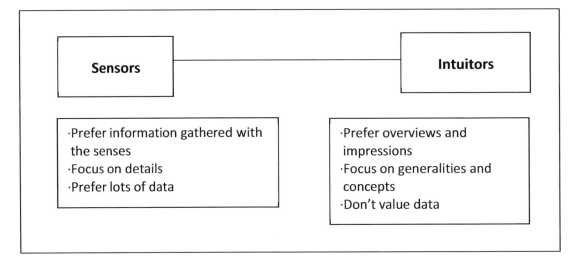

At one extreme are ***Sensors*** who value detailed, concrete, technical information. Generally, sensors have no preconceived idea of how relevant one piece of information will be, so they gather as much information as possible.

At the other extreme are ***Intuitors*** who prefer impressions and generalities to obtain a feeling or *hunch* about situations. They value information that goes beyond what the five basic senses can provide. In the following example, we can see the difference between sensors and intuitors.

An advisor at First Maritime met with Mr. Miner and Mr. Jackson on the same day. Even though their situations were similar, they were very different.

Mr. Miner had inherited a large sum of money from his father. He decided he needed some help in managing it. He asked the advisor for all the information on First Maritime's investment services. Mr. Miner had many questions about the rates of return on various investments, their risk levels, the kinds of reports the institution provided, the frequency of the reports, and he asked to see one. He also wanted to know about fees and the conditions under which they might vary. Armed with all this information, he left the branch.

Mr. Jackson also inherited a large sum of money. He, too, visited the advisor at First Maritime. He explained that he was not used to looking after investments and wondered what kinds of services they offered. He asked if they could help him manage his money. He also asked how their investment products had performed in the past and what their outlook was. He left feeling he could trust the advisor to provide a *good service*.

Mr. Miner is a sensor. He values technicalities and details, and lots of them. Mr. Jackson is more of an intuitor. He wanted a general impression of First Maritime's services. He asked no detailed questions and his objective was to come away with an impression of the service and the advisor. The advisor will have to relate to each in a different manner. With Mr. Miner, the advisor will concentrate on details such as service technicalities, rates of return, and fees. With Mr. Jackson, the advisor will talk in generalities and give him overall impressions of the services First Maritime can offer without being too specific about details. (Until the clients asks, or until the advisor fulfills his fiduciary duty or meets compliance requirements by revealing pertinent details.)

9.2.3 Reaching Conclusions

Information is evaluated and conclusions reached using two methods: ***thinking*** and ***feeling***. The range is seen in Figure 9.4.

Figure 9.4
Information Evaluation Mode

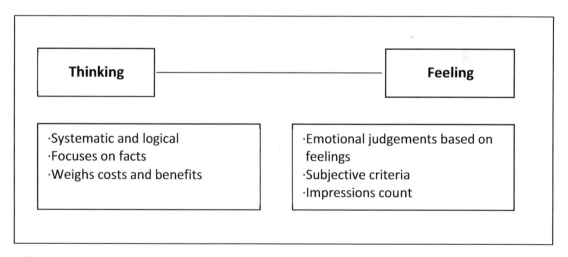

The ***thinking*** type likes to arrive at conclusions in a rational, systematic way. Thinkers usually conduct an orderly search for information and use logic to assess the data and to make decisions.

The ***feeling*** type makes judgments based not on logical and systematic thought, but on emotion and overall impressions. The feeling type relies on subjective rather than objective criteria to reach conclusions.

In purchasing a car, the thinking type will analyze the performance specifications and evaluate the features of one car versus another before deciding which one to purchase. On the other hand, the feeling type is likely to purchase the car that *feels* best.

Mr. Miner, in our example above, is likely a thinking type when it comes to reaching conclusions. Sensing and Thinking types frequently go together. The detailed information that Mr. Miner gathered will be analyzed in a systematic and logical way before he decides to do business with First Maritime. On the other hand, Mr. Jackson, who is probably a Feeling type, will make decisions by reviewing the impressions and feelings he gathered during his conversation with the advisor. Intuiting and feeling often go together, but sometimes they are situational.

Advisors must understand the different kinds of information individuals prefer and the ways in which they analyze information to make decisions. The advisor must be flexible enough to adapt to clients' preferred styles so that the presentation of services and products is done in a way that will be clearly received and fully considered.

9.4 CONCLUSION

The advisor must understand more than the client's words in order to communicate effectively. The advisor must understand the deeper constructs of beliefs, values, and needs that shape clients' preferences, goals, and attitudes. Knowledge of these personal dimensions creates a deeper understanding of clients and leads to stronger relationships. The advisor's communication with the client will also be more effective if the advisor understands the way clients like to receive information, the type of information they prefer, and the way in which they reach conclusions.

KEY TERMS

Auditory style. A learning style in which the person prefers to receive information by hearing.

Attitudes. Personality characteristics that are closest to action and predispose people to act in certain ways.

Beliefs. Strongly held propositions about the way things are or should be.

Feeling types. People who makes judgments, based not on logical and systematic thought, but on emotion and overall impressions.

Instrumental values. Ways we desire people to treat one another, or qualities we admire.

Intuitor types. People who prefer impressions and generalities to get a feeling or hunch about a situation.

Kinesthetic style. A learning style in which the person prefers to be physically involved and interact with information.

Needs. The tension people experience as a result of gaps between the way things are and the way they would like them to be.

Physiological needs. Needs related to biological functions.

Psychological needs. Needs related to emotional/intellectual functions.

Sensor types. People who prefer concrete, detailed, technical information.

Terminal values. Ends or goals we desire for ourselves or society.

Thinking types. People who like to arrive at conclusions in a rational, systematic way by weighing information and making logical decisions.

Values. Preferences for certain behaviours, ends, or outcomes.

Visual style. A style of learning in which the person prefers to receive information by seeing it.

CHAPTER 10

RATIONAL AND IRRATIONAL ASPECTS OF DECISION MAKING

10.0 DECISION MAKING

Each of the following clients is at a different stage in making a decision.

> Client A: *I am worried that by the time my children are ready for university, I won't be able to give them any financial support.*
> Client B: *I am interested in an educational savings plan. What does your institution offer?*
> Client C: *After I discuss your proposal with my accountant, I will get back to you.*
> Client D: *Thank you for your time. I will think about your presentation and call you.*
> Client E: *You have convinced me to invest in this fund and tomorrow I will courier money to you from my other bank.*
> Client F: *Why did I invest so heavily in equities when it was clear that the market was in a bubble?*

The previous chapter examined several important personal dimensions that shape people's behaviour and the kinds of financial services they seek and will accept. This chapter continues to explore people's cognitive and psychological processes by examining how individuals make purchase decisions, especially about financial products. In the first part of this chapter, we will assume people are logical and we will examine the decision-making process from a rational perspective, then we will consider the aspects of decision making that are less than rational and are often guided by faulty thinking and alluring emotions.

10.1 THE RATIONAL DECISION-MAKING PROCESS

In the opening incidents, each client is at a different stage in the decision-making process. Client A, at the beginning of the process, has recognized a need. Client B is searching for information about possible solutions. Client C wants to consult someone else to help evaluate the advisor's proposal. Client D is at the point of making a decision. Client E has made a decision, but has not implemented it. And Client F is having regrets about a past decision. The making of a decision is a complicated process and much can happen between the identification of a need and taking action to satisfy it. The rational decision-making model presented below assumes decision makers follow a logical sequence of steps. How they proceed through the process depends partly on whether the decision is *high-involvement* or *low-involvement*.

10.1.1 High and Low-Involvement Decisions

Depending on the perceived risk of making a wrong decision, the complexity of the decision-making process can range from careful analysis (high-involvement) to pure impulse (low-involvement).

Individuals do not put as much careful consideration into *low-involvement* decisions; they do not perceive there is much at risk and do not believe that wrong decisions will have adverse consequences. Purchasing a package of printer paper is a low-involvement decision. With low-involvement decisions, individuals move faster through each of the decision-making steps, or even skip steps. In low-involvement decisions, people tend to be ready to accept *satisfactory* decisions. They know that several options are acceptable and it is not worth the extra effort to find the perfect solution.

Most decisions about financial services are high-involvement decisions laden with financial and social risks – financial risk because a significant financial commitment may be required and social risk because a bad decision may create social embarrassment. Because it is difficult to foresee the future performance of financial products, individuals want to feel that at least they acted diligently and considered all factors thoroughly before they made a decision. In high-involvement decisions, people tend to look for the *optimal* solution, that is, **the** best solution. They may prolong a decision until they feel they have found the perfect solution. Advisors will find that generally clients are highly involved in their financial decisions and welcome guidance.

10.2 A SIX-STEP SEQUENTIAL PROCESS

Different models have been developed to explain the decision-making process. The one presented in Figure 10.1 has six steps. The process begins with the awareness of a need and finishes with the purchaser reflecting on the how well the purchase actually met the need.

Figure 10.1
The Purchase Decision-Making Process

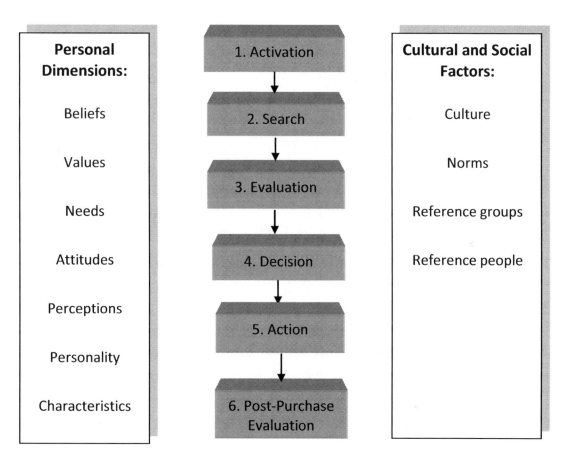

Consider, for example, the process you may go through to purchase a mobile phone. First you realize that you need a new phone (Step 1). Next, you probably will do some research and gather information on different brands (Step 2). Your research might consist of going on-line, consulting independent consumer organizations and friends for their recommendations, and visiting a few stores to try their mobile phones. You decide what features are most important to you – design, technical specifications, price, and reputation, for example – and then compare the options (Step 3). After all this information is evaluated, you decide to purchase what seems to be the best alternative (Step 4). Next, you follow through on your decision and purchase the phone (Step 5). Once you have purchased the phone, you assess whether it lives up to your expectations (Step 6). You might find that the phone is able to do what the manufacture promised, but the user interface is poor. You might decide that, overall, you made a bad decision and will never buy this brand again.

The same process applies to the purchase of financial services. Figure 10.1 not only depicts the six stages, but also the various internal and external factors that influence mental processing at each stage. We will concentrate on the activity at each stage, but we will also recognize the important impact personal, cultural, and social factors have on the process. (More will be said about cultural factors in Chapter 11.)

Figure 10.1 assumes people move intentionally and thoughtfully completing the tasks of one stage before moving to the next. However, in reality decision makers may jump ahead prematurely to another stage, or recycle to previous stages, especially if new information becomes available.

10.2.1 Activation Stage

At the initial stage, people become aware of a difference, or gap, between a current state of affairs and an ideal state. (This is similar to the definition of a need as defined in Chapter 9.) Individuals recognize a need and are motivated to do something about it. This tension between what is and what is desired motivates individuals to seek solutions.

> Jamal visited his neighbour to watch the World Cup football finals on his big-screen TV. He did not realize how small and inadequate his own TV was until he returned home and watched it. The next day, Jamal went shopping for a large flat-panel TV.

Financial examples of needs are dissatisfaction with the performance of a current investment, or the realization that nothing has been set aside to fund a child's education.

Needs can be sparked by advertisements, a crisis, self-reflection, or in the case of the big-screen TV, a comparison. The tension between the actual and the ideal state must be strong enough to motivate the person to seek a solution. Although many individuals may feel the need for personal financial advice, not everyone will actually seek help.

10.2.2 Search Stage

At this stage, individuals search for information about potential solutions. The search process tries to identify various feasible alternatives and their features.

The search for information is both internal and external. **Internal information** exists in the memory of past experiences with particular products. Standing in front of the candy rack in a convenience store, the shopper already has experience with various kinds of chocolate bars and will do a memory search to choose the most desirable one. Positive past experience usually leads to a limited search for additional information. Bad past experience will lead to a more extensive search.

> A customer first purchased an equity mutual fund three years ago. Before that, the customer had always invested in fixed-income securities. The first mutual fund purchase turned out well, so the customer decided to reinvest in mutual funds. Had the initial fund performed badly, it is unlikely that the customer would have invested in more funds. The customer felt no need to launch an extensive search for other investment alternatives.

External information is actively sought outside one's experience in publications, websites, and other people's opinions. The search process continues as long as the extra cost and time of gathering more information is felt to bring additional benefits. To go beyond this point is to experience *information overloaded* and to become weighed down.

The quality of information is perceived as the highest when it is internal rather than external, actively sought rather than unsolicited, and personal rather than general.

10.2.3 Evaluation Stage

Once an individual is satisfied with the collected information, each alternative is evaluated in light of criteria. There are several ways to evaluate alternatives, but two strategies commonly used are the ***compensatory model*** and the ***non-compensatory model.***

Using a **compensatory model**, individuals identify the advantages and disadvantages of each alternative. For example, the fact that segregated insurance funds sometimes charge a higher fee may be compensated for by the capital guarantee they offer. Using a compensatory model, individuals establish a hierarchy of desirable characteristics and weight them. Then they score the features of particular product solutions and the *winner* will be the product with the highest weighted average.

Using a **non-compensatory model**, individuals look for particular features and if they are absent, no other factors will offset this lack. For example, an individual may want an advisor with a financial services designation. Internet accessibility, fees, and other features will not be considered adequate trade-offs. Regardless of how impressive these other features may be, they will not make up for the lack of a designation.

10.2.4 Decision Stage

Napoleon is reported to have said, *nothing is more difficult, and therefore more precious, than to be able to decide.* After individuals evaluate the alternatives, they make decisions. At this stage, the advisor should be aware of any hesitancy or doubts that linger in clients' minds and be ready to explore them using such comments as: *It appears that you are hesitant to commit to this plan; do you mind explaining why?*

If the match between needs and products is good, and if clients perceive that selection of the product will add value, then they have a strong motivation to make a decision. However, this can be a frustrating stage for advisors if clients defer decisions. It is interesting that some people find it extremely difficult to make a decision and may waiver indecisively for a long time. (The author spent countless hours waiting for his teenage son to choose ball caps that gave him the right look.) The root of the word decision is to *cut off.* To decide, therefore, is to cut off the possibility of having all options and to be limited to only one. Some writers have suggested that indecision is basically greed – as long as a person does not decide the illusion is maintained that all options can be had. For some people, to have to decide is anxiety producing. The advisor needs to ascertain whether the client's reluctance is a sign that some part of the decision process needs to be re-visited – a fuller consideration of needs, a more thorough discussion of alternatives, or a more rigorous delineation of decision criteria – or whether this is just the client's personality and standard reaction to decisions in general.

Resistance to making a decision can also be tied to a fear of making a wrong decision (Neukam and Hershey, 2003), or as Harrison, Waite, and White (2006) point out, to a mistrust of financial advisors and their institutions.

One of the most frustrating situations for advisors to deal with is when clients will not make a decision and will tell the advisor: *you are the expert, you decide.* Beware! This can be a trap motivated by a psychological game that may end in the advisor being blamed for wrong decisions.

10.2.5 Implementation Stage

It is reasonable to assume that after clients have made a decision, they should feel relieved that their problem has been solved. Some people readily follow up a decision with action, while others hesitate, postpone, or never carry through. One explanation for this behaviour may be *regret avoidance* (see section 10.5.2.2 below).

It can be frustrating for advisors, who have put a lot of time and effort into helping clients find acceptable solutions, when clients do not implement their decisions. Implementation will not occur unless the motivation is strong enough to overcome inertia and inclinations that inhibit action. The failure to implement a decision could result from such conditions as a sudden change in circumstances (a promotion or relocation), last minute information (pro or con) about a product, risks the client decides are unbearable, or the client's perception that the advisor is applying pressure and seems to want the decision more than the client. In studying investment in pension plans, Olson (2008) determined that trust – defined as belief in the competence and integrity of advisors, their institutions and markets – can be a major factor in whether action is taken. If the client trusts the advisor, the probability is increased that the client's decision will be followed by action. Advisors should be ready to help strengthen their clients' resolve to take action and help them to turn intention into action. (See section 8.3 in Chapter 8.)

10.2.6 Post-Decision Evaluation,

The satisfaction individuals experience about their purchase decisions will vary.

> Mr. Harmond decided to finance 95% of the value of his new house. However, the day after negotiating the financing, he called the advisor to say he had not slept well and now realized the payments would put too much strain on his budget, and he should have financed a lower percentage.

The regret Mr. Harmond experienced, termed *post-purchase cognitive dissonance*, can occur as individuals review their choices and purchases. (My brother still wonders if he should have purchased the 40-inch big-screen TV instead of the 32-inch one.) To reduce this dissonance; some people seek reassurance, other people try to undo the decision – like Mr. Harmond. Some people mentally review the advantages and disadvantages of their choice to assure themselves that their decision was the best. Cognitive dissonance usually disappears as people adjust to their decisions.

10.3 THE ADVISOR'S ROLE

In Table 10.1, the characteristics of the six steps in the decision-making process are presented along with ways advisors can be helpful at each stage.

Table 10.1
Stages and Activities in the Decision-Making Process

Stage	Characteristics	The Advisor's Role
Activation	·Needs have been identified ·The current situation is no longer acceptable	·Listen to the dimensions and implications of clients' needs ·Identify unrecognized needs · Convey understanding by seeking feedback and verification ·Reinforce clients' motivation to find solutions to their problems ·Avoid premature solutions
Search	·Search for solutions that will best fulfil perceived needs ·Look for specific details about products and services	·Provide appropriate product information ·Help clients determine credible information ·Suggest appropriate product solutions
Evaluation	·Compare the advantages and disadvantages of various alternatives ·Use a compensatory or non-compensatory model	·Actively listen to clients' requirements ·Outline the features, advantages, and disadvantages of products and services ·Help clients decide how to evaluate alternatives ·Present the institution's products as solutions to needs ·Focus on the match between products and needs

Decision	·Alternatives with their advantages and disadvantages have been identified and now a choice must be made	·Inquire into the nature of any hesitancy and be ready to re-visit any aspect of the proposed solution ·Restate how the proposal will help meet clients' needs
Implementation	·Intention is turned into action	·Assure clients that decision outcomes will be evaluated ·Reinforce clients' motivation to take action ·Strengthen trust between the advisor and clients
Post-Decision Evaluation	·The client may have second thoughts – *cognitive dissonance* – and identify drawbacks to the decision ·The client is dissatisfied if the product or service does not meet needs or expectations	·Identify and discuss any doubts or regrets ·Identify the sources of any dissatisfaction ·Review clients' needs and the appropriateness of selected products and services ·Reinforce how the chosen options will help meet clients' needs ·Make changes where possible

10.4 Ethical Considerations

Of course, financial advisors hope clients will choose their institution's products and services. With the range of available financial products and services, it should not be difficult to match products with client needs. But as we have emphasized throughout this book, advisors create value for clients when clients' purchases or investments are in the clients' best interests and not primarily in the advisor's best interests.

At various points in the decision-making process, advisors may become aware of some of their clients' vulnerabilities such as distaste for detailed information or confusion about complex options. For the sake of maintaining a high ethical standard, it is important that advisors do not exploit client vulnerabilities or manipulate clients into making choices that put the advisors' interests above their clients'. These client vulnerabilities sometimes arise as a result of the complexity of financial products and sometimes from a lack of client sophistication. If advisors take advantage of their clients' lack of curiosity about details and withhold critical information, or exploit any lack of client knowledge to sell unsuitable products, they will squander any trust they have established – trust that is a critical factor in client decision making and implementation.

When advisors become aware of the criteria clients use to evaluate alternatives, they are handed a powerful tool that can be used to cast their institutions' products in a positive light. For instance, if an advisor becomes aware that one of the client's chief considerations is social approval, the advisor can describe the institution's products in terms of the prestige and status they bestow. The advisor might even cite examples of well-known people who have used the same products. This is not the value-creation model and puts the advisor's needs ahead of the client's. If the advisor has understood the client's needs and dealt with any client reservations, then products can be easily offered as solutions.

Knowledge of the various stages of the decision-making process is important to better understand clients' needs so that appropriate recommendations can be made to create value and build loyalty.

10.5 DECISION MAKING AND BEHAVIOURAL FINANCE

Despite the usefulness of the rational decision-making model, people are not always logical and rational in their decision making, especially with regard to investments. Recently, much attention has been paid to the irrational aspects of decision making, and the defective psychological and cognitive processes that lead to flawed investment decisions. The formal investigation of such imperfections by academics and practitioners, known as *Behavioural Finance*, is a recent development in the field of finance and has as its objective the identification and documentation of irrational investment behaviour.

There is considerable evidence that, contrary to rational economic theory, individuals make decisions based not on reason, but on feelings and hunches that are loaded with misperceptions and faulty thinking. Susan Trammell, who has researched the field, confirms this view: *Consumers are often irrational. Their decision-making process may be confounded by psychological stumbling blocks* (Trammell, 2008, p.41).

Academics have generated lists of irrational decision-making processes, but the categorization of these strategies and the way they are defined are somewhat inconsistent – there is no overall agreed-upon scheme. To help find our way through this topic and to select those strategies with implications for the six-step decision-making model presented above, we will use the framework developed by Hersh Shefrin (2000), who described two categories of strategies: *heuristics* and *frames*.

10.5.1 Heuristics

Heuristics are rules-of-thumb, or shortcuts, used to process large amounts of information in order to make decisions. However, these rules are often flawed and their use is driven not by sound financial principles, but by their psychological and cognitive appeal. An example of a rule-of-thumb is this line of thinking: *the 5-year performance record of mutual funds is the best predictor of future performance.* Using this rule as a selection criterion overcomes the necessity of having to do a thorough analysis of fund candidates, but it does not consistently predict future winners, nor is there any sound reason why it should.

The following are four examples of heuristic strategies.

10.5.1.1 Availability Bias. This heuristic puts the highest value on the most available information. Often that means information that readily comes to mind because of its recency, emotional vividness, or publicity. It has been shown that this effect leads to an overestimation of the probability of events. For example, consider this question: what is a more likely cause of death in the United States, being killed by a shark or by airplane pieces falling from the sky? As a result of their publicity and the fear they invoke, most people will answer that shark attacks have a greater probability. Yet, dying from falling airplane parts is actually thirty times more likely than being killed by a shark attack! The following exercise reinforces the point.

Consider these pairs of causes of death and from each pair, choose the one you think causes more yearly deaths in the United States, and then compare your choices with the facts.

- Lung Cancer vs. Motor Vehicle Accidents
- Emphysema vs. Homicide
- Tuberculosis vs. Fire and Flames

The selections of a sample of people and the actual number of occurrences are found in Table 10. 2.

Table 10.2
Subjective Assessment of Probabilities vs. Actual Results

Causes of Death	People's Choice	Annual US Totals	Newspaper Reports/Year
Lung Cancer vs.	43%	140,000	3
Vehicle Accidents	57%	46,000	127
Emphysema vs.	45%	22,000	1
Homicides	55%	19,000	264
Tuberculosis vs.	23%	4,000	0
Fire and Flames	77%	7,000	24

(Combs & Slovic, 1979)

The actual results show that in all cases, people tend to rate the causes highest that have the greatest media exposure. In 2 out of the 3 cases, *people's choices* would have been incorrect.

The availability bias has implications for investors' information search, especially the search for internal information. Those events that stick in an investor's mind may have the greatest influence on investment decisions rather than disciplined judgements reached after a rigorous search for, and analysis of, relevant information. Recent well-publicized market downturns or upturns, the spectacular short-term performance of individual securities, and startling news from individual companies – good or bad – can all have a disproportionate influence on investment decisions. Available information has an appeal even though its validity and reliability may not have been established.

As clients search for information, advisors should be ready to encourage them to consider relevant creditable information that is outside their recent experience, to which they have no particular emotional attachment, but which may be better indicators of longer-term performance.

10.5.1.2 Representativeness. When people become overwhelmed with large amounts of information, they may cope by selecting and reacting to only a small part of the information that they feel represents the entire situation. While representativeness helps the brain organize and quickly process large amounts of data, it is a shortcut that reacts to only select data, from which conclusions will be reached which are different from those based on a wider array of relevant data. Often, consideration is limited to past events, under the assumption that current and future events will mirror the past. Faulty parallels are drawn because people don't bother to examine the differences between the past, present, and future. One of the best examples of this phenomenon concerns the market meltdown of 1987.

In five trading days in October 1987, the Dow Jones average fell 742 points. Many people wondered if this was a repetition of the great market crash of 1929 and subsequent depression. People who were caught up in the false parallel turned to cash and missed the subsequent rally. The fact that the two crashes had only the remotest similarity was overlooked. A similar situation occurred in the United States in the period 2008-2009 when credit markets froze and frantic voices called for immediate government intervention to prevent a 1930s type crash and depression. In addition to the seriousness of the situation, fear of the past repeating itself convinced many to act.

It is a much easier mental manipulation to *freeze* one's view of stock markets or particular companies and project these into the future than reformulate new views based on new information. It has been shown that investors tend to be pessimistic when recent stock prices have been down and optimistic when past history has been bullish.

Emphasis on the past is a particular problem with the selection of fund managers. Faced with uncertainty, investors are tempted to invest in past winners, who, it is assumed, will be future winners. However, Figure 10.3 dispels this fallacy. The left-hand side of the figure shows that of the top 55 funds between 1998 and 2001, only 21 were top tier performers in the subsequent 3-year period. The remaining 34 funds were spread out amongst the other three quartiles. In fact, the top 55 performers in the 2002 to 2005 period came from all four quartiles in the preceding 3-year period.

Figure 10.3
Is Past Performance an Indicator of the Future?

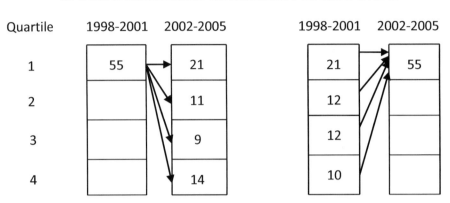

(In Wood, 2006, p.31 and based on data from the Frank Russell Company. Universe consists of 220 institutional managers in Russell's growth, market-oriented, and value universes with eight years of history ending 31 December 2005.)

Another aspect of the representative bias is that it leads to the making of decisions based on limited information, with the belief that some partial information represents the total reality of a situation. This can be seen in the following situation. As of 2009, the median correlation – based on a 10-year study – between Graduate Management Admission Test (GMAT) scores and first-year business school marks was only 26%. (GMAT Score Report, 2009). So why do business school admissions officers rely so heavily upon GMAT scores to make entrance decisions? Part of the answer is that a heavy weighting of GMAT scores makes the difficult screening of complex data and subsequent admission decisions easier. (I have some feeling about this matter because my application to a graduate business school was rejected with the explanation that my GMAT score was too low – but I had not written the test yet!)

The rational decision-making model does not differentiate between kinds of information. The existence of representative biases is a warning to advisors to be aware of the limited nature of some information and the making of unwarranted parallels in making investment decisions. Advisors should champion the search for relevant information, and discourage the grasping of one or two pieces of information assumed to represent the total picture.

10.5.1.3 Overconfidence. Investors can overestimate their abilities to make sound investment judgements. Terrance Odean found that average investors overestimate their ability to predict stock performance and erratically trade in and out of stocks, selling stock that later appreciated in price more than the ones they bought (in Vashisht, 2008). This overconfidence leads some investors to disregard many well-proven investment principles such as diversification.

The rational decision-making model makes no comment on whether people are overconfident when they make decisions. To guard against overconfidence in investment decisions, advisors should encourage clients to keep sound investment principles such as diversification in mind, to perform a proper risk assessment of securities, and to evaluate the risk-return trade-off of any investment. These considerations call for a *sober second thought* and should discourage overconfident clients from blindly picking securities without doing a proper evaluation.

The heuristic strategies discussed above have important implications for the rational decision-making process, especially with regard to steps 2, 3, and 4 – the search for and evaluation of information, and the making of a decision. The reliance on heuristic simplification increases with complexity and time constraints. The advisor can help by reducing the complexity of decisions and ensuring clients do not feel pressured to make decisions according to some artificial time line.

10.5.2 Framing

We have already discussed the process of framing with regard to the communication of information (see section 4.1.3.1). We discussed how opinions can be influenced not only by information, but also by the perspectives or views that are embedded in them. We referred to this embedded perspective as a frame. In the field of behavioural finance, the concept of framing is the same. In the context of this chapter, it refers to the influence on decisions arising from the way information is presented or framed, separate from the content of the information.

The power of framing prevails in many different aspects of life. Steven Lamb (2010) cited a study in which subjects were asked to decide between two medical procedures – one with a 90% success rate and one with a 50% success rate. The control group consistently chose the procedure that was successful 90% of the time. The experimental group was presented with the same options, but the researchers also revealed a negative anecdote about the more successful procedure, with no anecdote about the less successful procedure. In this group, only 39% of subjects chose the procedure with the 90% success rate, despite the better odds. The anecdote made the loss attached to the 90% option seem more real. The loss/gain framework in which opportunities are placed has a great impact upon the choices of decision-makers.

Trammel (2008) offers a prime example with regard to the presentation of retirement annuity products in citing a study in which researchers framed annuities first as a consumption decision and then as an investment decision. When annuities were presented as retirement consumption vehicles, they were judged superior by those in the sample, but when they were presented as investments, they were judged as inferior compared to other investment options. It matters how choices are framed.

The following are two examples of framing.

10.5.2.1 Loss Aversion. Psychological research suggests that people feel the emotional pain of a loss nearly three times more than the pleasure of a gain of equal size. Consequently, when stock prices increase, happiness is felt, but when prices fall by the same amount greater misery is suffered. The implication is that when making investment decisions, investors are more preoccupied with avoiding losses than with making gains. This helps explain the strong aversion some investors have to investing in equities and the attraction of guaranteed funds.

The following experiment points out the overriding effect of framing on rational decision making with regard to gains and losses.

> Subjects were faced with two options: accept $3,000 now with 100 percent certainty or accept the possibility of receiving $4,000 with an 80 percent probability of success. The majority of subjects chose the certainty of the $3,000.
>
> Framing the situation in terms of losses produced contrasting results. The two options were a $3,000 loss with 100 percent certainty, or a $4,000 loss with an 80 percent probability. Subjects took the greater loss with the 80 percent probability – unlike their inclination when the situation involved gains. In general, investors assume risk to avoid losses, yet avoid risk when seeking gains.

The loss aversion heuristic has some valuable insights for investment decision making. In the evaluation stage, advisors should be aware that clients may be heavily fixated on avoiding losses rather than fairly assessing alternatives. Despite the seeming rationality of the evaluation stage, there is an undercurrent of mental and psychological processes dominated by loss avoidance that work to undermine its rationality. Advisors may have to probe for verification of this possibility, and if present, engage in discussion of hedging, balancing and diversification strategies, and the proper assessment of risk-return trade-offs.

The loss aversion heuristic helps explain why clients may avoid decisions even after having given no indication that anything was disagreeable during the advisor's presentation or at the evaluation stage. The reading of nonverbal language and solicitation of client feedback become extremely important matters in this situation.

The loss aversion heuristic also helps explain a lack of follow-through from the decision to implementation stage. Not hearing from clients who earlier chose specific investment alternatives but made no attempt to execute them may be explained by the strong motivation to avoid loss. Faced with this situation, advisors should reconsider how the options were presented, and if while thoroughly assessing risk, potential gains were properly emphasized.

10.5.2.2 Regret Aversion. The desire to avoid regret is related to the motivation to avoid loss. Investors will try various strategies to avoid regrets about losses or missed opportunities.

Related to loss aversion and regret aversion is the ***disposition effect*** – the willingness of investors to sell investments with gains, but to hang on to losses. Barber *et al.* (2000) found that across a sample of investors' accounts, 15% of gains were realized against only 10% of losses. Odean (1998) discovered that, on average, investors are approximately 50% more likely to sell a winner than a loser. The disposition effect illuminates the tendency of investors to treat paper losses as unreal. This attitude leads to the holding on to losers too long hoping that they will pay off, or at least break even. Leroy Gross (1982) describes the problem this way: *Many clients will not sell anything at a loss. They don't want to give up the hope of making money on a particular investment, or perhaps they want to get even before they get out* (p.150).

Investors are often addicted to their losses and maintain the illusion that as long as they don't have a realized loss, they will have no regrets. A financial commentator on the cable news network CNN said that those who did not sell their stock in the fall of 2008 were smart because they did not *lock in their losses*. This is wonderful hindsight. At the time, many probably did not sell because they believed the current situation paralleled previous market downturns that were quickly followed by upturns (1987), or they did not want to turn paper losses into real losses.

The rational approach with all invested money is to ignore the past and to seek the best future returns. In order to encourage clients to adopt this view, advisors should confront their clients' tendencies to hang on to losers. Gross (1982) suggests that framing the issue in terms of *transferring* assets to another position, rather than selling losers, has the most chance of being accepted.

The regret aversion heuristic influences investors to evaluate winners and losers in their portfolios in a less than rational manner. Again, the evaluation stage is not always dominated by rational thinking and advisors should be ready to point out the influence of regret avoidance in the way clients assess their stock positions.

10.6 Conclusion

The six-step rational decision making model is a helpful way to view the process people go through as they make choices. It helps advisors become aware of how they can be most helpful at the various stages. One way they can be of help at any time during the process is to identify any faulty psychological and cognitive processes that interfere with the gathering and assessment of relevant data. Using knowledge of heuristic and framing strategies, advisors can help clients make sound investment decisions, even if there is no guarantee that their choices will always turn out right. The proof of a good decision is as much in the process as in the outcome.

Key Terms

Activation stage. The beginning step in the decision-making process in which people become aware of their needs and set out to fill them.

Availability bias. A tendency of decision-makers to rely on information that is readily available rather than search for relevant information.

Behavioural finance. The branch of finance that examines the psychological and cognitive factors that influence less than rational investment decisions.

Compensatory model. An information evaluation strategy by which decision makers assess the advantages and disadvantages of each alternative and search for the best trade-off.

Decision stage. The stage of the decision-making process in which individuals choose a solution.

Disposition effect. The willingness of investors to sell investments with gains, but to hang on to losses.

Evaluation stage. The stage of the decision-making process in which people use information to assess various alternatives.

External information. Information outside of a person's experience that decision-makers search for in such sources as publications, websites, and other people's opinions.

Framing. The influence the way information is presented has on investment decisions, apart from the content of the information.

Heuristics. Rules-of-thumb, or shortcuts, used to process and make decisions based on large amounts of information.

High-involvement decision. Decisions to which decision makers give careful and extend consideration because of the perceived risk of wrong decisions. Decision makers look for the best, or optimal, solutions.

Implementation stage. The stage of the decision-making process in which the decision maker actually buys the product or takes steps to put into operation the decision made at the previous decision step.

Internal information. Information about past purchases which resides within a person's memory.

Loss aversion. The motivation to avoid investment losses because of the greater pain attached to losses than gains.

Low-involvement decisions. Decisions made with minimal consideration because of the low level of perceived risk. Decision makers accept satisfactory solutions rather than look for optimal solutions.

Non-compensatory model. An evaluation strategy by which decision makers look for particular features in a product and if they are missing, no other factors can make up for their absence.

Overconfidence heuristic. An overestimation individuals make about their abilities to perform competently with regard to investment decisions.

Post-decision evaluation stage. The stage of the decision-making process in which purchasers assess satisfaction with their purchases.

Post-purchase cognitive dissonance. The dissatisfaction individuals may feel after they have purchased a product.

Regret aversion. Related to loss aversion. The extent to which investors will go in order to avoid regret about investment decisions.

Representativeness heuristic. A tendency by decision-makers to deal with only a portion of information relevant to a situation – the portion that they think represents or replicates the current situation.

Search stage. The part of the decision-making process in which the purchaser looks for information about potential solutions.

CHAPTER 11

CULTURAL AND SOCIAL INFLUENCES

11.0 THE INFLUENCE OF CULTURE AND SOCIETY

> Nan Zhou lived in the People's Republic of China until he was 18 years-old. In the 1980s, he studied in the United States, and in 1992 he immigrated to Canada. Today, he is a successful consultant for a large Canadian firm doing business in the Pacific Rim. He is married to a Canadian citizen and they have two young children. One day, a financial advisor suggested that he should prepare a will. As *westernized* as he is, Nan Zhou resisted the idea and was reluctant to talk about things that should not be discussed.
>
> Mr. Vibert applied for financing from First Maritime Bank to remodel his house to add a family room. He wasn't sure if he needs more room, but his neighbour just added a family room and highly recommended it.

Human behaviour is influenced not only by individual beliefs and values, but also by the beliefs and values of the surrounding culture and society. The important influence of culture was indicated in Figure 9.1 in Chapter 9 by the *dotted* background against which the personal dimensions of beliefs, etc. were set. The examples above illustrate how socio-cultural dimensions can affect a client's search for, and response to, financial services.

Nan Zhou does not want to discuss a matter that in his culture is considered taboo and bad luck. Mr. Vibert is strongly influenced by his neighbour's opinions. Advisors must understand how society and culture affect clients' beliefs, values, needs, goals, and attitudes toward financial services.

11.1 CULTURE AND SOCIETY

Culture is the sum total of ways of living developed over time, shared by a group of people, and passed down from generation to generation. Culture consists of many complex elements including religious beliefs and practices, political beliefs, customs, language, myths, music, tools, food, clothing, and art. Such daily habits as the way we dress, carry on social relations, and regard time are determined, to a large extent, by our cultural upbringing. Within cultures, there are also differences between smaller groups or **sub-cultures**. For example, those who live in urban areas often have values, attitudes, and practices different from those who live in rural areas. Canadians may be said to have a distinct culture, yet those who live in the *Maritimes* (Canadian provinces bordering on the Atlantic Ocean) have customs and attitudes quite different from those who live in western Canada. And those who live in one geographic area of the Maritime province of Nova Scotia – Cape Breton –

have their own distinct culture that is influenced by French and Gaelic customs and social values.

Cultures and sub-cultures may also be subdivided into smaller societal units made up of people who share a limited number of interests or characteristics. For example, members of a particular religious organization may come from many different cultures, but the church, synagogue, temple, or mosque to which they belong will impart a set of shared beliefs, customs, values, and interests.

11.1.1 Cultural and Societal Beliefs and Values

The shared beliefs and values of a societal or cultural group establish **norms,** which are acceptable attitudes, beliefs, values and behaviours. These may be in contrast to the norms of other cultures or societies. Edward VIII of Great Britain is purported to have said that the thing that impressed him most about American society was the extent to which parents obeyed their children. Underlying his statement was a different way of viewing the relationship between parents and children. Some cultures, out of respect, avoid eye contact believing that it conveys humility and respect for others, but in other cultures, it may be interpreted as a sign of guilt, deceit, or a significant lack of confidence. Norms may not only be different between cultures, but they may also clash. A student from an Eastern culture announced to one of my colleagues that she was repeating his university course. The professor commented that it was too bad she had failed. The student's response was interesting: *Oh, I didn't fail. I was sick at exam time and my twin sister wrote the final exam for me and she failed.* The professor was shocked by the student's admission, but her perspective was that she had followed an acceptable cultural practice in asking her sister to take her place at the exam – quite different from the professor's perspective.

Finding that my assigned seat on a long flight was at the rear of the plane and next to a passenger who had no hesitation to take up his space and mine, I looked around for a better option. I spied an empty window seat in a two-seat row, closer to the front of the plane. My inclination was to rush up the aisle, apologize to the person in the aisle seat, climb over him, and claim the window seat. But remembering my *manners,* I hesitated and remembered an important non-written rule of the air-travelling fraternity: passengers lucky enough to be in a two-seat row with an adjacent empty seat should be left to enjoy their good fortune. This injunction is not written anywhere nor is it announced by the airline crew; it is a norm understood amongst regular airline travellers, especially on long flights.

Based upon beliefs and values, specific groups of people within a culture are assigned roles and are expected to stay within the parameters of those roles. Western teachers often comment that their Asian students do not speak out in class. The root of this difference in role expectation can be traced to a belief that teachers are authorities and to question them is to show disrespect. In addition, differences in the respective roles of men and women represent some of the most prevalent cultural differences in human relationships. Role definitions dictate how men and women relate to each other, the responsibilities of husbands and wives to each other and to their families, and traditional occupations.

Despite significant cultural differences, social psychologists Christians and Traber (1997) propose that people of all cultures share certain *core values*. They suggest all cultures value truthfulness, respect for the dignity of other human beings, and compassion.

11.1.2 Dimensions of Culture

Hofstede (1980) proposed several dimensions along which cultures vary. Two with implications for the advisor's role are discussed here – Individualism vs. Collectivism and Power Distance.

11.1.2.1 Individualism-Collectivism.

Ting-Toomey and Chung (1996) suggest that *individualism* is the tendency of people in a culture to value *individual identity over group identity, individual rights over group rights, and individual achievements over group concerns* (p.239). The opposite of individualism is *collectivism* – the tendency of people in a culture to value *group identity over the individual identity, group obligations over individual rights, and intergroup-oriented concerns over individual wants and desires* (p.240).

Members of individualistic cultures tend to emphasize personal goals, to value independence and self-reliance, and to be direct in communicating with others. The influence of groups, such as family, school, and religion, is limited.

Collectivistic cultures emphasize conformity and interdependence. The focus is the group's welfare and success rather than individual needs and accomplishments. Members of a collectivist culture tend to avoid advancement of their own interests and shun direct confrontation. It is the group, and not the individual that has influence. Collective cultures include many Latin Mediterranean, Middle Eastern, African, and Asian cultures.

The difference between the two orientations of individualism and collectivism are reported in the findings of Imahori and Cupach (1994) who studied the types of situations United States and Japanese students found embarrassing. Japanese students were most embarrassed by social errors and expressed a sense of shame (an indication of their awareness of the importance of the group), while United States students were concerned about incidents that reflected their own stupidity (an emphasis on the self rather than the group).

In working with clients from an individualistic culture, advisors can expect clients to be more direct about their needs and preferences than clients from a more collectivistic culture. Clients from a collectivistic culture may require encouragement to express their reaction to suggestions and to verbalize their individual goals and aspirations. In addition, it should be kept in mind that those from a collectivistic culture may have goals that are more social and group-orientated, especially with regard to their extended families. The strong sense of shame members of a collectivistic culture often have may magnify their sense of loss aversion and regret (see Chapter 10).

The foregoing comments should be held as tentative hypothesis with the knowledge that to hold them unquestionably is to engage in stereotyping.

11.1.2.2 Power Distance. Power distance refers to the degree to which people accept authority, hierarchical organizations, and inequalities as a part of life. A culture with a strong power-distance orientation accepts and maintains inequalities between people. A culture that follows a caste system in which upward mobility is limited is a good example. Some members of the culture are expected to have higher status and more power than others. A more authoritarian style of communication accompanies this orientation. On the other hand, a low power-distance society minimizes differences in status, power and wealth, and values equality. Members of low power distance cultures are accustomed to questioning authority and confronting power. They also take pride in feeling that status and power, although impressive and admirable, are not barriers to social relations. In a low power-distance society, such as the United States, it is a great compliment to say that an important media personality, sports figure, or politician is *just like one of us.*

In an interesting investigation of airplane crashes and airline safety records, Malcolm Gladwell (2008) suggested that some crashes were caused by the reluctance of co-pilots of particular cultural backgrounds to express their safety concerns directly to pilots, whom they deferred to as authority figures. The co-pilots often observed pilot errors, but suggested corrective action only indirectly. The co-pilots' lack of forceful, direct confrontation of pilot error, Gladwell suggested, was a major factor contributing to several fatal crashes.

Clients from a strong power distance orientation may be more susceptible to the advisor's advice if they perceive the advisor as an authority. This condition makes for more cooperative clients, but it also may make the client more passive and willing to accept advice that can be later turned into blame. The challenge in working with clients with a high power distance orientation is to involve them in a discussion of options in which they feel free to give feedback and to encourage them to take responsibility for decisions. Again, these ideas are generalities, but they are useful for sensitizing advisors about these possible dynamics and their influence.

Individualism vs. Collectivism and Power Distance dimensions of culture lie on a continuum. There are really no pure types; most cultures lie in between the poles. The following diagram shows some of characteristics of the extreme positions and hints at the possibility of combinations in the areas between the extremes.

Individualism---**Collectivism**	
·Individual identify	·Group identity
·Individual rights & achievements	·Group achievements
Power/Distance *High*---**Power/Distance *Low***	
·People accept authority, status, and order	·Equality is important
·Authoritarian top-down communication	·Power is questioned

11.1.3 Overcoming Obstacles to Intercultural Communication

Although travel and electronic communication have brought world citizens into closer contact, communication across different cultures can still be awkward and difficult. When dealing with clients of different cultures, advisors should be aware that there will be differences. The best approach is to strive to understand the uniqueness of their clients, partially conditioned by individual personality traits and partially by cultural heritage. In addition, the advisor should give clear explanations, use the best communication skills, and always seek feedback and verification to assure there are no misunderstandings.

11.2 REFERENCE GROUPS

As well as being influenced by culture, individual preferences and practices may also be guided by smaller societal groups, known as **reference groups.** Out of a psychological need, individuals bestow the power of influence upon a group, and adopt that group's values and preferences. The reference group may be remote, but highly visible such as elite athletes or musicians, or it may be people whose notoriety is more local, such as colleagues, friends, societies, clubs, family, and neighbours.

11.2.1 The Power of Reference Groups

People adopt the behaviour and thinking of reference groups because they desire to emulate them, or as a means of *risk reduction*. For example, the purchase of goods or services can be a risky proposition and result in post-purchase dissonance and regret (as described in Chapter 10), but following the tastes and choices of an admired group, individuals may have more confidence in their purchase decisions and more easily persuade themselves that they made the right choice despite any later reservations. Reference groups can greatly influence the search for, and evaluation of, information as well as the recognition of a need in the first place.

Understanding the nature and power of reference groups gives advisors additional insight into clients' needs and motivations for seeking particular kinds of services. It is useful to know what is behind a client's interest in particular products and services so that an advisor can assess whether the client's expectations are realistic and products are appropriate. For example, if a client wants to invest in a foreign trust simply to emulate others at a social club, the client may be setting the stage for later dissatisfaction. It is the advisor's responsibility to make sure that clients understand the product features and that products meet clients' particular needs apart from what other people think.

11.2.2 REFERENCE PERSONS

Just as influential as reference groups are on individual decisions so is the influence of **reference persons**. Relatives, mentors, friends, celebrities, and salespeople can act as reference persons in an individual's decision-making process. People tend to seek advice from, or value the opinions of, others whom they believe have expertise or are models to emulate. Deceased people may influence individual needs and choices as much as living persons, especially if they were respected and left strong warnings and admonitions such as: *Don't let anyone else manage your money* or *Don't take any risks.*

I attended a financial planning seminar at which a lawyer made the general statement that no one should ever contract a financial institution to administer an estate because they were in it only for the fees (unlike lawyers?). Soon after, I wrote the lawyer and criticized her prejudice and lack of professionalism. My fear was that many at the seminar would accept the lawyer's opinion as an absolute rule because of her reference power.

It is quite possible that financial advisors may be reference persons because of their technical and product knowledge. Perceiving advisors as experts can instil trust. While this is positive, it also brings a significant responsibility. If the client perceives expertise in the advisor and relies on the advisor's advice in making financial decisions, the advisor is placed under a significant ethical obligation not to betray that trust and to give advice that is only in the client's best interests.

11.3 CONCLUSION

Beliefs, values, and attitudes exert a powerful influence over people's preferences and decisions. These dimensions of personality arise from people's uniqueness (Chapter 9) and from their shared cultural and societal experience. Culture shapes norms, attitudes towards roles, the degree to which people aspire to be independent, and the manner in which people communicate. A smaller unit of analysis, the reference group, and an even smaller unit of influence, the reference person, must also be considered when attempting to understand clients' preferences, constraints, and choices. Advisors who can set aside stereotypes and enter the cultural and societal world of their clients will be able to establish stronger relationships with clients and earn their trust and loyalty.

KEY TERMS

Culture. The sum total of ways of living developed over time, shared by a group of people, and passed down from generation to generation. Culture consists of many complex elements, including religious beliefs and practices, political beliefs, customs, language, myths, music, tools, food, clothing, and art.

Individualism-collectivism. The range of views cultures have about the importance of individuals and their rights versus groups and their rights. Individualism is the valuing of individual identity over group identity, individual rights over group rights, and individual achievements over group concerns. Collectivism is valuing of group identity over individual identity, group obligations over individual rights, and intergroup concerns over individual wants and desires.

Norms. Acceptable ideas and behaviours in a culture.

Power distance.   The degree to which people in a culture accept authority, hierarchical structures, and inequalities as a natural part of life.

Reference groups. Small groups within a society that have influence over an individual's values and preferences.

Reference persons. People in society who have a great deal of influence over the opinions and preferences of others.

Sub-cultures. Cultures within larger cultures.

MODULE V

MANAGING CLIENT RELATIONSHIPS

CHAPTER 12

MANAGING CHALLENGING RELATIONSHIPS

12.0 CHALLENGING RELATIONSHIPS

People can sometimes be difficult to deal with and we probably have some sympathy for the advisor in the incident below who is trying to understand the client, but meeting with resistance.

> **Advisor:** *I appreciate the time you have set aside for me this afternoon. I think I have a proposal that will be of great interest to you.*
> **Client:** *We will see.*
> **Advisor:** *After our last meeting, I reviewed the information you gave me, and before I begin, I would like to verify some of it.*
> **Client:** *Yes?*
> **Advisor:** *Your yearly income is two-hundred thousand dollars?*
> **Client:** *I don't remember telling you that.*
> **Advisor:** *Is that figure correct?*
> **Client:** *I make it a habit never to do two things: reveal my income and give my mobile number to salespeople.*

Some people are less cooperative than others, perhaps, as a result of their personalities or significant stressful experiences that have left emotional imprints. In this chapter we will examine types of difficult personalities advisors may often have to deal with, as well as people, who because of circumstances, raise relational challenges. This chapter hopes to answer the following questions:

- How can advisors deal with clients who are reluctant to share personal information?
- How can advisors deal with clients who are quick to find fault and complain?
- How can advisors deal with elderly clients whose post-retirement lack of enthusiasm and increasing hearing loss make them overly-sensitive and non-communicative?
- What can advisors say to clients whose spouses have just died and who are about to make rash, irrational financial decisions?
- How can advisors not only manage relationships with challenging clients, but strengthen their relationships with them?

12.1 PERSONALITY ISSUES

People's personalities can be described, but to account for them is a much more complicated matter. But we do know that personalities are the result of a confluence of a number of processes and factors such as beliefs, values, needs, experiences, attitudes, culture, genetic temperament, and physiological make-up. We also know there are some personality types we prefer more than others. In this section, we will describe and discuss some personality types that are likely to be challenges and suggest how advisors might relate to them more effectively.

12.1.1 The Resistant Client

As advisors attempt to gather personal information, some clients are cooperative and see the benefit in being open and forthcoming, while others are unwilling to reveal any information. In asking for personal information, the advisor must balance the need to know with the danger of being perceived as prying or being too personal. How comfortable clients feel about revealing personal information depends upon the client's personality, the client's attitude towards the advisor, the perceived quality of the advisor's help, the client's trust level, and the client's past experiences.

In responding to a request for information, clients will display a range of cooperative stances ranging from receptive to resistant. In between these two positions, the client may be cautiously neutral and unsure. Figure 12.1 indicates the range of possible attitudes that go with particular states of mind.

Figure 12.1
The Range of Client Reactions

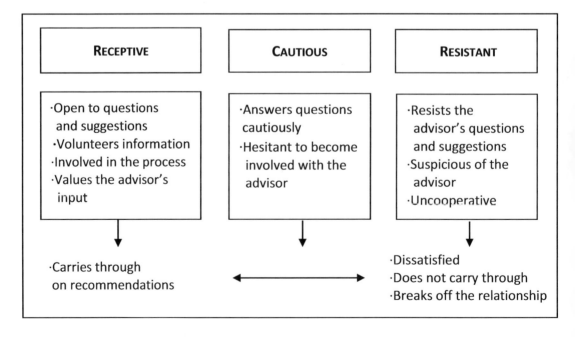

The ***receptive client*** freely volunteers personal information, feels understood, and believes the advising process will create value. It is highly probable that the receptive client will be satisfied with the relationship and commit to a recommendation.

The ***cautious client*** has not totally rejected the advisor or the advisor's help. There is enough personal gain in the relationship that the client stays involved. The cautious client could become more receptive, more resistant, or remain the same. If the client remains cautious, satisfaction will be limited. The advisor needs to bring the cautious client into the relationship by formulating and sending relevant messages (see Chapter 3), and by actively listening to the client's concerns (see Chapter 6).

The ***resistant client*** is defensive and doesn't want to get involved with the advisor. The client is guarded, secretive, and reluctant to reveal personal information. It is not always possible to determine why the client has this attitude. In addition to basic personality issues it could be something the advisor has said or done to make the client feel unappreciated or misunderstood, a negative perception the client has formed of the advisor, or a feeling that the proposed solutions do not meet the client's real needs. The resistant client may terminate the relationship. If the relationship continues, in all probability, the client will be less than satisfied and there is little chance that the advisor's recommendations will be followed.

Once the advisor has determined where clients are on the receptive-resistant scale, the receptive client can be supported, the cautious client encouraged, and the resistant client enticed into a relationship.

12.1.1.1 Strategies for Relating to Resistant Clients. In attempting to encourage the resistant client to be more cooperative, the following strategies are useful.

- **Read the nonverbal message.** The advisor must be aware of nonverbal cues that the client may be uncomfortable or resistant (see Chapter 5). Clients who hesitate too long before answering, or shift into guarded postures, or who answer with little forethought, or who change their tone during the conversation may be signalling that they are not at ease. Remembering that nonverbal language is a cue and not absolute proof of another's feelings, advisors should be ready to pursue the client's nonverbal cues and verify the perceived feelings behind them. Encouraging clients to talk about their reactions and reasons for resistance, is a significant strategy to get beyond clients' feelings and to draw them into a mutual relationship.

- **Set the context for the questions**. Sometimes all that is required to put the resistant client at ease is to explain at the beginning of the conversation that the advisor may need to ask personal questions. In attempting to secure the client's approval, the advisor should explain that this information is necessary to gain a complete picture of the client's situation so that appropriate solutions can be offered. In order not to provoke the client's resistance, the advisor should carefully select the questions and assess their importance before asking them. Sometimes, financial services personnel instinctively ask standard, and often intrusive, questions about such matters as the client's income and the location of investments, even though no further use is made of the information or the value of the answers are not apparent.

- **Use indirect questions** (see Chapter 6). If a client is threatened by a direct question, indirect questions may have more success. For example, if the advisor needs to know how much the client has already saved for retirement, the advisor may use a direct question such as *how much have you saved towards your retirement?* But if the client resists the question and responds: *I don't see why you need to know that,* an indirect approach may have more success. The advisor might ask, *Do you mind if I ask about your retirement savings?* or *In order to help you work out a retirement plan, I will need to know how much you have already saved towards your goal.* If the client does not readily respond, the advisor should solicit feedback: *is that too personal a topic?* If the client responds, *yes,* then the advisor can discuss the benefits of sharing that information.

- **Use open-ended questions** (see Chapter 6). Open-ended questions are perceived to be less threatening than closed-ended questions. The client may perceive the question, *what kinds of ideas do you have for your daughter's education?* to be less threatening than the question, *how much have you saved towards your daughter's education?*

- **Use a conversational style.** Resistant clients usually find answering questionnaires irritating, especially if they are not presented in a context. A flurry of questions asked from a standard form will feel like an interrogation to a resistant client. It is best if standard questions are asked in the context of a rolling conversation. The questions on the form can become points of conversation. For example, the question about yearly income might be approached in the following manner.

Advisor: *We have been talking about your job and the length of time you have been there. Has your salary increased over that time?*
Client: *No, unfortunately, not very much.*
Advisor: *You make about the same as you did when you first started?*
Client: *Yes, and I need an increase to meet my expenses and to have any hope of saving anything.*
Advisor: *This sounds like less than an ideal situation.*
Client: *It is.*
Advisor: *In order to put together a plan of action for you, at some point, we will have to talk about your actual income, expenses, and savings. How does that sound?*

In this conversation, the advisor used indirect questions, explained why the information was required, and then asked for permission to proceed. By the time the advisor focuses on the exact numbers, the client should feel more comfortable about revealing the information.

- **Timing of questions.** If a request for information is perceived by the client as intrusive, it is better if the advisor asks for the information after some rapport has been established, and after the client feels more comfortable with, and trusting of, the advisor. Highly personal information asked for later in the conversation has a higher probability of being provided.

12.1.2 Issues of Power and Control

At the root of many troublesome client relationships are issues of power and control. Some clients want to dominate and show that they are more knowledgeable or powerful than the advisor. At the other extreme are those clients who are eager to prove that they have little or no capability, especially compared to the advisor. (Eric Berne wrote a best seller in 1964 entitled *Games People Play* that is still very useful in understanding the psychological strategies some psychologically ill-adjusted people use to reinforce their feelings of supremacy or inferiority.) Heather Pengelley (1989) has provided a helpful approach to managing difficult people that recommends responding to them in ways they do not expect. Using a classification system created by Jim Murray, an organizational trainer, Pengelley describes three types of difficult people: *warriors*, *whiners*, and *wafflers*.

- **Warriors** are over-whelming, aggressive, hostile, and abrupt. They can be further classified into three sub-types: ***Bullies***, who want to intimidate; ***Know-it-alls***, who are aggressive and arrogant, and look for ways to convince others of their superior knowledge; and ***Grenades***, whose explosive outbursts and temper tantrums demand attention. For Pengelley, the key to coping with *Warriors* is to stay calm, be direct and firm, and refuse to be intimidated. Pengelley says the natural tendencies to be either submissive or combative will not work because these are the responses *Warriors* are used to evoking. When *Warriors* are trying to portray their vast knowledge, Pengelley suggests the use of statements such as: *It would appear that you know all you need to know and are capable of looking after your own finances, what, then, do you want from me?*

- **Whiners** are two types: ***Pessimists***, who see themselves as powerless and inadequate; and ***Blamers***, who blame their problems on anything and anyone but themselves. *Whinners* easily identify problems, but can't solve them. In Pengelley's view, the key to coping with *Whiners* is never to argue with them or try to convince them that things are not as bad as they think, and never to offer advice. *Whiners* will always find reasons to be negative. The best strategy, Pengelley suggests, is to get *Whiners* to take responsibility for their actions. For example, when a *Whiner* identifies a problem, the advisor should ask, *Well, what do you think we should do?* The advisor should be ready to suggest alternatives and ask for the *Whiner's* choices. If the *Whiner* resists, the advisor should be direct: *Well, I guess there is nothing we can do.* This usually shocks *Whiners* into action because they are used to people trying desperately to suggest solutions, which they can reject.

- **Wafflers** procrastinate and defer decisions. *Wafflers* feel that once they choose a course of action, they are exposing themselves to disappointment (regret aversion). The *Waffler* is the client who, in theory, is willing to consider reducing personal expenses, but can't decide which to cut. To encourage *Wafflers* to make decisions,

Pengelley suggests that advisors should always rank recommendations and never supply too many options. Situations usually have risk for *Wafflers*, therefore, it is important to discuss risk-reduction strategies.

12.1.2.1 Dealing with Difficult Clients – An Example. The following is an example of an advisor's encounter with a would-be difficult client. The conversation is in the left-hand column, and an analysis of the conversation is on the right.

Dialogue	Comment
Mr. Salmah: *After doing some careful analysis, I am convinced long-term rates are trending upwards. By the way, what is your opinion? I find you advisors are more preoccupied with daily details and don't have a good overall macro picture. My position in the Ministry of Finance has given me a good view of these matters through the years.*	The advisor has a potential a problem. It appears that Mr. Salmah may be a *Warrior*. His comment could be perceived as threatening.
Advisor: *I think you could make an argument for that. How did you arrive at your conclusion?*	To avoid a battle of opinions, the advisor decided to keep the focus on Mr. Salmah. He is sure that with Mr. Salmah, there is no such thing as a mutual discussion.
Mr. Salmah: *The US Government's stimulus plan is having some effect, but also putting pressure on the credit markets and inflation.*	
Advisor: *I see your point. (Pause.) How does this all affect you?*	The advisor feels that a discussion would give the client an opportunity to intimidate and he wants to avoid this. He decides to bring the focus back to the client's needs.
Mr. Salmah: *Well, I am thinking of repositioning my portfolio. What do you think?*	
Advisor: *I think it is a good idea to regularly review your portfolio, especially in light of your goals and objectives.*	The advisor raises the topic of goals in the hope that this will initiate more fruitful discussion with the client.
Mr. Salmah: *Yes.*	
Advisor: *If you don't mind me asking, what kinds of objectives and goals are you working towards?*	Sensing the client is somewhat resistant, the advisor has taken a more indirect approach to bringing up the subject of goals.

The advisor appears to have had some success in diffusing the client and getting closer to his interests and needs. The key has been the advisor's refusal to get into a battle of economic theories and to refrain from feeling intimidated.

12.2 RELATING TO CLIENTS WITH SPECIAL NEEDS

The financial advisor needs an understanding of the dynamics and service requirements of clients with special physical and socio-psychological needs – in particular, the elderly and the grieving. An understanding of the concerns and dynamics of the elderly and grieving makes it much easier to manage and deepen relationships with them.

12.2.1 The Elderly Client

> Mr. Moussa retired five years ago. During his working career, he was an international expert on under-water welding. After retiring, he stopped working and for the first two years, rested and enjoyed himself. Lately, however, he has felt empty and lost, and his friends and family would even say depressed. He has also shown signs of recklessness in his attitude towards investing. Usually a conservative investor, he now says, *what do I care? I just might strike it rich, and if I don't…who cares?*

Mr. Moussa's behaviour is puzzling and makes it difficult for his advisor to look out for his best interests. Aging brings about changes that sometimes result in attitudes and behaviour that are inconsistent with the person's past beliefs and values.

12.2.1.1 The Aging Process. There are some general changes associated with aging that affect clients' needs. During the later stage of life, significant physiological, cognitive, and psycho-social changes occur.

Physiological Changes. Physiological changes occur in sensory functions and the nervous system.

- **Sensory functions.** Gradually diminishing eyesight brings a sense of isolation and inadequacy. Frustration with a difficult-to-read form may cause some embarrassment when an elderly client is asked to complete one. Aging also impacts hearing. For many, it is not the volume that creates the difficulty, but the clarity of the words. (As my grandmother frequently reminded me.)   Some individuals have additional trouble following a conversation when background noise is significant. Consequently, some elderly people may avoid large gatherings where it is particularly hard to understand all that is being said. (I recently sat across from an acquaintance in a noisy dining area and carried on a conversation, much of which I admit I did not hear. Shortly afterwards, my acquaintance sent me an audio file through the Internet with the explanation that it was the excerpt from the radio show he had mentioned. I confess I did not hear that part of the conversation and his e-mail was a surprise, but, nevertheless, I enjoyed the *MP3* file.)

One advisor made these reflections after meeting with an elderly couple.

> *On more than one occasion I noticed Mr. Gingrich nodding off, so I continued my explanation to his wife. In hindsight, I should have kept my presentation shorter or suggested we take a coffee break. The meeting was long and no doubt affected Mr. Gingrich's comprehension level. I didn't ask if he had a hearing problem – something I should have expected given that he had always worked for the railway. I should have been more sensitive to the nonverbal clues.*

- **Nervous system.** An aging nervous system slows a person's reactions. This is particularly noticeable when new information is presented and a decision is expected. Elderly people may take longer to perform ordinary functions such as using a banking machine. Feeling that others are watching them blunder through common tasks, the elderly often feel embarrassed. One elderly person said his greatest embarrassment is standing in a line at a cash register and delaying people behind him while he fumbles through his change to make up the exact amount.

Cognitive Changes. Deterioration in the nervous system does not mean that intellectual abilities decrease. Elderly people may take longer to perform a task, but their ability to comprehend remains the same, unless they suffer from mental deterioration such as dementia or Alzheimer's disease. The same holds true for learning: elderly people can learn new things, but at a slower pace. Learning will be easier if new information is compared to what is already known or is presented within a familiar framework.

We know that the elderly usually have good long-term memories, but they often have difficulty with short-term memory. A person may recall money in various accounts, but not remember recent transactions. Difficulty in retrieving information can cause anxiety, which further inhibits memory retrieval. The elderly may be frustrated over not being able to perform mental tasks they once performed efficiently, or they may be upset by not being able to recall information, regardless of its degree of importance. Each memory lapse often seems like more proof to them that they are getting feebler.

Decisions are often made by relying on past habits, which can explain why elderly people are usually careful and conservative in their financial choices. In extreme cases, the person may appear inflexible when presented with new options. Elderly clients, who are concerned with maintaining and preserving the value of their capital, may need extra time to think through any decisions that suggest change and possible risk.

Psycho-Social Changes. As we age, we live through a number of major psychological and social crises such as changes in our identities, the death of family and friends, and changes in our relationships. These changes can stir up strong emotions such as anger, depression, and frustration. The main psycho-social changes experienced by the elderly involve identity, autonomy, a sense of belonging, and issues of integrity and despair.

- **Identity.** Our identity comes from our interests, beliefs, values, physical characteristics, and relationships. When any of these factors are modified, an identity crisis may result. It is not uncommon for identity issues to follow changes in career or marital status. Many retired elderly people feel that they have lost a major component of their identity.

Retirement, as well as bringing increased freedom, eliminates important components that gave life meaning: a professional identity, a social network, power, and prestige. Some retirees find it difficult because they are no longer known by their title, they are no longer at the centre of the business decision-making process, and their advice is not sought. The perception of many eager to retire is that it is a wonderful time of life. The truth is that many find it a difficult transition. In Arabic, there is a pun derived from the word for retirement that literally means *to die while sitting*. Another blow to one's identity is the death of a spouse or partner. Death transforms a person from being part of a pair, to being a single person.

- **Autonomy.** As people age, they are less able to do things for themselves such as driving a car or caring for themselves. This can be traumatic. People who lose their autonomy are faced with adapting to less freedom. Loss of dignity is an issue for many who have been used to commanding respect, or who have been free to go when and where they please.

- **Belonging.** Our social connections with family, friends, and colleagues give our lives meaning and generate happiness and fulfilment. In these relationships, we feel accepted and valued, and able to share deep and important parts of our lives. As we age, these relationships may dwindle because of death, retirement, or changing interest. As they do, we lose a feeling of connectedness and may even feel lost and alone.

- **Integrity or despair.** In the latter stages of life, we look back and make an evaluation about the meaning and value of our lives. Psychologist Erik Erikson (1993) suggests we arrive at the later stage of our lives either with a sense of integrity that it was all worthwhile, or with a sense of despair accompanied by regrets and disappointments. Erikson says those who achieve integrity live on with a positive outlook and a sense of peace, while those who arrive with despair are bitter and despondent over lost opportunities and unfulfilled dreams.

The changes outlined above explain the difficulty many people have adjusting to the aging process. For those of you who can't identify with these changes just yet – look at all you have to look forward to!

12.2.1.2 Adapting to the Elderly Client. Using the information presented above and the advisor's own experience, the advisor will have to find ways to adapt to aging clients, and offer supportive relationships that safeguard their clients' best interests.

> *When I met Mr. Abernathy, I was shocked to see that he must be over seventy years old. He sounded younger on the phone. I realized I would have to change my agenda and be more flexible. I leaned towards him as I talked to him. When I noticed his hearing aid, I lowered my voice.*

The incident above is an account of an advisor's meeting with an older client and an attempt to adapt to some assumed limitations. It is clear that before the meeting, the advisor had some stereotypes of older people, but it is not clear what the advisor meant by: *I realized I would have to change my agenda and be more flexible.* However, the advisor receives full marks for being ready to adapt to the client's limitations. The advisor also did well in being prepared to lean forward in response to the client's possible hearing loss, but being flexible enough to change demeanour when sight of the client's hearing aid gave evidence that it was not necessary.

- **Adapting to physiological changes**. A client taking more time than usual to read a document, adjusting the distance of the document, or squinting are indications that the person may have sight problems. When the client's vision has diminished, documents might be prepared in a larger font than normal and the intensity of office lighting increased. With hard-of-hearing clients, advisors will have to increase the loudness and clarity of their speech. Advisors will also have to be careful to create a quiet atmosphere, devoid of extraneous noise, to help clients concentrate. It will usually be appropriate to sit closer to elderly clients.

- **Adapting to cognitive changes.** The advisor may have to present information at a slightly slower pace, check if the pace is appropriate, and adjust the pace if it is either too fast or too slow. It is also helpful in presenting information to make explicit links to what the client already knows. The advisor should carefully choose words to avoid any problems with semantics. Simple explanations are better than complex ones. A slow and concrete presentation, with frequent summaries and verifications of understanding is very important. Despite the advisor's care in giving a clear presentation, the client may need more time before making any decisions. It may take more than one meeting and delays on the client's part should not be interpreted to mean the client is resistant.

- **Adapting to Psycho-Social Changes.**

> Life has changed dramatically for Mr. Moussa, whom we met before. First, he retired from his job and then his wife died – a loss of two important relationships. He has had difficulty managing these losses. His recent erratic investment behaviour has resulted in some major losses. Last year, he invested in all the stock recommended by his favourite financial news analyst. He is now thinking of switching allegiances to another investment *guru* on another TV channel. His advisor, who has known him for ten years, and out of concern, decided to confront his behaviour. The advisor, during a recent meeting in which they were reviewing Mr. Moussa's portfolio, said, *Mr. Moussa, you used to be a very cautious and conscientious investor, but now you don't seem to care. What has happened?*

The simple and direct way in which the advisor raised his concern about Mr. Moussa's behaviour, followed by active listening, could lead to a fruitful discussion. Empathetic listening is crucial for understanding and looking out for people's best interests as they go through periods of adjustment. Advisors are not psychological counsellors, but they do have an obligation to ensure that their elderly clients do not make rash financial decisions that jeopardize their financial well-being.

Elderly clients present special challenges to advisors. Advisors must confront their own misperceptions and stereotypes and get to know the dynamics and needs of their elderly clients. As well as being periodically challenging, many advisors find their relationships with older clients highly enjoyable and satisfying.

12.2.2 The Grieving Client

Grieving is the adjustment process people undergo when they are suffering the loss of a significant other. The loss does not have to be the death of a close friend or family member, as in Mr. Smitt's case, it can also be the loss of an important relationship, the loss of autonomy, or the loss of health.

> Mr. Smitt is grieving the loss of his wife to whom he had been married for 40 years. Prior to Mrs. Smitt's death, they had been preparing for a vacation in Costa Rica.

It is not uncommon for advisors to know clients who are suffering through their grief over the loss of someone close to them. In assisting those who grieve, advisors need to understand their roles, and the dynamics of grief that may affect the client's needs, attitudes, and behaviour. Relating to the grieving client will evoke the advisor's own feelings and memories of personal loss, and may challenge the advisor's patience and understanding, but the advisor's own experience of loss can be an invaluable resource.

12.2.2.1 Stages of Grief. Although each grief situation has its own circumstances, researchers (for example, Dr. Kubler-Ross, 1997) have identified a common sequence of reactions or stages people pass through. Here we will discuss three stages: denial, despair, and acceptance. These stages are of uneven duration and the entire process can last from a few weeks to years. Individuals go through the process at their own pace.

- **Denial.** The grief process begins with a state of shock. The survivor does not believe what has happened – it is all so unreal. *I will soon wake up and find that all this is just a nightmare* is the desperate hope. The numbness that accompanies this stage may exist for a time and the griever may try to continue to live as though nothing had happened and even plan activities involving the deceased. Denial of the event and the accompanying emotions may persist for some time.

  It is reported that Queen Victoria of England lived for three decades in a perpetual state of mourning over the death of her husband, Prince Albert. She wore only black satin and kept a plaster cast of his hand by her bedside so that she could hold it when she needed comfort (Larson, 2006).

  If the grieving process proceeds normally, this protective shell and denial only lasts for a short period of time. As the psyche is better able to cope with the loss, more and more of the loss becomes real. Various on-going events such as the burial ceremony or the visitation of friends will help the grieving person integrate the loss into reality. As denial gives way to awareness, feelings of sorrow and sadness begin.

> When he learned of his wife's death, Mr. Smitt was numb. He sat in his kitchen for an hour, holding a cup of coffee. When his daughter visited him, Mr. Smitt said nothing, then burst into tears. At the burial service, he cried and during the following days, he could hardly sleep. As the days passed, his sadness increased as ordinary things constantly reminded him of her. The day he found a Costa Rican travel brochure was particularly difficult because of the intended trip with his wife. He found it difficult to visit friends. Slowly, he began to realize the loss and all of its implications.

Disbelief gradually gives way to sadness, anger, apathy, a loss of energy, and despair. This next stage is despair.

- **Despair.** The grieving person gradually realizes the depth of the loss and may react with despair, and anger. When a partner dies, the survivor has lost a source of affection, a travel companion, an attentive ear, an advisor, and more.

The bereaved person's social identity changes. Some friends and acquaintances may change their attitudes towards the survivor. Some may become tentative and unsure about relating to others they once knew as part of a couple. They may even avoid the person. Social activities based on the survivor's marital status are gone. The person is no longer a spouse, but a widow or widower. What used to be *us* is now *me*.

During this stage, the person may feel abandoned, depressed, disorientated, and even resentful. There are a number of issues to deal with including reorganizing the daily routine to establishing new goals. In this *in-between time,* the person struggles with finding a purpose, a re-orientation to life, and the energy to deal with it all.

It is not uncommon to feel anger during this phase. Death and abandonment are personalized as being something that has been thrust upon the survivor and he or she may look for someone, or something, to blame. This blame may be directed generally at medical professionals who, it is believed, could have done more to save the deceased. Or the anger may even be turned towards the deceased for causing this anguish and distress: *why didn't he (or she) look after himself (herself) better?* Anger can also be displaced onto other people, such as friends who don't give enough support, children who did not have close relationships with the deceased, or even the financial advisor who seems to be concerned only about financial matters. Persons in grief may blame themselves for not having acted differently: *I should have made him (her) go to the doctor.*

The grieving person may have a tendency to retreat from society and neglect important relationships. A meeting might be missed because the survivor does not care anymore for money or material things. Alternatively, if the client has a good relationship with the advisor, then a meeting with the advisor can be a way to relieve loneliness, and start to rebuild one's life with a new identity.

> In the following weeks, Mr. Smitt had outbursts of rage, such as when the maintenance person didn't show up to fix the air conditioner. At one point, Mr. Smitt told his daughter that he was angry at his wife for not having taken better care of herself.
>
> Mr. Smitt had always been an active person, now he spends his days watching television. He has become less enthusiastic about life and is even falling behind in paying his bills and managing his investments – he recently failed to renew a matured time deposit.

During this period of instability, the person is vulnerable and susceptible to influence; any person who will lend a compassionate ear may have undue influence. Part of the advisor's role is to protect the client from bad advice and rash action. Life remains difficult until the acceptance phase begins.

- **Acceptance**. During this phase, survivors learn to live with and accept their losses, not that all is forgotten or that the loss is never felt again, but a new emotional balance is found. A new self-image emerges as grieving people start to reinvest in relationships and again take interest in activities. The process will take at least a year until all major events, such as birthdays, anniversaries, and holidays are re-lived and a new perspective about them is developed.

> Weeks have passed and Mr. Smitt has discovered new interests and is even considering taking Spanish lessons. His children come to visit him regularly and are helping out with maintenance around the house. At times, he still feels a great sadness, but he isn't as overwhelmed by his emotions as he once was. He is taking care of his financial affairs again, and is thinking of taking that trip to Costa Rica with one of his children.

Acceptance does not imply forgetting, but rather acknowledging that a past relationship has ended and a new life has begun. The successful outcome of grieving is the acceptance of loss and a renewed outlook on life.

12.2.2.2 Adapting to the Grieving Client. What is the role of the financial advisor when dealing with a grieving client? What attitudes and strategies are the most helpful?

Important Principles. When the client is grieving, the advisor can help by assisting with critical financial decisions, as well as being a source of understanding and support. Most importantly, the advisor should be comfortable with the grieving person's feelings and attitudes. Of major help will be the advisor's own personal experience with loss and reflection on how people were helpful at the time.

- **Be sensitive to the client's needs at various stages of the grieving process.** The advisor may see signs of denial, despair, and acceptance – and should feel comfortable with all of these feelings. During the **denial** stage, the advisor can listen patiently to the client's expression of disbelief. The advisor can be ready to react to signs that the client is ready to deal with the financial implications of the loss. There are many details to attend to connected with the settling of the deceased's estate, and the client will show varying signs of readiness to deal with them. The advisor must listen empathetically and when the client raises financial issues, the advisor should be ready to focus on them and give direction to the discussion. It is important not to push the client to deal with financial matters until it is clear that the client is ready. Until then, the advisor should protect the client from any impulsive decisions.

When it is perceived that the client is in the **despair** phase, the advisor should be ready to listen in a non-judgemental way. Here, as in all stages, the advisor's active listening skills and empathy are very important tools. If the grieving person is inappropriately angry at the advisor, the advisor should not take it personally, but realize that it is a normal part of the experience. One advisor, who felt very uncomfortable in the presence of a grieving client's sadness and tears, announced to the client: *Here are some tissues; I will leave the room and when you feel better and are ready to continue, just knock on the door and I will come back.* At a time when the client felt alone and abandoned, the advisor's actions likely reinforced those feelings and hurt the relationship.

As the grieving client comes to the point of **accepting** the loss, the advisor can listen and celebrate feelings of accomplishment as progress is made. The advisor can also help clients rearrange their finances to reflect their new needs and goals.

- **Find the balance between personal and technical matters.** In relating to grieving clients, the advisor must find a balance between technical and personal issues. If the advisor dwells exclusively on financial details, there is a risk of being perceived as *cold* and *uncaring*. A financial advisor said that one day a woman who had just lost her husband entered the branch to attend to some financial matters. The advisor said to her, *I am so sorry for your loss.* The client responded: *Thank you. I have been to six different institutions today and you are the first person who has offered me any sympathy.* On the other hand, if the advisor concentrates on the client's personal feelings, a chance will be lost to assist clients with financial matters that need attention.

- **Help the client with financial decisions.** Relationships with grieving clients are maintained and strengthened by active listening and empathy, but the advisor creates value for grieving clients by helping them with their financial concerns during a critical time when they may feel immobilized. At each stage of the grieving process, the advisor has something valuable to offer. One valuable service the advisor provides the grieving client is checking any impulses the client may have to make rash decisions with possible adverse long-term implications. During this period, the grieving person is susceptible to ignoring financial matters and vulnerable to unscrupulous financial salespeople.

12.2.2.3 Assisting the Grieving – An Overall View. After having read the proceeding account of the grieving process and how the advisor can intervene and assist, you should

disagree strongly with the following statement taken from a professional accounting organization's handbook: *[The] grieving can't deal with financial matters until they stop grieving....[The] best...[advisors] can do is help the person over their grief so new energy can be released.*

First, in response, we have seen how the advisor's awareness of the dynamics of grief can assist throughout the grieving process. We also know that it is a false expectation that the advisor can *help the person over their grief.* It takes time and much support from family and friends before the acceptance stage can be attained. Often, it is not possible to postpone dealing with financial matters until after grieving clients have achieved acceptance; in the meantime, the advisor should be ready to help with any financial concern, regardless of their clients' stage of grief, if clients indicate a need for assistance.

The following extended example of a relationship between an advisor and a client, who has just suffered the loss of her husband, is presented in two columns: the left-hand column presents details of the conversations. The right-hand column contains comments in light of the concepts of this and previous chapters.

Mrs. Lapierre is in her mid-forties. Her husband died recently after a short struggle with cancer. Mr. Lapierre was an entrepreneur who had established a construction business with an excellent reputation. In addition, he owned a diversified portfolio of other businesses including malls and restaurants. Mrs. Lapierre was left with five children all under the age of 18. Prior to Mr. Lapierre's death, Mrs. Lapierre had spent her time raising their family and managing the home. After her husband's death, she decided to become more involved in his businesses. The advisor contacted Mrs. Lapierre, based on a suggestion made by a friend of Mrs. Lapierre's, who was also a client of the advisor's. They met in the client's office.	
Advisor: *How is the construction business going in the local economy?*	A more personal acknowledgement of the client's situation and recent loss would have been a more helpful place to begin.
Mrs. Lapierre: *It is really hard to learn about something you have never dealt with before and especially when you are suddenly responsible for running it, but not ready to run it.*	
Advisor: *It is really hard when you have to learn about something you are not familiar with, especially when you don't feel ready.*	The advisor makes good use of reciprocal empathy.
The client and advisor talked generally about Mr. Lapierre's businesses. The meeting finished with an agreement to meet again to talk specifically about the client's financial needs and goals. The second meeting was also held in the client's office.	

Advisor: *I thought we had a very worthwhile meeting last time. We discussed a number of important issues related to your situation. (The advisor listed them). I am very impressed that you are facing such a large responsibility on your own. What I would like to talk to you about today are your banking needs and how I might be of help.*	The advisor conducts the opening phase well by reviewing what had been previously discussed and laying out the agenda for this meeting, but it could be friendlier.
Mrs. Lapierre: *Yes, you are right. A big part of our business depends on banking services, especially our import and export services.*	She assumes the advisor is referring to her business needs.
Advisor: *You probably have banking relationships set up now to manage your business interests. At some point, I would like to refer you to our commercial department to help review your business needs, but today, I would like to discuss how I might help you manage your personal financial concerns.*	The advisor acknowledged the client's business concerns, but then led the discussion to the personal services and products the advisor could provide.
Mrs. Lapierre: *Actually, I have been thinking about that lately especially since my husband left me a lot of cash as part of the inheritance, and I would like to do something about it. Maybe I should just dump it all in the stock market. My friends have been telling me about the large amounts of money they have been earning.*	
Advisor: *I can see how you could be tempted to do that just to get rid of the problem, but that action has a lot of risks. Maybe we should start by talking about what goals you might have for that money.*	The advisor discourages the client's rash impulses and brings the discussion back to the client's goals.
Mrs. Lapierre: *I certainly don't want to start any more businesses. Right now, I would like to invest the money rather than leave it in the current account with such a low interest rate, but my problem is that I do not know much about investments and I feel that I won't be able to make good decisions, and will lose the money he left us.*	
Advisor: *It sounds normal that without much experience in investing, you are a little afraid to make a mistake, especially when you see your money as a trust from your husband. I would like to help you sort through some of the options.*	Good additive empathy. The advisor listens to her concerns and then offers to assist.
Mrs. Lapierre: *There are so many products introduced by different banks; they all seem good, but I can't make up my mind. I want to pick one I can trust.*	

Advisor: *I would like to invite you to a seminar. It is about asset allocation and diversification. I think you will find it helpful.*	The client is looking for someone she can trust to give her good advice. As helpful as an invitation to a seminar might be, it does nothing to indicate what the advisor can do for the client. The invitation needs a context.
After attending the seminar, Mrs. Lapierre called and invited the advisor to meet her at her house. The client mentioned that the house was a gift from her late husband. The advisor noticed that much sadness appeared on her face.	
Advisor: *It seems it is still very difficult to talk about.*	The advisor is trying to be empathetic without being too personal.
Mrs. Lapierre: *Actually, I feel so lost and confused since he is gone. My children are still very young and I don't know much about the business and competition; besides that, I have a big responsibility towards my husband. I should be growing what he left to us, invest it for the children, and work hard not to ruin all that he did for us, by making wrong decisions.*	The client is under a lot of pressure. She perceives her wealth as a trust from her late husband that she must guard and safely enhance. She is struggling through the despair stage.
Advisor: *I can see how you feel. Did the last seminar help in opening a door towards learning more about investments?*	Not a very empathetic response. And no one can say that one can see what someone else feels, just as one cannot really say *I understand.* Rather than rushing to a discussion of the seminar, the advisor could actively listen to more of the client's concerns.
Mrs. Lapierre: *It gave me some confidence, but it is not enough. I need more than learning because no matter what I do, I always feel that I need an advisor to help me achieve my goals. I chose to deal with you because I can see that you are professional and many of your clients whom I know have a high regard for you.*	
Advisor: *Thank you for your trust. Where do you want us to start?*	The advisor brings the focus back to the client's concerns.
Mrs. Lapierre: *I think you are right; stock are too risky, but deposit rates are so low they hardly cover taxes.*	
Advisor: *Stock results vary. When you are ready, we can start to discuss these. Getting back to deposits, this sounds like a good place for your money*	The advisor curbs the client's impulse to invest all in equities.

right now until you decide what you want to do with it. There are different kinds. The longer the period of maturity and the less credit-worthy, the higher the return. What is the minimum return acceptable to you at this point?	
Mrs. Lapierre: *At least to cover taxes and a little bit more to cover inflation. I will invest for three to four years and use the money to build a small compound for my children after they finish college. I want each one to have a villa after they get married.*	The client has a goal for her money.
Advisor: *So, you want a deposit with a return of at least 5% to cover taxes and inflation, and one that can be booked for 4 years.*	Verification.
Mrs. Lapierre: *That is exactly what I want.*	
The advisor outlined the product that was most suitable for Mrs. Lapierre. The advisor was also careful in describing the kinds of risks it contained and how they could be managed. The advisor wrote out the details of the investment and gave it to the client for safe keeping. The next day the client visited the advisor with a cheque to open the account.	

Despite some flaws, the advisor was effective in dealing with Mrs. Lapierre. As well as a companion, her husband was the owner-manager of businesses that provided income and wealth for his family. Now, the task has passed to her. She feels that the businesses and the money he left have been entrusted to her for the benefit of her family. She feels under pressure not to make any mistakes and lose it. The advisor was able to understand her concerns, check her reckless impulse, recommend an appropriate product, and offer future help.

12.3 CONCLUSION

In an ideal situation, clients will readily supply all the information the advisor needs to construct appropriate solutions. Unfortunately, in the client-advisor relationship, the ideal does not always happen and the advisor may be faced with resistant or difficult clients. But here too, the advisor can master the competencies necessary to move the resistant client to an open stance, and to make troublesome clients more cooperative. Clients experiencing changes brought about by aging and the loss of someone close to them, need advisors to understand their dynamics and to formulate helpful and supportive responses.

KEY TERMS

Acceptance stage. The stage of the grieving process during which the grieving person gradually accepts what has happened, and builds a new life and identity.

Cautious client. A client who will reveal personal information to the advisor, but is hesitant to do so because of uncertainty about the advisor or the advising process.

Denial stage. The stage of the grieving process during which those who have suffered loss have not yet fully accepted it.

Despair stage. The stage of the grieving process during which those who have suffered loss are overwhelmed by feelings of sadness and hopelessness.

Receptive client. Clients who will readily reveal information to the advisor and cooperate with the advisor's attempt to know and understand them.

Resistant client. A person who is secretive and not forthcoming with information, and generally does not cooperate with the advisor's attempts to get an understanding of the client's situation.

Warriors. Difficult people who are aggressive, hostile, abrupt, and intimidating. Subtypes are Bullies, Know-it-Alls, and Grenades.

Wafflers. Difficult people who procrastinate and put off making decisions.

Whiners. Difficult people who easily see problems, but feel unable to deal with them. They tend to be negative and discount any solution to a problem. Two subtypes are pessimists and blamers.

CHAPTER 13

MANAGING CONFLICT

13.0 THE NATURE OF CONFLICT

> Mr. Helfert's wife died two years ago and since then Mrs. Rondeau has become a very important part of his life. She offers him advice about many matters. Lately, she has turned her attention to his portfolio and has a number of suggestions about how he should better manage his wealth. Even though she has no background in investments, she insists that he should make some changes to his portfolio that are clearly in her best interests. Mr. Helfert informed the advisor by phone that he will bring Mrs. Rondeau with him to their next meeting. Mr. Helfert told the advisor that Mrs. Rondeau had some strong criticisms about the way his portfolio is managed and he expects the advisor to follow her advice when they meet.

We have saved the topic of conflict management for the last chapter of this book because the relational skills and knowledge advocated throughout this book are put to their supreme test in managing conflict (such as the impending one above with Mrs. Rondeau). If advisors handle conflict well, their clients' trust and loyalty will be strengthened; however, conflict handled badly can jeopardize relationships. Part of the stress of conflict is the uncertainty of the outcome.

Conflicts can range from very minor issues that are easily resolved to major issues that are difficult, or impossible, to settle. Conflicts that are intense and difficult to negotiate usually result from individual differences where communication barriers already exist and where one party refuses to see the other party's point of view. People differ in their attitude towards conflict because of their psychological make-ups, cultural conditioning, beliefs, and experiences. Some people find confrontation and conflict distasteful, while other individuals actually enjoy the challenge and invigoration conflict creates.

Based on the principal that nothing hidden can be resolved, it is better if conflicts are expressed and resolved. Advisors should welcome client verbalization of complaints because only then can service improvements be made and impediments to relationships overcome. The advisor should read the signs of any conflict, encourage clients to voice their disagreements, and be ready to work towards resolutions.

Wilmot and Hocker (1998) suggest that all conflicts are about three things: incompatible goals, scarce resources, or interference by others in the achievement of one's goals.

Incompatible goals. If all parties' goals cannot be accommodated, potentially, there will be winners and losers. For example, a client may demand full compensation for portfolio losses, but the advisor, following the institution's policy, may not be able to accommodate the client. The advisor's and client's goals are incompatible; it is impossible to simultaneously compensate the client and to follow a *no* compensation policy.

Scarce resources. Clinton Bailey, a pre-eminent scholar of Bedouin culture, says that in the desert where water and grazing resources are limited, *everyone had to become a wolf and be prepared to survive at the expenses of the other tribe* (in Friedman, 1990, p.87). If two people each want to be promoted to their manager's vacated position, they will be in conflict over that one position.

Interference by others. If you want to study for the CFA designation to increase your knowledge and job prospects, but your manager is not supportive and in fact makes extra demands on your time, your manager will become a major obstacle to achieving your goals. Closer to home, have you ever sat down at the end of a busy day to relax, when a family member asks you to get up and do something you promised? If you have, you know the feeling of other people interfering with your goals.

One type of conflict advisors may experience involves client complaints. These are usually limited in nature, but must be handled skilfully to prevent damage to the larger relationship.

13.1 CLIENT COMPLAINTS

> **Client:** *I am really disappointed with my portfolio returns. They are much below those of my friend who invests with other institutions.*
> **Advisor:** *You shouldn't worry about that; we have the finest investment managers and they have very optimistic forecasts.*

The advisor's response in the example above is inadequate because it indicates the advisor did not try to understand the client's concern. Rather than listening, the advisor was defensive. Defensiveness and argumentativeness indicate that the advisor is more concerned with self-interests than client interests.

13.1.1 Handling Complaints

The advisor must be prepared to handle complaints – and the sooner, the better. Dealing immediately with complaints indicates that the advisor has listened, has respect for the client, and values the relationship. A general technique for handling client objections is the *H-A-I-R technique*. It is based on many of the concepts in this book.

Hear
Acknowledge
Identify
Rectify

- **H**ear the client: don't interrupt, don't be defensive, and actively listen to what the client says.
  Client: *I don't like the idea of only one person looking after all my investments.*
  Advisor: *Can you tell me more about your concern?*
- **A**cknowledge the objection by restating it.
  Advisor: *You don't like the idea that only one person will look after your investments.*
- **I**dentify the objection by asking an open-ended question.
  Advisor: *What is it about one person looking after your money that you don't like?*
- **R**ectify the situation, where possible.
  Client: *I just think that as a policy "more heads are better than one."*
  Advisor: *Actually, we work in teams and I will make sure that decisions about your portfolio will be a team effort.*

13.1.2 Price Objections

Client objections can be about many things including unmet expectations, the format of reports, hours of operation, returns on investments, and fees for service. Objections to fees and rates are sometimes the most difficult to handle because the cause and solution of the problem are often beyond the advisor's control. The challenge in providing a fee-based service is to understand what costs represent to clients, and to present products and services in a way that clients feel they are receiving significant value.

To some people, it is an ingrained value that they should receive any good or service for the least cost. They believe that they should never have to pay the full amount for anything. Even the wealthy may be obsessed with frugality. Mary Carter (2003), a family communications advisor, speaking at the Association for Investment Management Research said the following about the attitude of the wealthy: *Those who feel entitled to their wealth tend to be cheap and expect discounts and immediate service. In my experience, the wealthiest people are often the most reluctant to pay for what they want (p. 52).*

For other clients, attempting to negotiate fees and rates may be their way to handle anxiety about any later regret. If the cost issue is one of power, the advisor can attempt to negotiate with the client or decide that the cost of doing business with this client is too high.

One advisor gave the following report as a unique approach to the problem of costs.

> The customer insisted that I cut the yearly service fee in half before he would commit to the offer. I told him I couldn't. He was relentless in his demand and I was equally resistant. Finally, out of frustration, I picked up a pen lying on my desk, thrust it at him, and said, *here take this pen instead.* The client's response stunned me: *Sure, ok, where do I sign.* I lost a pen, but made the deal!

The issue here was obviously one of power and the pen became a symbol that the client had gained a concession from the advisor. As always in relationships, sometimes the creative and intuitive brings the unexpected.

And, of course, there are some clients for whom cost is a legitimate budgetary concern. With customers for whom cost is a genuine concern, advisors can work to find the most cost-efficient way to provide services and products. Advisors can also help clients view fees within a cost-benefit framework where the advantages gained are viewed in comparison to lesser costs. Another approach is to break down fees and costs into smaller units to put them in perspective, for example, dividing annual fees by 12 or by 365 results in a smaller fee that can be compared to a commonly purchased product, such as dinner at a restaurant or a cup of coffee.

In some cases, price objections may be the result of a comparison with competitors' fees. Advisors should know the market and make sure that clients' comparisons between providers are fair and evaluate equivalent features.

The way objections are handled will determine whether the client emerges satisfied with the service. All objections must be handled with respect. If objections and complaints cannot be resolved, it is important to exit relationships with goodwill, so clients feel there is no reason not to return.

13.2 CONFLICT RESOLUTION

The following incident is based on an actual experience in Saudi Arabia. No attempt has been made to remove the account from its cultural setting because the issues are universal, even though some of the details may be country-specific.

> Abdul Hassan is the son of a wealthy businessman. His father died recently and his brothers and sisters have given him their power of attorney to handle their inheritance. Abdul visited the bank to direct them to sell some local shares that were held in his deceased father's account. The bank refused explaining that the estate had not been settled and under the rules of the Saudi Arabian Monetary Agency (SAMA), it could not accept his direction at this time. As Abdul Hassan and the bank disputed the issue over a number of days, the value of the stock decreased. Abdul Hassan threatened to remove all of his and his family's significant business from the bank if he was not allowed to sell the shares immediately or if he was not compensated.

The incident involving the Hassan family is an example of a conflict over incompatible goals. Abdul Hassan and the bank have their own objectives: Abdul Hassan's is to quickly sell the shares and to freeze their value; the bank's is to follow SAMA's regulations. There is a dimension of interference with Abdul Hassan's goals because the bank will not carry out his instructions. This is an important matter to Abdul Hassan and to the bank.

Let us look at a model for dealing with this and other conflicts. For now, the following three-step strategy is presented in outline, but later each point will be expanded.

1. Understand the conflict – get the facts straight
    - *Position* vs. *objectives*
2. Choose an approach to resolution:
    Avoidance, accommodation, competition, collaboration, or compromise
3. Manage the interaction – in the presence of the parties.
    - Develop an understanding of all points of view.
    - Focus on common goals.
    - Keep personal feelings out of it.
    - Generate alternatives.
    - Evaluate alternatives and select a solution.
    - Follow up.

The first two steps in the process are issues the facilitator of the conflict resolution process must consider prior to meeting with the parties involved. The third step comprises guidelines to direct the facilitator's actions while managing the process in the presence of the parties. Note: the advisor may, in some situations, be one of the conflicting parties and the person attempting to resolve the conflict. In these cases, the advisor's task is more difficult and the advisor must have a high degree of self-awareness and control to be able to *rise above* self-interest to manage the process.

13.2.1 Understand the Conflict – Get the Facts Straight
To review the facts of the Hassan family's conflict with the bank: Abdul Hassam has demanded that the bank sell his late father's stock. The bank countered that under SAMA's, regulations it could not cooperate. Abdul tried to convince the bank to sell his father's shares because they were decreasing in value and to keep the proceeds in a closed account until the paperwork and legal issues were finalized, but the bank would not agree. Abdul has called the bank to arrange for a meeting.

The first step in the conflict-resolution process is for the facilitator to evaluate the nature of the conflict. This requires that the facilitator understand the events that preceded the conflict, the significance of the issues to the parties, the intensity of the parties' feelings, and the importance of reaching a resolution.

From the beginning, it is important to distinguish between **positions** and **objectives**. A position is a demand. Consider, for example, a conference room with 30 people, half of whom want the air-conditioning turned up (so it doesn't turn on until a higher temperature is reached, thus making the room warmer), and the other half who want the air-conditioning turned down (the room made cooler). The position of the first group is to request that the air-conditioner be turned up; the position of the second group is the demand to have the air-conditioner turned down. But what does each group *really* want – why have they made these demands? If the air-conditioner was not working, turning it up or down would have no effect and would not satisfy either party. Therefore, it is not the turning up or down of the air-conditioner that is really the underlying issue. This is why it is important to distinguish between positions and objectives. Considering objectives, the objective of the first group is to be warmer and the objective of the second group is to be cooler. The parties' objectives are what they *really* want; the result they desire after their demands are met. Redefining the problem this way opens up possible solutions – let the warm participants sit under the air-conditioner ducts and the cold participants sit in the sunlight, near the windows. The following table summarizes the situation.

Position	Objective
↑*Turn up the AC; it is cold!*	To be warmer
↓*Turn down the AC; it is too warm!*	To be cooler
Focusing on objectives makes it easier to think of solutions.	

The Hassan family's position is their demand that the bank sell the shares now. The bank's position is that they cannot and will not. Redefining the conflict in terms of objectives, the objective of the family is to make sure their wealth does not decrease while the estate is being settled. The bank's objective is to obey SAMA's rules (and to retain the Hassan family business).

13.2.2 Choose an Approach

The person whose responsibility it is to seek a resolution to the conflict (the advisor in our example) should be aware of the possible outcomes that can be sought. *Solving* a conflict can mean many different things. One of the best models for classifying the different ways in which conflicts may be resolved is proposed by Kilmann and Thomas (1975). Their model is illustrated in Figure 13.1.

Figure 13.1
Managing Interpersonal Conflicts

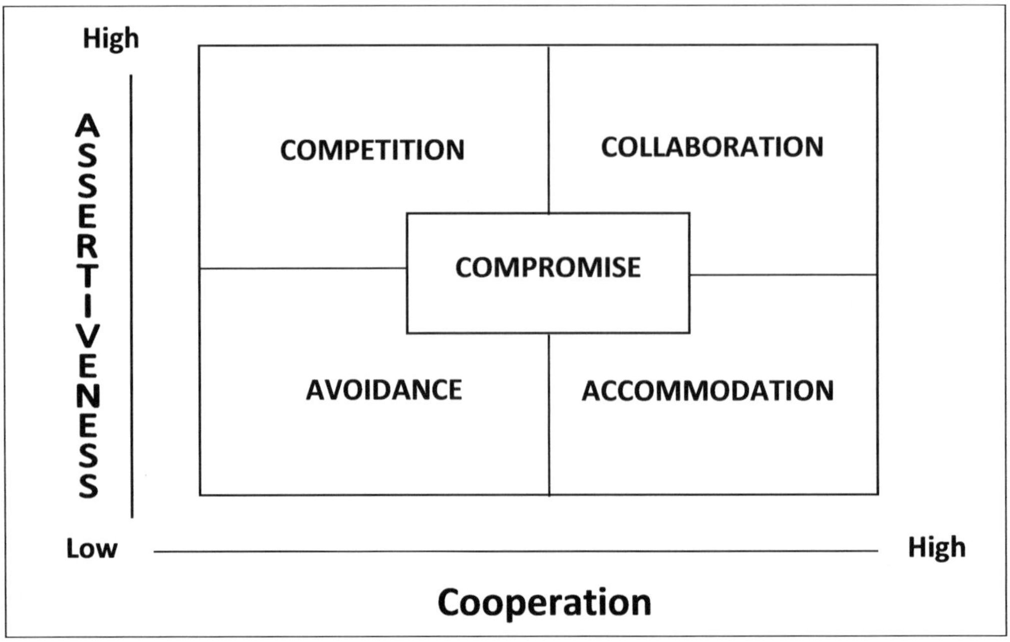

The five approaches pictured in Figure 13.1 – avoidance, competition, accommodation, collaboration, and compromise – differ in how the interests of the parties are balanced. Solutions high on the *assertiveness* scale (the vertical axis in Figure 13.1) seek the accomplishment of one party's objectives, over the other party's. Solutions high on the *cooperation* scale (the horizontal axis in Figure 13.1) allow for the achievement of the other party's objectives, even to the detriment of one's own objectives.

1) The **Avoidance** approach ignores the conflict and attempts no resolution; it is *a Lose-Lose* situation for everyone. The avoidance approach is based on the belief that it is best to ignore some conflicts. Sir Winston Churchill said that he and his wife decided at the beginning of their marriage that, if they were to remain married, they should never have breakfast together. In this case, Churchill believed avoidance of a discussion before breakfast, which might have led to conflict, was the secret of marital bliss.

The avoidance approach is also depicted by a cartoon character who said, *No problem is so big or so complicated that it can't be run away from.* John Turner, a former prime minister of Canada, is reported to have said, *There are two kinds of problems. Those that get better and almost solve themselves and those that get worse. You can afford to let the first type ride, but you better get the second fast.* Turner counselled avoidance as the proper approach to the first type of problem. Unfortunately, Turner did not say how one acquires the wisdom to know the difference.

During my involvement on an investment committee, the chair of the committee made a ruling that was to my disadvantage. I decided not to protest his ruling because I did not want to create any bad will in advance of the discussion of another matter that was even more important to me. I decided avoidance was the best approach, for the moment.

The first decision to be made is whether to deal with a matter or ignore it. Some people may feel that bringing issues out into the open will harm relationships and make situations worse – time will make things better. The disadvantage of the avoidance approach is that tensions may become stronger, distance between the parties greater, and issues larger. However, there can be situations in which avoidance is the best approach.

- When an issue is determined to be minor or temporary and other matters are more important, the avoidance approach may be appropriate. For example, an advisor may choose to ignore a client's comment about the size of investment management fees when the more important issue is how to stop the steep decline in the value of the client's portfolio.
- When taking time to gather more information is better than taking immediate action, the avoidance approach will accommodate this. For example, an advisor may decide not to discuss the mistakes that a client claims were made in his account until the facts are gathered.
- When a concern is important and may affect other issues over which the parties are presently in agreement, it may be best to let harmony prevail and avoid any conflict.

Avoidance is not the appropriate strategy in the Hassan situation. The bank is in danger of losing the family's business. If the issue is avoided, Mr. Hassan is sure to take his business to another bank. For the Hassans, something needs to be done, now. Both parties would agree that there is an immediate need to confront and resolve this situation.

2) The **Competition** approach is assertive and uncooperative. One's objective is to win *at all costs*. It is a *Win-Lose* situation. Those who adopt this approach focus on satisfying their needs without trying to find solutions that meet any of the other party's objectives. For example, it appears that Mr. Helfert, in the opening incident, is intent on getting his way and including Mrs. Rondeau in decisions about his portfolio despite the reservations of his long-time advisor. Competition runs the risk of harming relationships, but there are instances in which the competitive strategy may be appropriate.

- When the advisor is convinced of the importance of following an important regulatory or institutional guideline, the advisor may feel bound to prevail in the dispute.
- When the advisor cannot afford to give in to a client's demand because it might set a precedent, the advisor has a good reason to insist on winning.

In the conflict between the bank and the Hassan family, the bank has adopted a competitive approach because it believes the cost of not following SAMA's regulations is too high. The bank can *win* by staying committed to its position, but it will surely lose the family as clients. This is not an acceptable strategy if the bank wants to retain the Hassan family account.

3) Accommodation is the opposite of competition. In this approach one party disregards its own interests and co-operates fully with the other party to secure the other's party's objectives. It is a *Lose-Win* situation. Because conflict can generate stress and discomfort, some people will give in to eliminate friction and to secure harmony. An accommodation strategy may be appropriate in the following situations:

- When a party feels there is no possibility of satisfying its own interests, the party may accommodate the other person's interests. (In the incident at the beginning of this chapter, the advisor may adopt an accommodation approach out of a fear that if Mrs. Rondeau is not listened to, Mr. Helfert may move his business to another institution.)
- When the issue is more important to the other party and the first party wants to show goodwill in maintaining a climate of cooperation, accommodation may be appropriate. Cancelling a service fee that a client vigorously objects to in order to gain the client's future business is an example of an accommodation approach. Ken Lay, Former CEO and Chairman of the Board of the late energy company Enron, came into conflict with Enron's Board of Directors in arguing that the company's auditing firm and management consulting firm should be separate parties. After many arguments, Lay decided to accommodate the Board's demands to use one firm in order to buy goodwill and secure future advantages (Eichenwald, 2005).

If the bank had accommodated Abdul Hassan's requests it would have run the risk of violating SAMA's rules and incurring penalties and sanctions. Accommodation is not a satisfactory approach in this situation.

4) Collaboration is both assertive and co-operative. It involves an attempt to find a solution that satisfies everyone's interests. It focuses on identifying the objectives of the parties and finding an alternative all parties can accept. This *Win-Win* outcome is the ideal, although it may not always be possible to achieve. Collaboration is appropriate in certain situations.

- Collaboration is the best approach when the interests of both parties are too important to ignore or abandon.
- To eliminate negative feelings that interfere with interpersonal relationships, a collaborative approach is best.
- To combine different points of view in order to reach a consensus, the collaboration approach should be used.

The collaborative approach focuses on **WE** rather than **ME** or **YOU**. The approach views individual differences as normal and worthy of an attempt to accommodate. Creativity is a key component in the ability to find collaborative solutions that meet everyone's needs. The collaboration approach is the one with the best chance of preserving relationships.

One of the best examples of a collaborative solution involves the late United States industrialist Howard Hughes. In 1945, Hughes promised to pay a business associate one million dollars for previous services. When it was time for payment, Hughes informed his associate that he had *cash flow* problems and, unfortunately, could not make the payment. After the associate verified this statement to be true, they worked out an agreement. Hughes agreed to pay his associate an annuity over the next 20 years which would be the time value equivalent of one million dollars at the time. This was better for Hughes' cash flow situation and was also more advantageous for the associate's tax situation.

Collaboration is always the goal; however, in Abdul Hassan's dispute with the bank, given the regulatory framework, it appears, at least on the surface, that it is impossible to meet SAMA's requirements and those of the Hassan family at the same time, unless a creative solution can be found.

5) Compromise lies between assertiveness and co-operation, and between competition and accommodation. It is a *Half-Win–Half-Win* situation. By engaging in mutually agreeable trade-offs, the parties seek to find equally acceptable solutions that partially satisfy the needs of all sides. Compromise requires a give-and-take approach. In the semi-agricultural community where I live, a strong disagreement exists between those who what to preserve farm land for agricultural use and those who want to open it up to residential development. A local county council decided in favour of development, but when their decision was sent to the provincial government for review, the government decided that the land in dispute would be *cut in half* and development would be allowed on one half and the other half maintained for farming. No one is happy with this pure compromise solution.

The following circumstances dictate the use of a compromise approach.

- When the objectives are important, but do not justify extended efforts or the additional risks associated with a more competitive approach, compromise is the best approach. For example, a client wanted to spend half of his accumulated capital on a risky investment, but the advisor recommended against it. The advisor, recognized that it was the client's decision, but wanting to save the client from financial distress, suggested the client should risk only 25% of his capital.
- As a final solution when no other approach promises to yield the desired results, a compromise approach should be used. Settling out of court before a trial is a good example of the use of a compromise approach.

The greatest disadvantage of a compromise approach is that the solution is not optimal for either party. For example, if two brothers disagree over the other's suggestion for the proper type of investment for their joint inheritance, they may be able to agree on a third alternative. The third alternative may not be particularly attractive to either, but at least it has prevented a more serious conflict and the designation of a *winner* and a *loser*.

Given that the bank does not feel that it can violate SAMA's rules and that Mr. Hassan is threatening to withdraw his business, the best approach may be a compromise. Each party may have to give some in an effort to reach a solution that satisfies both. How the bank and the advisor will negotiate with Mr. Hassan during the meeting is the next matter to consider.

13.2.3 MANAGING THE INTERACTION
In managing the interaction between the conflicted parties, the facilitator should follow these principles:

- Develop an understanding of all points of view
- Focus on common goals
- Keep personal feelings out of it
- Generate alternatives
- Evaluate alternatives and select a solution
- Follow up

13.2.3.1 Develop an Understanding of all Points of View. The facilitator will ask each party to explain the problem from its perspective, while the other parties are asked to withhold any comment or criticism. When a party is not talking, it should be actively listening and trying to genuinely understand and develop empathy for the other party's point of view. Each party is then asked to summarize the other party's version of the problem, without prejudice. The use of feedback and verification techniques can help lessen the emotional intensity of the event and create a feeling of trust. Phrases that allow the parties to explore the thinking of the other parties and to deepen their understanding without being argumentative are:

- o   *Correct me if I am wrong…*
- o   *Let me see if I understand what you are saying…*
- o   *Here is where I have trouble following your reasoning…*

In our example, Mr. Hassan should be allowed to express his opinion about what happened, how it affected his family, and interfered with his objectives. Then the bank should explain the reasons for its actions (or lack of action) and its objective. At this point, the purpose is not to prove who is right, but to make sure all parties understand how each party sees the situation. This is an important part of the negotiation process and will do much to diffuse strong feelings and establish a climate of good will.

13.2.3.2   Focus on Common Goals. After the parties have described the conflict as they see it and have identified the issues that keep them apart, the facilitator should focus attention on what all parties can agree upon – common goals. In the Hassan example, the common goal is a solution that will be acceptable to both parties. The bank should express the hope that Mr. Hassan will not feel he has to withdraw his business and will feel that his objectives have been met. Mr. Hassan may express his desire to maintain his business with an institution that has served him well and that he will not have to go through the inconvenience of setting up new accounts at an unfamiliar institution. A focus on common goals shifts attention away from the parties' positions towards their common interests.

It is critical to create a climate of good will. It is important that the facilitator portrays the attitude that the issues at stake are important to all parties and must be solved without destroying their relationship. In an incident in which the author was involved, the senior management of an international food processing company was in conflict with a competitor over a copyright issue. One senior manager suggested that they should cut off all business with the competitor until the issue was settled. (The food processor was a major customer of one of the competitor's products.) The president disagreed saying, *we may be at battle, but we are not at war.* He refused to let the one contentious issue contaminate the entire relationship.

13.2.3.3 Keep Personal Feelings out of it.

> *Speak when you are angry and you will make the best speech you will ever regret.*
>
> Ambrose Bierce

It is important that the dispute is discussed in a rational and civil manner without either party becoming overly-emotional or personal. Mutual respect is encouraged and insult and sarcasm banned. Each party should at least try to remain emotionally neutral toward the other party, even though they may disagree strongly over the issues. It is the facilitator's role to *keep the lid on* personal emotions and attacks.

In negotiation with Mr. Hassan, it will be the facilitator's responsibility to make sure that neither Mr. Hassan nor anyone representing the bank makes personal attacks on the character or motives of the other. To help maintain a positive rational atmosphere, the facilitator should suggest a break when strong feelings emerge. The facilitator should model the proper behaviour by speaking slowly and calmly at all times.

13.2.3.4   Generate Alternatives. After the issues have become clear and each party understands the other's perspective, the facilitator should ask for suggestions regarding possible solutions. These suggestions should be offered freely and without comment by anyone, no matter how inadequate they may appear – evaluation comes later. The term often used for this process is *brainstorming*. The facilitator will call for, and list, all suggested solutions. The more alternatives generated, the greater the chance of success. In this atmosphere of freedom, creativity can occur and, as often is the case, someone's wild idea may contain the kernel for another idea that later becomes the favoured solution.

13.2.3.5   Objectively Evaluate Alternatives and Choose a Solution. If the meeting has proceeded successfully, all parties will be able to evaluate the options objectively without a concern for their sponsor. If Mr. Hassan is willing to look at solutions, it means his mind is still open and the possibility of retaining his business remains. Roger Fisher and his colleagues (1991) at Harvard University call this ***principled negotiation.*** What this means is that the parties are willing to evaluate alternatives based on their merits and set aside a win-lose mentality.

The parties should agree on the criteria that will be used to evaluate the alternatives. These could be feasibility (the ease with which the solution can be implemented to achieve the intended results), consequences (the avoidance of negative results that could create bigger problems), and *appeal* (the surface acceptability of the solution).

Possible solutions to Mr. Hassan's problem might turn out to be an offer by the bank to wave all service fees for a period of time during which they will try to help him regain any losses, or the bank also might offer to assign its best investment advisors to his portfolio. Or a way might be found to liquidate the stock portion of the account and freeze it in *escrow*, within SAMA's rules.

13.2.3.6   Follow Up. Hopefully, as a result of negotiations, the parties will be able to adopt a mutually agreeable solution. But after a solution is implemented, the decision must be followed up to assure that it has been implemented and that it is working.

13.3 CONCLUSION

Fisher *et al.* (1991) summarize the essence of *principled negotiations* by offering these four rules that should guide negotiations. These guidelines parallel what we have advocated regarding management of the negation process.

1. Separate people from the problem.
2. Focus on interests, not positions.
3. Invent mutual options for mutual gain.
4. Use objective criteria.

Throughout the attempt to resolve conflicts, the advisor as facilitator is called upon to use exemplary listening and relationship management skills. At all times, clients must feel understood and respected, and if they do, the chances of resolving issues and maintaining good relationships are enhanced.

KEY TERMS

Accommodation approach. An approach to conflict resolution in which one party gives in to the demands of the other party.

Avoidance approach. One or all parties decide to ignore the conflict.

Collaboration approach. All parties involved in the conflict work to find a solution that satisfies the objectives of everyone.

Competition approach. An approach to conflict resolution in which one party refuses to give up its demands and strives to win.

Compromise approach. An approach to conflict resolution in which all parties decide to give up some of their objectives and accept a less than perfect solution.

H-A-I-R technique. A method for handling client complaints. The letters of the acronym stand for *Hear, Acknowledge, Identify,* and *Rectify*

Objectives. What a party to the conflict really wants to achieve.

Positions. What a party to a conflict demands from the other party.

Principled negotiation. Parties to a conflict are willing to evaluate alternatives based on their merits and set aside a win-lose mentality.

A Last Word

Exchange Theory and Client Loyalty

Thibault and Kelley (1959) theorized that relationships between people can be understood in terms of the exchange of rewards and costs. **Rewards** are outcomes that are valued by the receiver such as good feelings, prestige, economic gain, and fulfilment of emotional needs. **Costs** are outcomes that the receiver does not wish to incur such as time, energy, and anxiety. Thibault and Kelly propose that clients will look for the best reward-to-cost trade-off. For example, clients will drive half-way across the city to visit a financial institution, passing several others on the way, if they feel that the effort to get there is less than the personal service received once there.

If, over an extended period of time, people's net rewards (rewards minus costs) in a relationship are above a certain level, they will judge the relationship as satisfactory. But, if the net rewards are lower than the standard they set, they will be dissatisfied. Moreover, if people have a number of high net-reward relationships, they will set the standard higher, and they will be less satisfied with low or negative net reward relationships. This has important implications for financial advisors. The average financial consumer deals with three financial institutions at any one time. If a client is satisfied with two of these relationships, then, the client will be less likely to deal with a third institution that gives less than adequate service. Clients are continually comparing services they receive from all institutions they deal with.

As we know, in today's financial service industry many alternatives exist. This puts the pressure on advisors to do all they can to assure that net rewards are high for their clients. According to exchange theory, **your customers will remain loyal if the rewards in dealing with you outweigh the costs – and by a greater degree than what they might receive elsewhere.**

The costs of dealing with financial institutions are largely a function of time and energy spent, and frustration incurred. The availability of personnel in a branch to serve clients is a significant component of cost, as is the location of the branch, and available parking. Once inside, costs to customers are in terms of delays, frustration in getting representatives to understand their needs, and dissatisfaction with the way they are treated.

The rewards today's consumers of financial services are looking for are an understanding of their concerns, timely personal attention to their requirements, comfortable relationships, knowledgeable product information, technical competency, financial solutions that meet their specific goals, and overall creation of value for them. The focus on value creation as stressed in this book is an efficient and effective way to quickly identify clients' needs and to help them find suitable products and services that meet those needs. One significant cost that a value-creation focus eliminates is the fear that the advisor may to try to persuade them to buy products and services they do not need. A reason customers sometimes feel tentative or guarded is that they fear they will not be able to say *no* to any pressure and that they may end up purchasing something which is not in their best interests.

A friend of mine, who owns a furniture store, told me that in all of his retail experience, my wife and I were the only customers who told him exactly what they were looking for. All other customers either did not know or would not say. His guess was that they would not tell because they were afraid they would then be vulnerable to pressure. They feared the salesperson might try to force products on them that really did not meet their needs, or that they simply did not like. Your clients should have no fear that revealing their concerns and aspirations makes them vulnerable to pressure and manipulation. They should realize that you are there to discover and discuss their concerns so that together you might find workable and appealing solutions.

If advisors concentrate on creating value through relationships, relational costs should be minimized and the balance of net rewards increased.

BIBLIOGRAPHY

Adler, Asa. (1995). "Utilizing Market Segmentation Techniques to Target Affluent Clients." *Marketing Wealth Management Services to High Net-Worth Individuals*. Toronto: The Strategy Institute.

Adler, Ronald B., Rolls, Judith A., & Towne, Neil. (2001). *Looking Out/Looking in: Interpersonal Communication*. Toronto: Harcourt College.

Anand, V., Ashforth, B.E., & Joshi, M. (2005). "Business as Usual: The Acceptance and Perpetuation of Corruption in Organizations." *The Academy of Management Executive*, 19(4), 9-23.

Ashenbrenner, Gary L., & Snalling, Robert D. (1988, April). "Communicate with Power." Business Credit, 90(4), 39-42.

Axtell, Roger E. (1991). *Gestures: The Do's and Taboos of Body Language Around the World*. New York: Wiley.

Bandler, Richard, & Grinder, John. (1975). *The Structure of Magic*. Palo Alto, CA: Science and Behavior.

Barber, Brad M., Odean, Terrance, & Zheng, Lu. (2000, September). *The Behavior of Mutual Fund Investors*. Retrieved from http://faculty.haas.berkeley.edu/odean/papers/MutualFunds/mfund.pdf

Berne, Eric. (1964). *Games People Play: The Psychology of Human Relationships*. New York: Ballantine.

Beyer, Charlotte. (2009). "Toward a New Science of Private Client Psychology." *CFA Magazine*, 20(6), 10-13.

Blomfield, John, & Hamil, Sharla D. (2003, Nov.). "Who Puts Clients First?" In *Financial Advisor*. Retrieved from http://www.fa-mag.com/component/content/article/796.html?issue=38&magazineID=1&Itemid=27

Buchta, Dirk, Erazo, Fernando, Garbois, Cyril, & von Pock, Alexander. (2008, August). "GCC Banks Losing Hundreds of Millions of Dollars a year due to Poor Customer Service." In *AMEInfo.Com*. Retrieved from http://www.ameinfo.com/165430.html

Buller, D., & Aune, K. (1992). "The Effects of Speech Rate Similarity on Compliance: Application of Communication Accommodation Theory." *Western Journal of Communication*, 56(1), 37-53.

Byrne, Alistair, & Brooks, Mike. (2008). "Behavioral Finance: Theories and Evidence." Charlottesville, Virginia: The Research Foundation of CFA Institute.

Callahan, Michael. (2008, Dec.). "Growing Grey." In *Advisor.Ca*. Retrieved from http://www.advisor.ca/advisors/mypractice/clientrelationships/article.jsp?content=20090120_135046_45152

Carter, Marty. "The Psychology of Wealth." (2003, July). *AIMR Conferences Proceedings: Investment Counselling for Private Clients V*, 52-57.

CFA Standards of Practice Handbook. (9th ed.). (2005). Retrieved from http://www.cfapubs.org/doi/pdf/10.2469/ccb.v2005.n3.4000

Chisholm, Patricia. (2009). "How will you Fare if a Client Sues?" *Investment Executive*, April, 1-4.

Christians, Clifford, & Traber, Michael. (Eds.) (1997). *Communication Ethics and Universal Values*. Thousand Oaks, CA: Sage.

Churchill, John. (1996). *Servicing the Client*. Montreal: The Institute of Canadian Bankers.

Churchill, John. (1990). *Financial Goal Counselling*. Montreal: The Institute of Canadian Bankers.

Combs, B., & Slovic, P. (1979). "Causes of Death: Biased Newspaper Coverage and Biased Judgments." *Journalism Quarterly*, 56: 837-843.

Cormier, Sherry, & Cormier, W.H. (1985). *Interviewing Strategies for Helpers: Fundamental Skills and Cognitive-Behavioral Interventions*. Monteray, CA: Brooks Cole.

Covey, Stephen. (1990). *The 7 Habits of Highly Effective People*. New York: Simon and Schuster.

Daft, R.L., & Lengel, R.H. (1984). "Information Richness: A New Approach to Managerial Behavior and Organizational Design." *Research in Organizational Behavior*, 6, 191-233.

Dalhousie University (2008, April 24). "Lying? The Face Betrays Deceiver's True Emotions, But In Unexpected Ways." In *ScienceDaily*. Retrieved from http://www.sciencedaily.com/releases/2008/04/080422200952.htm

Deep, Sam, & Sussman, Lyle. (1998). *Yes You Can!* Reading, MA: Addison-Wesley.

DuPlessis, Dorothy, Enman, Steven, O'Byrne, Shannon, & Gunz, Sally. (2008). *Canadian Business and the Law*. (3rd ed.). Toronto: Nelson.

Egan, Gerard. (1994). *The Skilled Helper: A Problem-Management and Opportunity-Development Approach to Helping*. (5th ed.). Pacific Grove, CA: Brooks/Cole Publishing Company.

Eichenwald, Kurt. (2005). *Conspiracy of Fools*. New York: Broadway Books.

Erikson, Erik. (1993). *Childhood and Society*. New York: W.W. Norton & Co.

Financial Planning Standards Council (2010). *Financial Planning*. Retrieved from http://www.fpsc.ca/financial-planning

Fisher, Roger, Ury, William, & Patton, Bruce. (1991). *Getting to Yes: Negotiating Agreement Without Giving In*. (2nd ed.). New York: Penguin.

Friedman, Thomas. (1990). *From Beirut to Jerusalem*. New York: Anchor Books.

Freud, Sigmund. (1963) "Fragment of an Analysis of a Case of Hysteria." In *Dora: An Analysis of a Case of Hysteria*. *New York: Collier Books*.

Gibson, James W., & Hanna, Michael S. (1992). *Introduction to Human Communication*. Dubuque, IA: Wm.C.Brown Publishers.

Gladwell, Malcolm. (2008). *Outliers*. Little, Brown and Company: New York.

GMAT® – Graduate Management Admission Test® Official Score Report – Test Taker Copy, (2009, July). Retrieved from http://www.mba.com/NR/rdonlyres/105C7177-7A89-4D1D-B285-7F1400360055/0/SampleScoreReport2009.pdf

Goleman, Daniel. (2005). *Emotional Intelligence*. (10th ed.) New York: Bantam Dell.

Gross, LeRoy. (1982). *The Art of Selling Intangibles: How to Make Your Million ($) by Investing Other People's Money*. Wappingers Falls, NY: New York Institute of Finance.

Hall, Edward T. (1966). *The Hidden Dimension*. Garden City, N.Y.: Doubleday.

Hammond, Corydon D., Smith, Veon G., & Dean H. Hepworth. (1977). *Improving Therapeutic Communication*. San Francisco: Jossey-Bass.

Harrison, T., Waite, K., & White, P. (2006). "Analysis by Paralysis: the Pension Purchase Decision Process." *International Journal of Bank Marketing*, 24(1), 5-23.

Hartman, George E. (1998). *Risk Is a Four Letter Word : the Asset Allocation Approach to Investing.* Toronto: Stoddart.

Heath, Chip, Huddart, Steven, & Lang, Mark. (1999). "Psychological Factors and Stock Option Exercise." *Quarterly Journal of Economics*, 114(2), 601-27.

Hess, Eckhard. (1965). "Attitude and Pupil Size." *Scientific American*, 212, 46-54.

_____. (1975). *The Tell-tale Eye: How Your Eyes Reveal Hidden Thoughts and Emotions.* New York: Van Nostrand Reinhold.

Hollenbeck, John R., Williams, Charles R., & Klein, Howard J. (1989). "An Empirical Examination of the Antecedents of Commitment to Difficult Goals." *Journal of Applied Psychology*, 74(1), 18-23.

Imahori, T. T., & Cupach, W.R. (1994). "A Cross-Cultural Comparison of the Interpretation and Management of Face: U.S. American and Japanese Responses to Embarrassing Predicaments." *International Journal of Intercultural Relations*, 18(2), 193-219.

"Is your Behaviour Affecting your Decision Making? A Guide to Behavioural Finance." (2006, January). *Mercer Investment Consulting.*

Jennings, Marianne. (2003, May 14). "Restoring Trust Following the Perfect Storm in Financial Reporting and Analysis: The Ethical Eight." A talk delivered at the CFA Annual Conference, Phoenix, Arizona.

Johns, Gary. (1996). *Organizational Behavior: Understanding and Managing Life at Work.* New York, NY: HarperCollins College.

Kahneman, Daniel., & Tversky, Amos. (1979). "Prospect Theory: An Analysis of Decision under Risk." *Econometrica*, 47(2), 263-92.

_____. (1982). "The Psychology of Preferences." *Scientific American*, 246,160-73.

_____. (1984). "Choices, Values, and Frames." *American Psychologist*, 39(4), 341-50.

Kilmann, R.H., & Thomas, K.W. (1975). "Interpersonal Conflict-handling Behavior as Reflections of Jungian Personality Dimensions." *Psychological Reports*, 37(3), 71-80.

Kindra, Gurprit S., Laroche, Michel, & Muller, Thomas Edward. (1994). *Consumer Behaviour: the Canadian Perspective.* Scarborough, Ont.: Nelson Canada.

Klapstein, R.E. (1994). *Legal Aspects of Financial Counselling.* Montreal: the Institute of Canadian Bankers.

Kubler-Ross, Elisabeth. (1997). *On Death and Dying.* New York: Macmillan.

Lamb, Steven. (2010, June). "Understanding Behavioral Finance." In *Advisor.ca.* Retrieved from http://www.advisor.ca/advisors/news/industrynews /article.jsp?content=20100614_095154_7344

_____. (2009, Nov.). Investor Illiteracy: Advisors can do Better." *Advisors Edge*, 6.

Larson, Erik. (2006). *Thunderstruck.* New York: Three Rivers.

Locke, E.A., Saari, L.M., Shaw, K.N., & Latham, G.P. (1981). "Goal Setting and Task Performance: 1969-1980." *Psychological Bulletin,* 90, 125-152.

"Please, Please Mr. Postman." (2009, July). *Macleans Magazine*, p. 8.

Madonik, Barbara Haber. (1990). "I Hear What You Say, but What Are You Telling Me?" *Canadian Manager* 15 (Spring), 18-21.

Maslow, Abraham H. (1954). *Motivation and Personality.* New York: Harper.

McIntyre, Grant. (2004, Dec.). "Strengthening your "Soft" Side. In *Investment Executive*. Retrieved from http://www.investmentexecutive.com/client/en/News /DetailNews.asp?IdPub=100&Id=24425&cat=30&IdSection=30&PageMem= &nbNews=

Mehrabian, Albert. (1981). *Silent Messages*. (2nd ed.). Belmont, Calif.: Wadsworth.

Moore, Don A., Tetlock, Philip E., Tanlu, Lloyd, & Bazerman, Max H. (2006). "Conflicts of Interest and the Case of Auditor Independence: Moral Seduction and Strategic Issue Cycling." *The Academy of Management Review* 31(1), 10-29.

Morris, Desmond, Collett, Peter, Marsh, Peter, & O'Shaughnessy, Marie. (1979). *Gestures, Their Origins and Distribution*. New York: Stein and Day.

Moulton, Donalee. (2008, October). "Placing People before Products." In *The Investment Executive*. Retrieved from http://www.investmentexecutive.com/client /en/News/DetailNews.asp?Id=46235&cat=30&IdSection=30&PageMem =&nbNews=&IdPub=168

Neukam, K.A., & Hershey, D.A. (2003, Jan.). "Financial Inhibition, Financial Activation, and Saving for Retirement," *Financial Services Review*, 12(1), 19-37. Also found online: http://www2.stetson.edu/fsr/abstracts/vol_12_num1_p19.pdf

Odean, Terrance. (1998). "Are Investors Reluctant to Realize Their Losses?" *The Journal of Finance*, 53, 1775-1798.

Olsen, R. A. (2008). "Trust as Risk and the Foundation of Investment Value." *Journal of Socioeconomics*, 37(6), 2189-2200.

Partnoy, Frank. (1999). *F.I.A.S.C.O.: The inside Story of a Wall Street Trader*. New York: Penguin.

Pengelley, Heather. (1989). "Coping with Difficult People." *The ICB Exchange*. Montreal: Institute of Canadian Bankers.

Pervin, Lawrence A. (1989). "Self-Regulation of Motivation and Action through Internal Standards and Goal Systems." *Goal Concepts in Personality and Social Psychology*. Hillsdale, N.J.: L. Erlbaum Associates.

Prince, Jeffrey T. (2009). "Credit Default Swaps and Structured Credit: A Primer for Wealth Managers. *CFA Conference Proceedings Quarterly. Charlottesville,* Virginia: CFA Institute, 26(4).

Prince, Russ Alan. (1995). "The Nine Profiles of Wealth." *Marketing Wealth Management Services to High Net-Worth Individuals*. Toronto: The Strategy Institute.

Pusateri, Leo. "Exploring the Value Ladder." (2002). Retrieved from http://www.pusatericonsulting.com/files/May_2002ExploringVL.pdf

Redhead, Keith. (2009). "A Behavioral View of How People Make Financial Decisions." *Economics, Finance and Accounting Applied Research Working Paper Series, Coventry University RP09-6, 1-19*. Also found online: In *Journal of Financial Planning*. http://www.fpanet.org/journal/BetweentheIssues/LastMonth/Articles /ABehavioralViewofHowPeopleMakeFinancialDecisions/

Rogers, C.R. (1951). *Client-centered Therapy: Its Current Practice, Implications and Theory*. Boston: Houghton Mifflin.

Rokeach, Milton. (1973). *The Nature of Human Values*. New York: Free Press.

Sandburg, Carl. (1936). *The People, Yes*. New York: Harcourt, Brace and Co.

Shefrin, Hersh. (2000). *Beyond Greed and Fear: Understanding Behavioral Finance and the Psychology of Investing*. Boston, Mass.: Harvard Business School.

Smith, David. (1998). *Financial Goal Counselling.* (revised ed.). Montreal: the Institute of Canadian Bankers.

Solomon, Michael R. (1996). *Consumer Behavior: Buying, Having, and Being.* Englewood Cliffs N.J.: Prentice Hall.

Soskin, W. F., & Kauffman, Paul E. (1961). "Judgement of Emotion in Word-Free Voice Samples." *Journal of Communication,* 11, 73-80.

Stewart, John Robert (Ed.). (1999). *Bridges Not Walls: a Book about Interpersonal Communication.* Boston: McGraw Hill College.

Taleb, Nassim. (2007). *The Black Swan: the Impact of the Highly Improbable.* New York: Random House.

Ting-Toomey, Stella, & Chung, Leeva. (1996). "Cross-Cultural Interpersonal Communication." In William B. Gudykunst, Stella Ting-Toomey, and Tsukasa Nishida (Eds.) *Communication in Personal Relationships Across Cultures.* Thousand Oaks, CA: Sage.

Thibault, John W., & Kelley, Harold H. (1959). *The Social Psychology of Groups.* New York: Wiley.

Trammell, Susan. (2008). "The Pool and the Stream." *CFA Institute Magazine,* 19(2), 40-45.

_____. (2007). "Applied Science: How to Jump Start a Quantitative Investment Process." *CFA Institute Magazine,* 18(2), 50-53.

Tubbs, Stewart L., & Moss, Sylvia. (2000). *Human Communication.* Boston: McGraw-Hill.

Tversky, Amos, & Kahneman, Daniel. (1986). "Rational Choice and the Framing of Decisions." *Journal of Business,* 59(4), 251-278.

U.S. Department of Labor, Employment & Training Administration. (2010a) *O*Net OnLine Details Report for: 13-2052.00 – Personal Financial Advisors.* Retrieved from http://online.onetcenter.org/link/details/13-2052.00#Skills

U.S. Department of Labor, Employment & Training Administration. (2010b) *O*Net OnLine Details Report for: 41-3031.02 – Sales Agents, Financial Services.* Retrieved from http://online.onetcenter.org/link/details/41-3031.02

Van Zutphen, Neal. (2007, June). "Interpersonal Communication Skills Matter More than Technical Expertise. In *Journal of Financial Planning.* Retrieved from http://www.fpajournal.org/BetweentheIssues/LastMonth/Articles /InterpersonalCommunicationSkillsMatterMorethanTech/

Vashisht, Kanupriya. (2008). "Buy and Hold." Retrieved from http://www.advisor.ca/advisors/mypractice/clientrelationships/article.jsp?content=20080924_094852_7972

Williams, George. (2000, Feb.). "Question, then Listen – and Learn." In *Investment Executive.* Retrieved from http://www.investmentexecutive.com /client/en/News/DetailNews.asp?IdPub=24&Id=7615&cat=30&IdSection=30&PageMem=&nbNews=

Wilmot, William W., & Hocker, Joyce L. (1998). *Interpersonal Conflict.* (5th ed.). Boston, Mass.: McGraw-Hill.

Wood, Arnold S. (2006, Dec.). "Behavioral Finance and Investment Committee Decision Making." *CFA Institute Conference Proceedings Quarterly,* 23(4), 29-36.

Wood, Julia T., Sept, Ronald Edward, & Duncan, Jane. (1998). *Everyday Encounters: an Introduction to Interpersonal Communication*. Toronto: ITP Nelson.